DATE DUE

THE MUTUAL FLAME

BY THE SAME AUTHOR

On Shakespeare

THE WHEEL OF FIRE
THE IMPERIAL THEME
THE CROWN OF LIFE
THE SHAKESPEARIAN TEMPEST
THE SOVEREIGN FLOWER
PRINCIPLES, OF SHAKESPEARIAN PRODUCTION

On Other Writers

THE STARLIT DOME (WORDSWORTH, COLERIDGE, SHELLEY, KEATS)
THE BURNING ORACLE (SPENSER, MILTON, SWIFT, POPE, BYRON)
CHARIOT OF WRATH (MILTON, PROSE AND POETRY)
LAUREATE OF PEACE (POPE)
LORD BYRON: CHRISTIAN VIRTUES
LORD BYRON'S MARRIAGE
THE GOLDEN LABYRINTH (BRITISH DRAMATISTS)

Poetry and Religion

THE CHRISTIAN RENAISSANCE (THE NEW TESTAMENT, DANTE, GOETHE)
CHRIST AND NIETZSCHE (CHRISTIAN DOGMA, GOETHE, THUS SPAKE ZARATHUSTRA)
HIROSHIMA

General

ATLANTIC CROSSING
THE DYNASTY OF STOWE

Drama

THE LAST OF THE INCAS

The Mutual Flame

on Shakespeare's *Sonnets*
and *The Phoenix and the Turtle*

by

G. Wilson Knight

Professor of English Literature in the University of Leeds
Formerly Chancellors' Professor of English at
Trinity College, Toronto

> Our happiest earthly comradeships hold a foretaste
> of the feast of salvation and by thatt virtue in them
> provoke desire beyond them to out-reach and surmount
> their humanity in some superhumanity
> and ultimat perfection: which, howe'er 'tis found
> or strangely imagin'd, answereth to the need of each
> and pulleth him instinctivly as to a final cause.
>
> *The Testament of Beauty*, IV, 1408

> Phoenix and the Turtle fled
> In a mutual flame from hence.
>
> *The Phoenix and the Turtle*

METHUEN & CO. LTD. LONDON

 BARNES & NOBLE, Inc., New York
Publishers · Booksellers · Since 1873

First published in 1955

Reprinted with minor corrections 1962

822.33
X K

45306

July, 1963

1.2

CATALOGUE NO. 2/5727/10

Made and printed by offset in Great Britain by
William Clowes and Sons, Limited, London and Beccles

FOR

ANNE M. WOOLCOTT

who laid the foundation of my work

WITH GRATITUDE

CONTENTS

PREFACE

IT is many years since I first wrote on Shakespeare's Sonnets in an article called 'The Theme of Romantic Friendship in Shakespeare', which appeared in *The Holborn Review* during the year 1929 (xx, new series). That was a slight sketch only and, apart from the scattered comments in my subsequent books, nothing more was done on them until the Summer Vacation of 1953, when I began to get together what was to be my last Shakespearian volume. In this it seemed reasonable to include a short essay on the Sonnets, and I set to work.

But, as so often happens, the essay quickly developed beyond its intended proportions and, though it was completed in about a month, I already had in it the making of a book. It was set aside until the autumn term, when I decided to add a few pages on *The Phoenix and the Turtle*. It seemed as well to take a dutiful glance at *Love's Martyr*, which I had not read; but here again, an exciting set of significances started to unroll, and I was soon involved in a number of enquiries which I had hoped to avoid. Nevertheless, and though the autumn was busy, with the normal run of University work and a number of lecture excursions, the complete text was in the publishers' hands by the end of term. This I mention since, the work having been done under pressure, I am only too well aware that it may contain, here or there, a slip, if not a blunder, the more likely because the second part of the book enters fields of social history new to me. But the significances that cluster about the Phoenix were multiplying so fast that I dared not let the work expand; had I lingered over it into another term it would have been, not twice, but six times its present length, and might not have reached publication.

In the following pages I have tried to maintain my usual concentration on the timeless poetry without altogether avoiding secondary considerations of biography and event. These I could, of course, have ignored, but in a matter where so many theorists have engaged themselves to the point of disaster, it would have been rather unkind to refuse the same risks myself. Besides, so much personal theory has clustered round Shakespeare's Sonnets that to treat them in isolation might be to leave the reader in a state of anxiety.

Strangely enough, the most important of earlier theorists did not come to my attention until after the book had gone to press, when Mr. Arnold Freeman reminded me of A. C. Bradley's remarks on the Sonnets in his essay 'Shakespeare the Man', in *Oxford Lectures on Poetry*. I cannot recall whether I had ever read this essay, but on referring to it was gratified to discover that on a number of cardinal points, such as the reasons for supposing the Sonnets to be autobiographical, the social status of the Fair Youth, and the improbability of his being Shakespeare's patron, his conclusions were the same as my own. Since these are questions of judgment rather than of knowledge, the importance of the correspondence is little affected by whatever unconscious influence from a forgotten reading may have been at work. I have done what I could to incorporate references to Bradley in my text.

I would express my gratitude to all those who have helped me: to Prof. Bonamy Dobrée for the loan of books; to Prof. Kenneth Muir for telling me of Carleton Brown's important work; to Miss Dallas Kenmare, Prof. J. A. Davison, Mr. Harold Fisch, and Mr. Alan Over, for notes respectively on D. H. Lawrence, Hesiod, the Book of Job, and Walter Whiter; and to Mr. Peter Mann for a timely reminder.

To Mr. Arthur Creedy I am indebted for bringing to my attention certain passages of Donne which I might otherwise have missed, for reading and discussing the text, and also, more generally, for his constant sympathy, understanding, and encouragement; and to Miss Patricia Ball for her invaluable assistance in critical comment, proof-reading, the checking of references, and the making of the index.

Acknowledgment is also due to both publishers and author for permission to quote a passage from J. Duncan Spaeth's *Old*

English Poetry brought out by the Princeton University Press in 1921.

Scene and line references to Shakespeare's dramas follow *The Oxford Shakespeare*. The letter 'p.' always indicates my own page numbers.

May, 1954.

The central theme of this study has been recently extended in the section 'The Seraphic Intuition' added to *The Christian Renaissance* (1962).

A valuable commentary on Shakespeare's Sonnets forms part of Mr. Francis Berry's *Poets' Grammar* (1958).

March, 1962   G. W. K.

Part I

THE SONNETS

I

FACTS AND PROBLEMS

There are many footprints around the cave of this mystery,
none of them pointing in the outward direction.

WALTER RALEIGH

SHAKESPEARE'S Sonnets raise a number of problems.
We do not know when they were written, to whom they are
addressed, nor even if they are certainly autobiographical.

What might be called the orthodox view has placed them
somewhere within the first half of Shakespeare's writing career,
the choice of dates being usually influenced by the identity
attributed to the young man who is the subject of most of them,
and who may, or may not, have been the mysterious 'Mr.
W. H.' ('Mr.' to be read 'Master', not 'Mister') named as their
'only begetter' in the first edition printed by Thomas Thorpe
in 1609. Academic opinion has for many years now been
divided between the Earls of Southampton and Pembroke. If
the favoured youth were the Earl of Southampton, born in
1573, to whom Shakespeare dedicated *Venus and Adonis* and
The Rape of Lucrece, the Sonnets should start about 1590 or
1591; if the Earl of Pembroke, born in 1580, about 1598. But
this view has not gone unchallenged. Towards the end of the
last century Samuel Butler argued strongly for a less distinguished friend and an earlier date. His *Shakespeare's Sonnets
Reconsidered*, first published in 1899, was reprinted in 1925 and
1927. I shall quote from the 1927 edition.

Much controversy has developed about the date of Sonnet
107, which runs:

> Not mine own fears, nor the prophetic soul
> Of the wide world dreaming on things to come,
> Can yet the lease of my true love control,
> Suppos'd as forfeit to a confin'd doom.
> The mortal moon hath her eclipse endur'd,
> And the sad augurs mock their own presage;

3

Incertainties now crown themselves assur'd,
And peace proclaims olives of endless age.
Now with the drops of this most balmy time
My love looks fresh, and death to me subscribes,
Since, spite of him, I'll live in this poor rhyme,
While he insults o'er dull and speechless tribes:
And thou in this shall find thy monument,
When tyrants' crests and tombs of brass are spent.

(107)

This sonnet has often been taken to refer to the peaceful succession of James I, following Elizabeth I's death in 1603; it has also been thought to refer to the queen's illness in 1596, but Butler (xi, 133–45) argues that it refers to the Spanish Armada in 1588. Recently Leslie Hotson, in his *Shakespeare's Sonnets Dated* (1949), has followed Butler.

'Mortal moon' for Butler means Queen Elizabeth and for Prof. Hotson the Spanish Armada itself (with mortal = deadly). 'Endur'd' will mean either 'lived through', the natural Shakesperian meaning,[1] or 'suffered' (for Elizabeth's death). That Prof. Hotson's enlisting of Antony's 'terrene moon' *Antony and Cleopatra*, iii, xi, 153) in his support is, as I have elsewhere (*T.L.S.*, 14 July, 1950) shown, inadmissible, does not in itself invalidate his main reading. However we read 'mortal moon', the general argument for the Armada is unaffected, and it certainly lends point to the powerfully placed phrase, 'tyrants' crests'; though it is difficult to see why the mere threat of defeat should constitute an 'eclipse'. If the succession of James I is meant, it is strange that it is not mentioned. Line 5 tells us of the queen's death, and we pass immediately to the augurs' relief: surely the poetic run-on forces us to regard 'mock' as a natural result of 'endur'd'?

No certainty has as yet been reached. In the *New Variorum* edition of the Sonnets (1944), Hyder Edward Rollins calls this sonnet 'a weak prop to support so strong a burden as the dating'

---

[1] Compare *King Lear*:

> Men must endure
> Their going hence, even as their coming hither.
> Ripeness is all.

(v, ii, 9)

Here 'endure' = 'live until'. That is, 'men must put up with life', not 'put up with death'. This is made quite clear by the context.

(II, 61), but when in his *Literary Genetics of Shakespeare's Poems and Sonnets* T. W. Baldwin insists that it 'merely answers the questions posed in Sonnet 65, usually in its own figures, with no possible allusions to contemporary actualities, unless there be an allusion to an eclipse of the moon' (XI, 311), the statement appears too extreme, contradicting the poetic impact (and see p. 114 below).

Butler uses other arguments to substantiate his timing of the Sonnets from 1585 to 1588 (his table is given at XI, 148), and Hotson claims to find contemporary references in two more Sonnets, 123 and 124, in support of his conclusion. In *The True History of Shakespeare's Sonnets* (1933) Lord Alfred Douglas agreed to Butler's dating.

Hotson's conclusions, though at first accorded a measure of agreement, were soon opposed on both sides of the Atlantic. Alfred Harbage and Edward Hubler offered incisive criticism in *The Shakespeare Quarterly* (I, ii; April, 1950); and so did F. W. Bateson and J. M. Nosworthy in *Essays in Criticism* (I, i, Jan., 1951; II, iii, July, 1952), Nosworthy using some original vocabulary tests which lead him to suggest a date as late as 1606 for the crucial sonnet. Middleton Murry, in 'Problems of the Shakespeare Sonnets' (*Countries of the Mind*, II; 1931), does not think any of the sonnets show sufficient mastery for a date later than *Hamlet*. He also (Notes, 201–6) discusses the date of Sonnet 107 with a careful analysis of its meaning and context, concluding with 1596 as a likely year.

If the poet's complaint in Sonnet 102 (p. 114 below) that, though he was the first to sound the strain, he now recognises that 'that wild music burthens every bough', refers in general to the cult of sonneteering during the 90's, and it certainly sounds like that, we have an earlier date for this piece than has usually been supposed. Nor is it an early sonnet in the sequence. George Wyndham, in his important and scholarly edition *The Poems of Shakespeare* (1898), draws an interesting distinction between the earlier and the later sonnets in point of—among other things—'metaphysical speculation' (250).

We cannot, of course, be sure that the Sonnets as we have them were all composed at even roughly the same period of Shakespeare's life, and any one of them may contain layers of work done at different times. Francis Meres' *Palladis Tamia*

(1598) refers to Shakespeare's 'sugred sonnets', but does not describe them, and only two (138 and 144) were printed in *The Passionate Pilgrim* in 1599. In the introduction to his edition of the Sonnets (Cambridge, 1924), T. G. Tucker thinks that some may be quite early and some composed at any time up to Thorpe's publication in 1609. I have little to add except to remind investigators that Thorpe's volume included *A Lover's Complaint*, which contains a study of a young man very like the young man of the Sonnets. If he be the same, and if we date this poem early, we must suppose that *the events of which the Sonnets treat* were also early. Of their date of composition, we shall have more to say later (pp. 107–9 below).

Early dating tends to disqualify Southampton as a candidate for Shakespeare's friend and finally disqualifies Pembroke. The initials 'W. H.' suit Pembroke, whose name was William Herbert, and Tucker (xlv-xlvi) gives reason, and quotes authority, for regarding 'Mr.' as natural, even though he had become 'earl' at the date (1609) when Thorpe used it; but Butler (VIII, 78, 84) and Hotson (36) regard it as a disqualification for a man of rank. Marchette Chute in *Shakespeare of London* (1951; App. I, 300) adduces an obsequious dedication by Thorpe to this same Earl of Pembroke only a little later to underline a significant contrast.

It has usually been supposed from internal evidence alone that the youth addressed was a man of high birth. But Samuel Butler insists, with an especial emphasis on Sonnet 25, that there is nothing in the poetry to suggest that he was of higher status than Shakespeare himself (III, 28; VIII, 78–85); and Lord Alfred Douglas agrees with him (*The True History of Shakespeare's Sonnets*, 15). Here we come up against an insuperable difficulty, since the Sonnets regularly express love through metaphors from royalty and its derivatives, using such phrases as 'my sovereign' (57), 'thy glory' (37), 'lord of my love' (26), 'embassy of love' (45), 'commanded by the motion of thine eyes' (149). In such a context the lover naturally admits 'duty so great' (26) and calls himself his love's 'vassal' (58), or even 'slave' (57). These terms do not necessarily hold social implications.

Whereas the greater part of the academic profession has for long settled down to the conviction that either Southampton

or Pembroke was the person addressed, our more specifically creative writers seem to have taken a rather different
direction.

In 1889 Oscar Wilde, building on a suggestion made by
Tyrwhitt to Malone in the eighteenth century (*New Variorum*,
II, 181) that Sonnets 20, 135 and 136 together showed that the
young man's name was Will Hughes, composed a story *The
Portrait of Mr. W. H.* arguing from Sonnet 25, as did Butler
later, that the youth was no nobleman, and insisting instead that
he was the boy who took the feminine parts in Shakespeare's
plays and indeed did much to inspire Shakespeare's dramatic
work. Butler regards the name 'Will Hughes' as a 'plausible
conjecture' (VIII, 85). Lord Alfred Douglas, though he prefers
Butler's dating, goes a long way with Wilde, and tells us that
Wilde himself believed the thesis apart from fiction (34–5).
Wilde's story seems to have influenced John Masefield, who
in his Romanes Lecture *Shakespeare and Spiritual Life* (1924)
suggested that the 'lovely boy' of Sonnet 126 was a boy who
remained small enough to play diminutive parts from Moth to
Ariel, and symbolised for Shakespeare his own genius (14, 27).
A character in James Joyce's *Ulysses* (Mr. Best) calls Wilde's
'the most brilliant' of all the theories (quoted Rollins, *New
Variorum*, II, 184, referring to *Ulysses*, 1922, 190; in my,
1936, edition, 187). In 1931 André Gide told Julian Green
that Wilde's was 'the only, not merely plausible, but possible,
interpretation' (*Personal Record*, trans. J. Godefroi, 1939; 66;
quoted *New Variorum*, II, 184).

The poet 'A. E.' (G. W. Russell) in his *The House of the
Titans* (1934, 46–55), imagines the Dark Lady commenting on
Shakespeare's love:

> I grew sick
> Seeing the dawn of an unnatural love,
> The kind that marred the Grecian genius.

So she sets her own attractions to work as an alternative
(quoted Rollins, *New Variorum*, II, 238). Butler thought the
quality of Shakespeare's love 'more Greek than English' (XII,
159). In *The Lion and the Fox* (1927), Wyndham Lewis, going
perhaps farther than the evidence strictly warrants, considered
that the Sonnets proved Shakespeare to be one whose 'wits and

senses had been sharpened and specialised in the school of
Sodom' (iv, ii, 153–4).

It is perhaps natural that academic enquirers have tended
to read the Sonnets in terms of patronage and advancement,
and that the creative writers have concentrated rather on art
and erotics. Though the distinction might be said to tell us
more about the theorists than about the mysterious youth, it
would certainly seem that in such a matter the opinions of the
more creative minds should be accorded a high measure of
respect (pp. 105–7, below).

The poet's friend does, however, appear to be generally
popular and admired. He is a youth 'so gazed on' (2), and it is
natural to expect others to write of him (32). He could 'honour'
the poet with 'public kindness' (36). We hear of his 'bounty'
(53). He is copied by the society in which he moves (67), 'the
world's eye' is on him, and 'all tongues' speak his praise (69).
He appears to be a man of some 'knowledge' (82). It is unlikely that other poets, including one of learning (78), should
write verses to a youth of no distinction. Butler (vii, 67–8)
appears to underrate the significance of these lines:

> For whether beauty, birth, or wealth, or wit,
> Or any of these all, or all, or more,
> Entitl'd in thy parts do crowned sit,
> I make my love engrafted to this store.
>
> (37)

Tucker, who tends to favour Pembroke, admits that the youth
may have been merely 'a private gentleman'; but he is surely
right in thinking that there must have been something of 'the
glass of fashion and the mould of form' about a man said to be
the theme of other poets who 'under thee their poetry disperse'
(78). Tucker gets the general impression of a nobleman (xlii–
xliii); but in 'Shakespeare the Man' (*Oxford Lectures on Poetry*,
1909) A. C. Bradley offers (332) good reasons for supposing
him to be a gentleman, but no more.

Shakespeare's own social status is felt to be low. He is one
whom 'fortune' has barred from 'public honour and proud
titles' (25). One sonnet records a general sense of inferiority, in
part social, in contrast to his one kingly consolation of love (29).
He feels himself 'poor' and 'despised' (37), but his love is 'better

than high birth' (91). He has made himself—and this probably refers, in part at least, to his stage work—'a motley to the view' (110). Being merely a man of 'public means' he must be excused for 'public manners' (111). Shakespeare's status appears to be depicted much as we would expect.

Little can be proved regarding the young man. But one thing appears certain. Before Bradley, Butler also adduced reasons why Shakespeare's tone and themes of address do not indicate a great nobleman as their object (VIII, 79–84). These we may extend by suggesting that he cannot well have been Shakespeare's principal patron. Shakespeare, we must suppose, had some worldly wisdom; and we know that he possessed business instincts. It is scarcely conceivable that he ever complained to his patron that nature had 'added one thing to my purpose nothing' (20) to his lordship's physique; that he could have accused him of being 'fond on praise' (84) and snub him with the line 'lilies that fester smell far worse than weeds' (94); or that he should be found in the later sonnets (pp. 113–28) persistently warding off the great man's pursuit of his, Shakespeare's, favours. Elizabethan poets did not rise by such methods. If such pieces were ever addressed to a patron, we may be sure that they were never sent, nor even circulated in private. I understand that Prof. Hotson has in preparation a suitable candidate: should he turn out to be a law student at the Inns of Court, we might suppose him to be in some measure responsible for Shakespeare's love of legal metaphor.

Then there is the question of age. But here again we come up against a difficulty. Shakespeare regards himself as old. Now we know from the plays, which present a succession of apparently old, generally tyrannical, men with young daughters or sons (Egeus, Capulet, York, Leonato, Shylock, Polonius, Lear, Polixenes, Prospero), that Shakespeare's views on age were queer. Hamlet and Macbeth appear from their texts to grow with lightning speed during the action. We can say that people aged rapidly at this period, but difficulties remain. 'Forty winters' may, at a stretch, be allowed to constitute some sort of 'age' (2, 3); and we can pass 'my glass shall not persuade me I am old' (22); we can allow the young Shakespeare to 'summon up remembrance of things past', including 'old woes', buried 'friends' and 'old loves' (30, 31). But that he should see

himself in a glass as 'beated and chopp'd with tann'd antiquity'
(62) seems at first beyond all reason. So does this:

> Against my love shall be as I am now
> With Time's injurious hand crush'd and o'erworn,
> When hours have drain'd his blood and fill'd his brow
> With lines and wrinkles; when his youthful morn
> Hath travell'd on to age's steepy night . . .
>
> (63)

He says that he is at the age when bare boughs 'shake against
the cold' (73). He does, however, admit that his mistress 'thinks
him young', although 'she knows my days are past the best'
(138). He can also refer to his 'pupil pen' (16), and speaks of
his style growing 'with his growing age' (32).

Poets do tend to regard themselves as old in their verse.
C. Knox Pooler in his Introduction to the *Arden* edition of the
Sonnets (1918) quotes (xxxv) a passage from Barnfield's *Affectionate Shepherd* (1594), where the poet, in terms certainly of a
pastoral fiction though otherwise in a similar context to Shakespeare's, makes an even more exaggerated claim to age, though
he was only twenty at the time. Byron at thirty-six wrote 'my
days are in the yellow leaf' (stanzas on his *Thirty Sixth Year*),
and his prose contains similar thoughts: 'Would not one think
I was sixty instead of not quite nine and twenty? To talk thus
——' (To Augusta Leigh, 28 October, 1816; and see Journal,
2 February, 1821). T. S. Eliot compares himself to an 'aged
eagle' in *Ash Wednesday*. But Byron rapidly lived through the
experiences of a lifetime; and Eliot's poem is highly symbolical.

Butler argues that these statements are as unsuited to a
man nearing the thirties as for one in the early twenties, and
more likely to be used by the latter (x, 122). The net result
is that such phrases are useless as factual evidence, though
they assist the poetry. We shall later (pp. 45, 71) discuss the
nature of the poetic pressure that appears to have prompted
them.

As for the poet's friend, his youth is clear. He is called
'sweet boy' and 'my lovely boy' (108, 126). But after only three
years' acquaintance Shakespeare expects his beauty to be going
(104), and writes in terms of 'wrinkles' and 'antiquity' (108).
The logic, if there be any, is imaginative.

I do not propose to settle any of these problems in factual and biographical terms. I do, however, think that Butler's very able arguments should be reconsidered in the light of Hotson's theory; and yet the arguments from style and vocabulary supporting a later date—though neither Middleton Murry (p. 5) nor L. C. Knights discussing the Sonnets in *Explorations* (1946) are willing, on literary grounds, to put them any later than the end of the century—are as strong, or stronger. A possible synthesis might be arrived at by supposing that the facts of the story, in so far as they are facts, together with some first versions of the poetry, were indeed early, but that Shakespeare, like Drayton, revised or rewrote many of his pieces later. They probably meant much to him. Some were, as we know from Meres, circulated among his friends, and may have been only withheld from publication because of their intimacy and boldness. The main body of Thorpe's collection certainly gives the impression of what had once been a structured work of art, whatever details—if any—have gone wrong with it afterwards. Let us now glance at his arrangement.

As Thorpe printed them, we have a long series addressed to the Fair Youth followed by a shorter series most of which are concerned with a dark mistress. Whether the youth was what we should call 'fair' remains doubtful: Butler argues that the word means no more than 'good-looking', and supports his contention with a number of quotations (vii, 72–3). Similarly, the Dark Lady may not have been so 'black' as the poetry makes her. Tucker is prepared to see both meanings in 'fair'; 'black' he equates with 'dark' (liii–lv). The two persons concerned appear to be real individuals, and they are firmly contrasted. The very similar young man of *A Lover's Complaint* has 'browny locks' (85). We may regard it as unlikely that the youth was dark and the lady golden-haired.

Samuel Butler has worked out a rearrangement. Though most of the first series appear to be in a sensible and significant order, it is rather strange that some of them refer to the youth's association with the Dark Lady before we know anything about her. For a definite statement about the association we have to turn to the second series. Butler, quoting Wyndham's *Poems of Shakespeare* (cx, cxi, and 325), notes that 40, 41, 42 all refer to this association (and he also adds, rather questionably, 35).

He regards it as strange that the intimacy should not be touched on in the first series after 42 and then, after a lapse of three years, be handled with passion in the last group. He shows good reason why 143 and 144 cannot well come after 134. Some redistribution within the second series may be needed, but he is on less secure ground when he inserts Sonnets 147 to 150, which are generally taken to be addressed to the lady, within his main series as poems to the youth (ix, 87–8). Tucker (xv) says that the two affairs 'seem', from a comparison of Sonnets 133, 134 and 144 with 41, 'to have gone on together'.

It seems that someone, perhaps Shakespeare himself, had originally arranged the first series as a unit, thinking that Sonnets 40 to 42 were enough to shade in the secondary theme of the Dark Lady and rejecting the rest, even the great sonnet on the 'soul' (146), as irrelevant to the artistic unity aimed at; but that Thorpe, having got hold of the rest, bundled them in at the end.

We cannot subscribe to all Butler's details. When he interposes Sonnet 121 *of the first series* between 32 and 33 in order to explain certain troubled pieces in terms of a trap or practical joke played on Shakespeare to lure him on to attempted vice and subsequent mockery, we must withhold our assent. The evidence is not there; and it is a pity that he should, in his more general remarks, appear to regard this as proved. It is not fair to Shakespeare, and still less so to the Fair Youth, whom we have no reason to suppose an ungenerous friend. Butler's conclusion that the publication of the Sonnets in 1609 must have been 'exquisitely painful' to Shakespeare is, of course, possible on other grounds (xii, 152). Middleton Murry, in 'Shakespeare's Dedication' (*Countries of the Mind*, ii; 1931), thinks that it may have had some effect on Shakespeare's more bitter dramatic works (e.g. *Timon of Athens*), but 1609 is rather late for that.

We may conclude these prefatory remarks by admitting that Tucker may be right in thinking that the Sonnets as we have them may include poems addressed to more than two persons (xvi). But the sequence, as we have it, holds together so well that we are justified in regarding such a possibility as irrelevant. The poems, as they stand, tell us, rightly or wrongly, a story. Let us now see what that story is.

Shakespeare, addressing a young man of good, though not, it seems, great, social standing, starts (1–17) by imploring him to marry in order to perpetuate his beauty. Next, he asserts and reiterates the thought that the youth will be immortalised by the poetry.

But there are complications. The poet suffers moods of depression and abasement, and in these moods invokes his love as a support (29, 37, 88, 110, 112). He also appears to suffer ill-fame, his name receiving a 'brand' for his *deeds*—a word which seems throughout the Sonnets to denote some sort of sexual vice (111). He is the subject of 'vulgar' (i.e. popular) 'scandal' (112). Similar suggestions of, it would seem, some well-known 'shame' occur elsewhere (36, 71, 72, 109, 121). He appears to vary, rather like Byron, between humility (88, 111) and the self-assertion of 'I am that I am' in despite of all charges and shames (121).

Sometimes he complains of the youth's deserting him (87–93, 120); and he shows pain, both at his mixing in a false society (67) and at his association with the Dark Lady (40, 41, 42, 133, 134, 144). He also, more generally, complains that the young man is ruining his own good name by what appears to be some variety of 'sport', which probably means sexual vice (95, 96). It appears to be 'sensual', in our sense of the word (35); 'lascivious' is twice used (40, 95); the references are various (41, 67, 69, 70, 94). Why Butler disclaims any 'sensuality' on the youth's part (ix, 94) is not clear. Though at first 'unmoved, cold and to temptation slow' he certainly appears to have succumbed in some sense to what the poet calls 'base infection' (94).

There is also a rival poet, and Shakespeare is hurt by his friend's acceptance of his praise:

> Was it the proud full sail of his great verse
> Bound for the prize of all too precious you . . .
>
> (86)

The rival appears to be one of some 'learned' set in strong contrast to Shakespeare's 'rude ignorance'; one who wields a 'worthier pen' than Shakespeare's 'sick muse'. He is called 'a better spirit', Shakespeare's own poetry being a 'saucy' and 'inferior' bark as against one 'of tall building and of goodly

pride' (78, 79, 80). He is also said to be a man of occult
practices:

> Was it his spirit, by spirits taught to write
> Above a mortal pitch, that struck me dead?
> No, neither he nor his compeers by night
> Giving him aid, my verse astonished.
> He, nor that affable familiar ghost
> Which nightly gulls him with intelligence,
> As victors of my silence cannot boast;
> I was not sick of any fear from thence . . .
>
> (86)

Tucker's notes take 'spirits' to be the 'disembodied geniuses of
the past' from whom a man of learning naturally derives assistance; and 'compeers' as simply other learned men with whom
he associates by night; 'affable' he translates 'obliging'. But the
massed associations point rather to occult practices. I owe to
my brother the translation of 'affable' as 'talkative' or 'approach-
able through direct conversation'. Tucker's general commentary on the sonnet offers little but confusion. Dowden's
introduction to *The Histories and Poems of Shakespeare* in the
three-volume Oxford edition of the works refers to Chapman's
statement that he was visited by 'skill' coming 'like a heavenly
familiar'; and points to Acheson's *Shakespeare and the Rival
Poet.*[1]

There appear (78) to have been other rival poets, but there
was only one main rival ('both your poets', 83). Shakespeare
continually, as we shall see (pp. 18–20), urges that his own
compositions are sincere, and the other's artificial. Butler, indeed, thinks that his jealousy was primarily a literary jealousy
(IX, 100).

Our romance concludes, at first sight rather unromantic-
ally, with a number of sonnets from 100 onwards in which
Shakespeare excuses himself for the silence of his muse. Butler
(IX, 101) notes that Sonnet 97 shows no trace of the earlier
'sense of injury' and 'remonstrance'. It is now Shakespeare
who feels himself somehow at fault; though in 121, a sonnet
Butler quite unjustifiably removes from this section and places
between 32 and 33, he asserts a kind of beyond-good-and-evil
claim for himself. Of 108 Butler writes: 'It is tolerably plain

---

[1] See, too, Rollins' discussion in the *New Variorum* edition, II, x.

that Mr. W. H. has been taxing Shakespeare with want of constancy, and has especially galled him by repeating the accusation that Shakespeare had ceased to care for him now that he
had got to look old.' Shakespeare, he says, 'seems to have been
stung to the quick' (ix, 104–5). There are, however, some
magnificent recoveries of poetic rapture, including 'When in
the chronicle of wasted time' (106). The natural conclusion is
that Shakespeare has been giving his attention to other matters,
probably the stage, and at the same time indulging in 'public
manners' (111). He admits inconstancy in giving way to
'appetite' and so troubling his friend (110). But it is clear that he
has not lost contact with his ideal of love, though less ready to
write directly of it: to this problem we shall return (pp. 113–36).

The Sonnets addressed to the Dark Lady are very different
in tone. They are characterised by harsh criticism of her looks,
and considerable evidence of self-conflict in the poet. It is
clearly a physical relationship (138), and given sharp physical
expression (151). But it is called a matter of the 'heart' and
distinguished from the senses, all of which, and his eyes in
particular, she repels (141). He is uncertain whether the fault
lies in his eyes or in his judgment (148; and see pp. 37–9).
Certainly love must be a 'blind fool' to put 'fair truth upon so
foul a face' (137). A dark colour was conventionally supposed
to be unbeautiful, as in *A Midsummer Night's Dream*:

> The lover, all as frantic
> Sees Helen's beauty in a brow of Egypt.
> (v, i, 10)

He knows, rationally, that she is not beautiful (130), but he can
write lyrically of her 'raven' hair and 'mourning' eyes in contrast to artifice and decoration (127). The action of her eyes is
of deep concern to him (139, 140). To him she is not black,
save—dubious compliment—in her 'deeds' (131). 'Eyes' are
repeatedly emphasised. The attraction appears to have been
finer than lust and cruder than love. We may perhaps call it a
'magnetic' attraction.

The relationship is illicit and sinful (142). She is a bay
'where all men ride'; she is 'the wide world's common place'
(137). She runs after someone else, and Shakespeare after her
(143). She has 'seal'd false bonds of love' as often as the poet

himself (142), but he continues to love her, even 'in the very refuse of thy deeds' (150). 'Sin' is admitted (141, 142), and the great sonnets on lust as 'the expense of spirit in a waste of shame' (129) and the body as 'sinful earth' (146) find here a natural place. Her one redeeming feature, as she appears in the poetry, is her playing of music (128), an art which the Fair Youth does not like (8).

Sometimes the sentiment is more gentle, as when the poet refers to 'thy sweet self' (151), or develops a comparison of himself to a child with the lady as his mother: 'And play the mother's part, kiss me, be kind' (143). But in the main these are dark, sin-impregnated sonnets, as those to the Fair Youth are not. They are summed up in one grim outburst:

> My love is as a fever, longing still
> For that which longer nurseth the disease,
> Feeding on that which doth preserve the ill,
> The uncertain sickly appetite to please.
> My reason, the physician to my love,
> Angry that his prescriptions are not kept,
> Hath left me, and I desperate now approve
> Desire is death, which physic did except.
> Past cure I am, now reason is past care,
> And frantic-mad with evermore unrest;
> My thoughts and my discourse as madmen's are,
> At random from the truth vainly express'd;
>   For I have sworn thee fair and thought thee bright,
>   Who art as black as hell, as dark as night.
>
> (147)

There is nothing like this said with reference to the Fair Youth. Where such torment is there suggested (e.g. in 119), it is related to other, contrasted, engagements

As we have seen, Butler (ix, 87–8) reads this last piece, 147, and also 148, 149 and 150, as written to the Fair Youth. Since it may be that those sonnets which seemed best to fit the Dark Lady were abstracted and put at the end by someone who knew little more about them than we do, Butler might conceivably be right. No final certainty is possible, but on internal evidence we shall disagree. The sonnets to the youth are not marked by this particular unrest.

Whether Shakespeare's relations with his friend remained

idealistic and non-physical we cannot say. Butler has no good warrant for regarding Sonnet 23 as an invitation in response to encouragement, and few will subscribe to his fanciful story of the trap (IX, 90–1; see p. 12). There is nevertheless direct evidence of desire in the thought of 'nature' as having 'defeated' the poet by 'adding' to his friend 'one thing to my purpose nothing', with the following resignation of the youth to 'women's pleasure' (20); and on another occasion the poet, confessing 'that we two must be twain', regrets, in the manner of Marvell's *Definition of Love*, the 'separable spite' which cuts them off from 'sweet hours of love's delight' (36); though here the reference may be quite general. There may be recollection of a rebuff in the description of the youth as one of those 'who, moving others, are themselves as stone' (94). If it were so, we can be grateful to him, since, had he given way, we should probably have had no sonnets thereafter, the best pieces clearly flowering from instincts that have been forced into the eye and mind. Shakespeare's actions cannot be known, and are not here our concern. What we can say is this: within the poetry the love is realised for us as a principle of light and truth in contrast to the tormented and lustful quality of the other series.

Much of our story may appear, at first sight anyway, rather sordid, with a goodly assortment of mysterious and presumably vicious 'deeds', the word being applied variously to the poet himself (90, 111, 121), his friend (94), and his mistress (131, 150). But these are countered by so fine an idealisation in the main romance that we feel them rather as a dark background from which 'like a star i' th' darkest night' that central splendour may, as Hamlet has it, 'stick fiery off indeed'.

But, we may ask, are these sonnets honest records, or merely the conventional exercises that some critics have thought them?

Well, those to the Dark Lady are so strangely outspoken, so burdened with passion and paradox, with sin and sickness of soul, that they can hardly be considered in any normal sense conventional. No one would indulge in them for fun, to please himself; and we can scarcely suppose that they could have pleased the lady. They must be either true records or poetic fantasies possessing a high degree of personal validity. But what of those to the Fair Youth?

3

Some of these are, indeed, very flattering, and there are
clear instances of thought-structures which may be called 'conventional', as when the poet persuades the young man to marry
or promises him a poetic perpetuation. Many of Shakespeare's
themes are found in Barnfield's *Affectionate Shepherd*, where the
boy Ganymede is told that his beauty will pass, advised to
marry, warned against profligacy, and so on; and though Barnfield's work, published in 1594, might be supposed to copy
Shakespeare, it is safer to admit a single pattern used by various
poets for a similar purpose. After all, there is a limit to the
number of things you can say on such occasions. But Shakespeare's sonnets do it in their own way, telling a partly obscure
story of uneasy and insecure love, of separation, jealousy, misunderstanding, recrimination and criticism. There are those yet
stranger, inhibited, pieces explicitly reacting from convention
and apologising for being unable to continue playing variations
on the one theme. The Sonnets' contents, if they are all
addressed to the same person, make it most unlikely, as we have
(p. 9) seen, that they could have been addressed to a patron
whose favour was being sought. They are clearly, in the main,
sincere enough, with at least the kind of sincerity we expect
from poetry. They are perhaps sometimes too sincere to be
graceful, as though the poet were labouring under difficulties
to express his exact meaning, though we need not deny that this
is done through a variety of tricks, conceits, fancies and word-
play that may all, as tricks, be called 'conventional'. But these,
as Tucker notes (xxx), would not necessarily seem insincere at
the time. They were well-known tricks of communication, and
if they be conventions, we can consider them such almost in the
sense in which all words and grammatical structures are conventional. The substance of meaning, at least in the most
important asseverations, which, as we shall see (pp. 76–7), may
sometimes be linked together by certain less important mechanisms, is surely, to a critical judgment, as sincere as the love-
poetry of Donne or Tennyson. Again, if they do not constitute
a factual record, they at least hold some kind of inward and
spiritual authenticity. And this is all that we need to justify our
attention.

Not only may we call them sincere, but we may observe
that sincerity is one of their leading themes. Even in one of the

early adulatory sonnets the poet says that he will not compare
the wondrous youth to sun, moon, and stars—though he does
so elsewhere—since, being 'true in love', he will 'truly write',
calling him as fair 'as any mother's child', but no more (21). He
resents all adornment, almost, we may say, all poetry, rather as
did Wordsworth. He sees his own poetry as a crude, unlettered,
attempt drawing its power from genuine feeling, a thing of
'poor rude lines' compared with those of 'better poets' (32);
others have learning in comparison with his 'heavy ignorance',
but his poetry is yet 'thine and born of thee', for 'thou art all
my art' (78); others employ 'strained touches' of 'rhetoric',
whereas his is made of 'true plain words' by a 'true-telling
friend' (82). The thought is Antony's in *Julius Caesar*:

> I am no orator, as Brutus is;
> But, as you know me all, a plain, blunt man
> That love my friend.
>
> (III, ii, 221)

He even has to apologise, for his silence: 'I think good thoughts
while others write good words'; he is like an 'unletter'd clerk'
(85). We may compare Theseus' lines in *A Midsummer Night's
Dream* on his valuation of those 'clerks' who stumbled in their
welcome, with its conclusion:

> Love, therefore, and tongue-tied simplicity
> In least speak most to my capacity.
>
> (V, i, 104)

'Truth needs no colour' (101); too much publicising of emotion
kills its object, which itself surpasses 'all invention' (102, 103).
As Brutus in Julius Caesar, speaking of 'a hot friend cooling',
says: 'There are no tricks in plain and simple faith' (IV, ii, 22).
   The jibes at any sort of artificiality are, as in the plays,
where all exaggerated fashions are so regularly attacked, here
also both strong and insistent. Social decoration, make-up,
wigs, are criticised. 'Art's false borrow'd face' (127) is rejected.
Wigs, 'bastard signs' of beauty, decorating a 'living brow' with
'golden tresses' that are 'the right of sepulchres', are denounced
(68), exactly as in *The Merchant of Venice*, where Bassanio,
looking at the deceptive gold casket, compares it to 'golden
locks' whose proper head is 'in the sepulchre' (III, ii, 92–6). To

all such false art, the loved youth, relying on no ornament but
'self and true', is a living contradiction (68). These thoughts
are summed up in a fine quatrain from a sonnet complaining of
the society with which the youth was mixing, and which had
been guilty of imitating by poetry, painting, or make-up, the
young man's beauty:

> Why should false painting imitate his cheek
> And steal dead seeming of his living hue?
> Why should poor beauty indirectly seek
> Roses of shadow, since his rose is true?[1]
>
> (67)

He himself does not need 'painting', and Shakespeare's poetry
has not offered any (83); let others indulge in the 'precious
phrase by all the muses fil'd' (85); but 'best is best if never
intermix'd' (101). The poet must, if we believe him, be grouped
with Timon himself as against the Poet and Painter in *Timon
of Athens*.

Shakespeare's adoration is to be distinguished from such
superficialities. It is not 'idolatry', like the false intuitions
attacked by Hector in *Troilus and Cressida* (II, ii, 51–8; *The
Wheel of Fire*, III, 53); for he and his love are 'still constant in
a wondrous excellence' (105). He can be tongue-tied and silent,
like Troilus on his first meeting with Cressida (III, ii, 63; *The
Wheel of Fire*, III, 64), and ask that his eyes alone may speak for
him (23). The loved one's eyes are themselves beyond all
poetry:

> There lives more life in one of your fair eyes
> Than both your poets can in praise devise.
>
> (83)

It is just this 'simple truth' that is not present in the affair with
the Dark Lady (138). The effect is that of Troilus' asseveration:

> I am as true as truth's simplicity
> And simpler than the infancy of truth.
> (*Troilus and Cressida*, III, ii, 176)

'Fair, kind and true' is his own argument (105), and the youth's
'constant heart' the basis of his faith (53).

[1] I follow Capell's emendation of 'seeing' to 'seeming'.

Some of our evidence is drawn from the later sonnets when Shakespeare is apologising for a cessation of love-poetry. The truth appears to be complex: his love had, it seems, projected him into a state where it had itself, without its quality being lost, become more impersonal, and less readily phrased. This problem we shall discuss later (pp. 113–29).

But can we accept any of these assurances as true? We have only Shakespeare's word for it, and the Fair Youth might tell a very different story; and so might the Dark Lady. All we can say is, that, within the context of the Sonnets, Shakespeare's love is of this sort; what the Sonnets insist on repeatedly must be for us, in so far as we are attempting to elucidate their meaning and value, the truth.[1] After all, the whole sequence may be a work of art devised as deliberately as Nietzsche's *Thus Spake Zarathustra*; if, indeed, that *was* deliberately devised. We can put it like this: if the poet is not sincere, the poetry is. And what more, at this hour, concerns us? Whether or not he has exactly recorded a section of his autobiography we can never precisely know; but he has certainly left us a poetic record of considerable interest.

[1] This has in the past been my method when dealing with Pope's satires in *The Burning Oracle* (the essay in question now re-published in *Laureate of Peace*); and Wordsworth's *Prelude* in *The Starlit Dome*.

II

THE INTEGRATION PATTERN

He who, being a man, remains a woman, will become a universal channel.

LAO-TZE

WHATEVER we think of the story, in so far as there is one, there flowers from its soil some of the world's greatest love-poetry. From this nettle-bed of vice, we pluck the flower, genius. Nor is the poetry itself anything but healthy: throughout there breathes an air of simplicity, honesty and purity, shirking nothing and somehow finally establishing a spiritual principle of the kind which we naturally associate with the noblest literature. What exactly is this 'principle'?

Before proceeding to a discussion of it, a word or two on Shakespeare's language may be helpful. The Sonnets are not easy. In the plays we have a clear context and can interpret the words accordingly. But each sonnet is an independent statement; we have no certain context, and are thrown back on the words alone, which too often offer us little foothold. Shakespeare's words have unsuspected meanings: 'modern' means 'commonplace'; 'shadow' is used for a pictured likeness or reflection; 'lovely' can mean not merely 'pretty', but also 'lovable'; 'passion' may mean what it means to us or may mean 'emotional poem'; 'crime' signifies little more than 'fault'; 'sport' usually suggests sexual indulgence; 'will' can carry obscene connotations. We must be constantly on our guard.

T. G. Tucker, who seems to have pushed verbal analysis of the Sonnets further than anyone, is often an excellent guide. Here are some of his translations: 'thy dear virtue'='the virtue on which you set so high a value' (142); 'base infection'='contamination from lower things' (94); 'gentle sport' is construed 'wanton behaviour becoming to a gentleman' (blending notes to 95 and 96). Subtle intricacies may be involved, as when 'to every wandering bark' is rendered 'to any bark, if ever it wanders', and for 'within his bending sickle's compass' we are given 'within the curving sweep of his sickle' (116). Tucker's analysis is always scholarly, and his reasons clear. Again and again he corrects the unwary and inexpert. Even those most saturated in Shakespeare's language are in danger of the most undignified blunders: Shakespearian scholars continually mis-interpret Edgar's 'Men must endure . . .' in *King Lear* (see p. 4, above). The trouble is, there is so often a perfectly clear sense according to our modern meanings as well, and you may have to discipline your mind to avoid them. I know no better preparation for an understanding of Shakespeare's language than Tucker's commentary on the Sonnets.[1]

He is nevertheless not always, and for all purposes, reliable. His very concentration on archaic syntactical exactitudes seems sometimes to blind him to an obvious intention, and he surely misreads the general meaning of certain sonnets badly (pp. 49–52, 96, 131). Though he is sometimes ready enough, as was Wyndham, to observe duplicate meanings in word or phrase, he probably also misses some valid alternatives where a student of William Empson's 'ambiguities' would allow them as over-tones. He works with the most extreme caution, studying the language to get the context of meaning, and rarely assuming a context to interpret the language. He is not aware of—and herein lies much of his value—the kind of contexts-of-meaning which I shall myself be developing. He is also, in the manner of his generation, liable to write off as fancies or 'conceits' passages in which we, today, may be tempted to find pro-fundities. That is inevitable. But when this is said, it remains true that no commentator of the modern school can afford to assert a meaning without testing it against Tucker's commentary.

We now proceed to our analysis. The Sonnets we shall discuss as a semi-dramatic expression of a clearly defined pro-cess of integration pointing towards the realisation of a high state of being ; a process rather like that announced by Words-worth in his *Recluse* fragment, printed in the Preface to *The Excursion*. My recent reference to Nietzsche's *Thus Spake*

---

[1] I may here record my own debt. Since the early days of my work Tucker's com-mentary has lived in my mind as a perpetual warning against forgetting the difficulties of Shakespeare's language.

Zarathustra may have looked like an intrusion, but since that is our greatest document of the process we are to analyse, references to it are not merely in order—they are forced. For a more widely documented discussion of the matters discussed in my present section, I must point to my book *Christ and Nietzsche* (iv and v), where the whole theory of the bisexual integration with, as its furthest aim, the Superman, is developed and explained.

Our main attention must concentrate on the poet's love for the Fair Youth. There is nothing strange about this, since throughout the ages such attachments can be observed, as Hugh Ross Williamson has recently argued in *The Arrow and the Sword* (1947, v, 80), in persons of literary and other genius. In the records of great literature we have David and Jonathan, Homer's Achilles, Plato's *Phaedrus* and *Symposium*, Vergil's *Eclogues*, and much else in Latin poetry. Among English poets we have examples in Gray; in Byron, whose various friendships, in particular those with the chorister Edleston and Nicolo Giraùd, were 'passions' (*Lord Byron: Christian Virtues*, ii, 66–73); and Tennyson, whose *In Memoriam* aroused concern in Victorian England. The greater the poet, or perhaps we should say the more he is given to human, or humanistic, themes and actions, the more likely is this emphasis to recur. Browning's central and perhaps greatest poem, *Saul*, cannot be deeply received without some such understanding; nor, perhaps, can Marvell's *Definition of Love*. The strain continually recurs. The great ages of the humanistic imagination in ancient Greece and Renaissance Europe are rich with it: names such as Michelangelo, Leonardo da Vinci, Montaigne, Sir Thomas Browne, come to mind. It is significant that the terms 'friend' and 'lover' were in Elizabethan England interchangeable. I am not referring specifically to physical vice, but rather to what might be called 'romantic tone', or 'romantic colouring'. There was romance in friendship; and by 'romance' I mean something that expresses itself naturally in such poetic idealisation as Shakespeare devotes to it.[1]

We must not deny a strong sexual impulse. Of Shakespeare's

---

[1] An account of such idealisations is given by Friedrich Gundolf in his *Shakespeare*, I, 167ff., and a passage of it quoted by Rollins, *New Variorum*, ii, 236. See also my articles on *Don Leon* in *The Twentieth Century*, July, 1954 and June, 1956.

actions we know nothing. We are concerned not with what Shakespeare did or did not do, but with what the poetry says. Now the poetry does, very clearly, say in Sonnet 20, and perhaps, though less certainly, in Sonnet 36, what amounts to this: 'I am sorry that normal sexual intercourse between us is impossible.' In so far as sexual intercourse is considered as a necessity of the richest love-life, the romance remains one, to quote Marvell's *Definition of Love*, 'begotten by despair upon impossibility'; and the balance of the lovers' 'one respect', or single spiritual direction, against 'separable spite' in Sonnet 36 does, indeed, correspond closely to Marvell's figure of parallel lines that 'never meet'. Nevertheless the love, at its finest moments, does not seem tragic; we somehow feel it the grander and more perfect in that physical intercourse goes no farther than 'eyes' (pp. 37–42). That is not to say that the poetry is unphysical, or spiritual in any limited and doctrinal sense. The Sonnets show as fine a physical ardour as *Venus and Adonis*, but it is less a matter of desire than of adoration. There is no lust, no sense of sin, as with the Dark Lady; no lasciviousness, as may be subtly felt within Marlowe's *Hero and Leander* and in *Edward II*. The youth functions as the poet's 'better part' (39). It appears to have been an exacting relationship on both sides, and when either of the partners indulged in loose behaviour in the outer world, there appears to have been trouble from the other (pp. 13, 28, 43, 52, 67, 79, 115–18, 124–9).

The love poetry of Shakespeare's contemporaries is couched for the most part in heterosexual terms; but that, among a number of sonnet sequences supposedly at least celebrating the love of a lady, we should find Shakespeare directly confessing love for a young man, is not strange. It is what, having regard to the psychology of his peers, we should expect.

Beside the homosexual [1] idealism, we have a heterosexual passion, or lust, together with all the extraordinarily rude things said about the lady. These we shall naturally group with Dante's marital bitterness, and with Milton's, together with his ugly remarks on women in *Paradise Lost* (IX, 1182–6;

[1] The term is used to preserve honesty. It may be worth stating, since confusion is fairly general, that 'homo' derives from the Greek, and means 'like', or 'similar'. It does not derive from the Latin word for 'man'. Nor does it signify physical vice: 'homosexual' is defined in the *Oxford English Dictionary* as 'having a sexual propensity for persons of one's own sex'. 'Propensity' is defined as 'inclination'.

x, 137–56 and 867–908; xi, 628–32), and throughout *Samson Agonistes*; with Swift's uneasy sexual associations; with Pope's feminine studies, Atossa especially (*Moral Essays*, ii); with Byron's marriage disaster and subsequent invectives against his 'moral Clytemnestra'; with the succession, despite his own success, of futile marriages in Ibsen's plays; with the less strong, but relevant, anti-feminine strictures in Nietzsche's *Thus Spake Zarathustra*; with Strindberg's peculiar dementia. Sometimes the dark substances occur in the man's work, sometimes in his life, but there is certainly a goodly amount of it. Much of our greatest drama turns on dark feminine figures: Clytemnestra and the Erinyes, or Furies, in Aeschylus; Medea in Euripides; Shakespeare's Margaret of Anjou, Tamora, Lady Macbeth, the Witches, Goneril and Regan, Dionyza, the Queen in *Cymbeline*, Sycorax; Racine's Hermione, Phèdre and Athalie; Ibsen's Furia, Hiordis and Hedda Gabler; and throughout Strindberg.

There are, of course, good women too, in Shakespeare preeminently; and to these we shall return. But first we must face this dark and feminine evil, from the Book of Genesis on; though with a woman writer of comparable stature, we have, in *Wuthering Heights*, a man. Against this evil we shall balance the masculine idealisation.

The balanced antithesis within Shakespeare's Sonnets accordingly compresses wide areas of Western literature. It is, very exactly, an expression of those two root principles of Nietzsche's *Birth of Tragedy*, the Dionysian and the Apollonian.[1] These are principles of widest application. The one suggests all that is darkly mysterious, the creative origin and end; the numinous, mystic, orgiastic, mad, and un-moral, or rather a-moral; the sub-conscious, or the mass-consciousness, death. Its typifying art or language is *music*. The other is light, has intellectual clarity, is a vision of shapes and figures, individualistic, suggesting the created rather than the creative; is sane, moral, political, ideal, and of the conscious mind. Its typifying language is *sculpture*, and also *epic*, as opposed to dramatic, poetry. Greek drama Nietzsche reads as a union of Dionysian

[1] These, the terms used in the standard translation, may, I think, be properly reserved for Nietzsche's scheme in distinction from the terms 'Dionysiac' and 'Apollinian' in general use among classical scholars.

chorus with Apollonian stage-persons, fusing music and epic. In this fusion lies its greatness, for the fusion of these root principles is the supreme achievement.

Dionysus is an effeminate God, Apollo a figure of masculine beauty. In Aeschylus' *Oresteia* you get the balance: on the one side Clytemnestra and the Erinyes, or Furies; on the other, Apollo, the rights of husband against wife, and Orestes; Athena and the Council of the Areopagus symbolising some higher synthesis.[1] In the Christian scheme, God the Father is Dionysian; God the Son, especially at the transfiguration—for the Apollonian is visionary—Apollonian; and the Holy Spirit, the Divine Sophia, the poetic fusion, Aeschylus' Athena. You could say that Nietzsche was, without knowing it, reformulating Christian dogma and simultaneously showing its relation to Attic drama. These are inexhaustible categories: once you understand them, you find them everywhere.

You certainly find them in the Sonnets. The Fair Youth is continually, as we shall see (p. 39), realised in pre-eminently *visual* terms, with much talk of 'eyes', 'image' and painting. He is exactly defined by calling him an Apollonian conception. The Dark Lady is visually repellent, but exerts a fascination and a magnetism which eludes intellectual definition (p. 15). The youth enjoys Apollonian 'praise' of his beauty (84), and appears to have been the willing centre of a poetic cult (78); and he is blamed for mixing in a society whose 'painting' imitates the roses of his good looks (67). He is always *colourfully* depicted, with metaphors from painting (101). But he significantly feels, like Jessica in *The Merchant of Venice* (v, i, 69), ill-at-ease with music:

> Music to hear, why hear'st thou music sadly?
> (8)

A comparison of music to family love is next developed, urging the youth to marry, and suggesting a relation of his Narcissistic chastity, unmoved, at first anyway, by sexual attraction (94), to his dislike, or fear, of the otherness, the depths, of the, in Nietzsche's scheme, non-Apollonian art, music. In sharp distinction, the Dark Lady, like Ibsen's Hedda Gabler, a strictly

---

[1] See W. F. Jackson Knight's account in *Greece and Rome*, v, 13; Oct., 1935.

Dionysian conception whose thoughts dwell on 'vine-leaves',
is a musician:

> How oft, when thou, my music, music play'st
> Upon that blessed wood whose motion sounds
> With thy sweet fingers, when thou gently sway'st
> The wiry concord that mine ear confounds,
> Do I envy those jacks that nimble leap
> To kiss the tender inward of thy hand . . .
>
> (128)

The correspondence is exact.

The Sonnets show us Shakespeare, who has left, tempor-
arily at least, the normal life of a married man, being plunged
into two contrasted experiences of love and lust, light and darkness, and moving through these to some higher integration. To
him it is, pretty nearly, a contrast of good and evil, of *Venus
and Adonis* as against *The Rape of Lucrece*:

> Two loves I have, of comfort and despair,
> Which, like two spirits, do suggest me still:
> The better angel is a man right fair,
> The worser spirit a woman colour'd ill.
> To win me soon to hell, my female evil
> Tempteth my better angel from my side,
> And would corrupt my saint to be a devil,
> Wooing his purity with her foul pride.
> And whether that my angel be turn'd fiend,
> Suspect I may, yet not directly tell;
> But being both from me, both to each friend,
> I guess one angel in another's hell:
>   Yet this shall I ne'er know, but live in doubt,
>   Till my bad angel fire my good one out.
>
> (144)

The words (e.g. 'my female evil') suggest an almost allegorical
meaning. The balanced antithesis recalls one of Michelangelo's
sonnets:

> The love of that whereof I speak, ascends:
> Woman is different far . . .
>
> (53)

One 'the soul lights', the other 'the senses stir'.[1] The two

---

[1] I am using J. A. Symonds' translation of Michelangelo's Sonnets (London, 1950).

persons are aspects of Shakespeare's soul, whatever they may
have been in their own right; and he is further involved in
their relationship with each other. The use of 'hell' in such a
context recalls *Othello*, as also does the horror of living in
doubt (see *The Wheel of Fire*, v, 114–15; and *Othello*, III, iii,
336–8, etc.) Line 12 must be allowed its vivid physical impact.
It refers to sexual intercourse between the youth and the lady,
the use of 'hell' pointing on to Lear's

> But to the girdle do the gods inherit,
> Beneath is all the fiends'.
> There's hell, there's darkness, there is the sulphurous pit,
> Burning, scalding, stench, consumption . . .
> (*King Lear*, IV, vi, 129)

Of lines 12–14 Tucker observes: 'The allusion is (with an
equivoque) to the fire of passion and the burning of concupis-
cence.' On line 12 Edward Hubler, in *The Sense of Shakespeare's Sonnets* (1952), notes (50) that 'the reference is to that
story in *The Decameron* usually left in Italian'. Neither comment
is as explicit as one might wish.

The horror of lust found in the Sonnets is continued, with
variations, throughout Shakespeare's work. Here we have a
peculiarly intriguing complex of disgust roused by the thought
of the Apollonian ideal being tainted by the Dionysian horror.
We are aware, in the relationship of youth to lady, of the inter-
twining of good and evil, and it would be an error to regard
the evil as, in the last resort, an intruder. They are necessarily
involved in each other, and somehow both must be assimilated.
Our final aim must always be the blending of Dionysian and
Apollonian celebrated in *Thus Spake Zarathustra*. Whether or
not it ever happened, it is right that the lady should be sus-
pected of having seduced the youth.

We can see how fascinatingly the Sonnets hold in embryo
the more expanded works to follow. And here we may face the
problem, for in this context it *is* a problem, of Shakespeare's
many fine and lovable women. How do they fit in?

Edward Hubler, though admitting that in a purely general,
Freudian, sense, a sexual element may be included in all
varieties of love (98), nevertheless argues against any suggestion of a 'homosexual' attachment in the Sonnets (App.,

151–61). It is, of course, as he says, a question finally of words. 'Homosexual', as I use the term, is not intended to signify physical intercourse. But it does involve, and I think Shakespeare's Sonnets do also, physical and sexual attraction. Surely some distinction must be drawn between this richly expressed devotion and what someone once called, in a clever if cruel phrase, the 'sexless camaraderie' of certain modern Christian gatherings. It is clearly nearer *eros* than *agapé*. 'Sex' is not only within it, but a large and valuable part of it.

Prof. Hubler finds no significant homosexuality in the plays, and observes that the love-interests are normal. But this is a dangerous simplification. When Shakespeare as lover of the Fair Youth shows jealousy of the Dark Lady he is, in this regard, functioning as a female partner; we can say that the female element in his personality is engaged. About this 'female element' there is a great deal to be said.

In *The Lion and the Fox* Wyndham Lewis argued that Shakespeare was 'a sort of feminine genius' (IV, i, 149), who had been 'turned into a female at an early age', and, though by nature 'sexually aggressive', was so 'constituted' that heterosexual experience was repellent to him (IV, ii, 153). His general attitude was accordingly 'that of a woman' (IV, ii, 158). But there was gain as well as loss, since this 'reversal of sex' may, according to Lewis, be related to 'Shamanism' and 'occult powers' (VI, iv, 222). Much of the 'perfection' of the plays is due to it (IV, ii, 154), for it is precisely this 'female nature' in him which empowers the poet's majestic praise of his 'warlike demigods', especially Antony (IV, 11, 154). Aptly for his purpose Lewis quotes (VII, iv, 261–2) Achilles' statement in *Troilus and Cressida* (III, iii, 238) that he is 'sick' with 'a woman's longing' to see 'great Hector in his weeds of peace'. We may remember that Achilles is presented as, in part, a homosexual type, Thersites, who *would* go to extremes, referring to Patroclus, with extreme scorn and disgust, as one 'thought to be' his 'masculine whore' (V, i, 18–28).

Wyndham Lewis does not stand alone. John Cowper Powys tells us that both Shakespeare and Dostoievsky had 'the magic power of *becoming women*' and complains that modern critics do not take this into account; and he records similar 'Druidic' experiences of his own (*Autobiography*, x, 528). Byron once observed that we could not properly be supposed to understand the desires of the opposite sex, 'unless, like wise Tiresias', we had been able to become that sex (*Don Juan*, xiv, 73). Such, too, is the significance of Tiresias in *The Waste Land*, symbolising the total consciousness at work. Our greater writers all have their share of this supersexual understanding.

Both *A Lover's Complaint* and *Venus and Adonis* recount a heterosexual passion from the woman's view. Shakespeare wrote them; and in so doing he was expressing a similar experience to that of the Sonnets, while *The Rape of Lucrece*, in all its agony of lust and guilt, clearly reflects the darker elements of the poet's association with his mistress. Once we see this, we can see that, though there are in the plays clear examples of homosexual feeling, as in the two Antonio's of *The Merchant of Venice* and *Twelfth Night*, Shakespeare's normal love-poetry may also be relevant. It is always his women, rather than his men, whose love-poetry is most convincing: *Romeo and Juliet* and *Antony and Cleopatra* offer expanded examples of a general tendency, seen in the contrast of Viola and Orsino as lovers (analysed in *Principles of Shakespearian Production*, iii), and in the exquisite love-poetry and strange story of *All's Well that Ends Well* (see p. 54; and compare Helena here with the other man-chasing Helena of *A Midsummer Night's Dream*, whose abandon in humility, as at ii, i, 203–10, recalls Sonnets 57 and 58). Again and again the men ride callously over the love of women; *they* are fine in action and tragedy, the women in love. Where love-poetry is our concern, we look for it in Shakespeare's women; they are his voices, and this, as we shall see (pp. 55, 141), is precisely why Prospero is shown as giving his Miranda, the feminine aspect of his own self, or soul, to mankind. Shakespeare is always 'within' his women, as lovers; the men are, as lovers, presented objectively and critically.

These women may be said to represent the feminine aspect of Shakespeare's own self, or soul. Many writers have observed something strangely wonderful in them. In *Don Juan*, Byron, after calling his Aurora Raby 'a young star', 'too sweet an image' for life's glass, 'a rose with all its sweetest leaves yet folded' (xv, 43), one who 'gazed upon a world she scarcely knew' (xv, 47), passes to a phraseology directly recalling

Shakespeare's description of Marina as 'crown'd Truth' and
Patience (p. 102):

> There was awe in the homage which she drew;
> Her spirit seem'd as seated on a throne
> Apart from the surrounding world, and strong
> In its own strength—most strange in one so young!
>
> (xv, 47)

The comparison is explicit, later on, when she is called 'more
Shakespearian' than Adeline, since

> The worlds beyond this world's perplexing waste
> Had more of her existence, for in her
> There was a depth of feeling to embrace
> Thoughts boundless, deep, but silent too as space.
>
> (xvi, 48)

So, too, Shelley, in *Julian and Maddalo*, writes of Maddalo's
daughter as 'a wonder of this earth' and thing of 'transcendent'
value, 'like one of Shakespeare's women' (590–2).

Their quality is defined by an at-first-sight hostile comment
when Kenneth Muir and Sean O'Loughlin in *The Voyage
to Illyria* (1937) refer to their 'unreality and doll-like character',
adding: 'The Bawds have the sex of women; the heroines only
the virtues' (ii, 26). Rosalind, Viola, and Portia, are called
'magnificent', but 'not human', being portraits of Shakespeare's
'ideal', and we are told that 'the reason is that the heroines
were not drawn from life, but from an idealization of Southampton' (vi, 180). This, with Willie Hughes for Southampton,
had been Wilde's thesis. To Hughes, as actor, were entrusted
the presentation of Shakespeare's 'noble heroines', his 'physical
beauty' being 'the very cornerstone of Shakespeare's art' (*The
Portrait of Mr. W. H.*, 1). James Joyce's Mr. Best was also
probably thinking of Wilde when he remarked of Shakespeare: 'His boy-women are the women of a boy. Their life,
thought, speech, are lent them by males' (*Ulysses*, ed. 1936;
179).

Shakespeare's ladies can indeed be related to his love of the
Fair Youth. Pictorially, they may have been the more inspiring
to him for their frequent use of a boy's dress, and also the easier,
perhaps, for the boy, whoever the actor was, to act. Rosalind

is at one point a boy acting a woman disguised as a boy (significantly named Ganymede) pretending to be a woman! That they
are somehow even the more satisfactory as women for the
nature of the inspiration at work and the manner of their
original performance may be suggested by Mrs. Basham's
remark in Shaw's *In Good King Charles's Golden Days* regretting
the passing from fashion of boy-actors for feminine parts, since
'they could make you believe', as the new actresses could not,
'that you were listening to real women'. Women themselves
regularly accept Shakespeare's women as ringing true. 'Generation after generation', writes Wyndham Lewis discussing this
problem in relation to Shakespeare's Sonnets, 'has marvelled
at the truth and delicacy of Shakespeare's women' (*The Lion
and the Fox*, IV, ii, 154). I would therefore return to my first
statement that they represent *the feminine aspect of Shakespeare's
soul*. That is why they are, despite all idealization, real enough.
I think that Middleton Murry had the truth of it when, in
Adam and Eve (III, ii, 172), he suggested that 'Shakespeare
replaced Our Lady in Heaven by a galaxy of divine and natural
women on earth'.

The tendency to feel love from the woman's standpoint is
not unique to Shakespeare. We find it in Milton, whose Eve
speaks a love-poetry unknown to his Adam; and in Pope, whose
one great love-poem, *Eloisa to Abelard*, is written from within a
woman's experience; and in Byron's exquisite love-descriptions
of Juan as seen from Haidée's standpoint—though there are
good descriptions of Haidée too—in *Don Juan* (Canto II; and
see *The Burning Oracle*, VI, 262–4). Of course, we can say that
this is just one result maturing from the creative, beyond-sex,
consciousness; the consciousness that creates and enjoys any
love-story as a whole. It is so, but with the emphasis we have
noted; and this leads us on.

The creative consciousness is bisexual; otherwise there
could be no creation; and in representing the poet's engagements with both sexes, the Sonnets describe steps on the path
towards the creative integration. They are also the richer for the
further complication of the rival poet, with the accompanying
contrasts of true and false art. The total content is not confined
to love and lust: we are shown these in relation to each other,
and to poetry, true and false (pp. 18–20, 82–3, 94). Every

conceivable ramification of this difficult subject is adumbrated, and all without losing contact with close, human actuality.

The drama of these sonnets may accordingly be known as a workshop, 'the quick forge and working-house of thought' of *Henry V* (v, Chor., 23), widening out to that specific integration, or wholeness, from which the plays were composed. At the moment of artistic creation one is, as Shelley put it in his *Defence of Poetry*, beyond 'every base desire'—lust, ambition, and so on. But the desire is nevertheless within, contained though not apparent. The hair-breadth distinctions and delicate balances involved are exactly symbolised, as I have elsewhere (*Christ and Nietzsche*, v, 179) observed, by Irene in Ibsen's *When We Dead Awaken*. Poetry and all the arts are pointers to that higher state of being momentarily glimpsed in Marvell's *The Garden* ('Two paradises 'twere in one, to live in Paradise alone'), and exactly defined throughout *Thus Spake Zarathustra*; but that is not to say that the artist, as a man, has attained such a state except in and through his art; if he had, he would not be an artist at all. He attains it at moments of creation, that is all, and so do we in responding. At other times, he may fall far below it (p. 128). Such experiences are experiences of wholeness. The perfectly integrated state, which we may call the Christ-state, is necessarily unmarried, since no partner can, for the bisexual integration, be needed, both sexes being complete, and at one, within. The Sonnets show the way towards this state of being. Their poetry, like all poetry, at its best reflects it; but also the contained experiences may be known as stages in the pilgrim's progress recorded.

The integration must clearly use the whole complex content, good and evil, all of it; but nevertheless we can point to certain high moments of positive experience that appear to be the ideal striven for. Such are found in the poet's love for the youth. And yet this ideal, to be an ideal, must itself somehow contain the whole; must have at least something of the Dionysian as well as the Apollonian; and it has, in various ways. There is, if not lust, at least desire, within the poet's love (20, 36; p. 25); the affair we can call pure in action—I am relying on the account as we have it—but saved from limitation by being impure in fantasy. Next, the young man himself gets involved with the siren lady of music, magnetism and lust, and

in himself has, as we shall see, attributes which we may call
'bisexual'. Though mainly Apollonian, he accordingly comes
as near as may be to covering the whole within his own personality, and Shakespeare's love of him is a comprehensive matter.
The best moments are moments of unity when the poet feels
at one with his friend; but his friend possesses also a peculiar
unity; and Shakespeare is bound for another unity. In so far
as there is a union, it is a union not of parts but of unities.

The young man, when we first meet him, is on the youthful
side of sexual maturity. He possesses what might be called the
'lower integration' of youth, and is nearing what might be
called the 'lower maturity' of sexual activity. He is at first
shown as chaste, 'contracted' only to his 'own bright eyes',
feeding his 'light's flame with self-substantial fuel'; as a 'tender
churl' 'niggarding' the world by not marrying (1). Later we
hear how he has presented 'a pure unstained prime', passing
untainted the temptations of youth (70). He has been one
'unmoved, cold and to temptation slow', like Angelo, husband-
ing his 'riches' from 'expense' (94).[1] He enjoys, if only tem-
porarily, a state of self-dependent unity, which is a kind of
'self-love' (3). And he is fond of praise (84). His completeness
is Narcissistic. It is also bisexual. Male youth naturally attracts
in that blend of sexual attributes which Tennyson found in
Hallam as one in whom 'manhood' was 'fused with female
grace' (*In Memoriam*, cix).[2] So Shakespeare writes:

> A woman's face, with Nature's own hand painted,
> Hast thou, the master-mistress of my passion.
>
> (20)

He is both Adonis and Helen (53), and compared to a 'throned
queen' (96). Such comparisons are not absurd for a youth of
refinement and grace. After all, Milton was called 'the lady of
Christ's', and Byron regarded by his friends as a partly feminine
personality, Hobhouse feeling for him as for a 'froward sister'
(*Lord Byron: Christian Virtues*, ii, 95). Byron's Juan is described

[1] Michelangelo's Sonnet 35, telling of a 'cold face' making the poet 'burn', like the
Sun which, though 'temperate', 'inflames the world', develops a conception similar to
Shakespeare's.

[2] The quotation is aptly, if rather reservedly, used by Prof. Hubler writing (97) of
Sonnet 20. The implications, as I see them, go farther than his treatment would allow.

in similar, expressly bisexual, terms, suggesting a blend of
strength and gentleness, as in the pregnant irony of the line,
when he is put in uniform by the Empress Catherine, like
'love turned a lieutenant of artillery' (*Don Juan*, IX, 44). He is
compared to Vergil's Camilla (*Don Juan*, XIV, 39). Once he is
dressed as a girl (*Don Juan*, V, 73–80). Byron's greatest single
human creation, Sardanapalus, is an effeminate type. Or it can
happen the other way round. The bisexual appeal can, dramatically at least, flower from either sex. Whenever, as so often
in Shakespeare's plots, girls appear, to quote Lorenzo, 'in the
lovely garnish of a boy' (*The Merchant of Venice*, II, vi, 45), we
are close to the Sonnets; and as I once, in a note to my discussion of Orsino's love of Viola in *Principles of Shakespearian
Production* (III), suggested, the discovery of the girl beneath the
boy's dress may hold a considerable meaning in answer to
Sonnet 20. Shaw favours effeminate boys such as Marchbanks
and Bentley (in *Candida* and *Missalliance*), and women of action
like Joan.[1]

In, or through, such youthful figures the poet glimpses a
visual objectification, or symbol, of the higher, bisexual, integration which he himself at moments of composition enjoys.
Poetry is itself a bisexual awareness, or action. We have already
referred to the use of Tiresias by Byron and Eliot. Eliot tells
us in his notes that *The Waste Land*, a poem composed largely
of sexual relationships, represents what is *seen* by the bisexual
Tiresias; and Tiresias was used by Byron to signify a resolution
of the conflict of lust and love (*Don Juan*, XIV, 73). Shakespeare's loved youth accordingly represents an ideal beyond the
opposition of biological desire and moral reason so torturingly
present in Sonnet 147. True, the youth shows only the lower
integration, and it is a transient thing. But the poet is bound
for the higher integration, though this has, as in Plato's
Socrates, a far less obvious, and no necessary visual, appeal.
One is young, the other, as the Sonnets keep insisting, old in
comparison. In any ordinary love-affair the male finds completion in the female. Here a completed unit, for at choice
moments the poet attains to such a state, sees its soul-state

[1] The substance of this section has been carefully argued and elaborated in my
Christ and Nietzsche (IV) to which I must refer my readers. It is impossible to cover all
the relevant subtleties and adjustments here.

reflected in a physical embodiment of its own unity; and from that unique experience flower our supreme pieces.

These are, like the comparable sonnets of Michelangelo, simultaneously sexually impregnated, and indeed burning with sexual, or homosexual, passion, yet chaste; as when Socrates in *The Symposium* is shown as refusing physical contact with Alcibiades. The lover may even compare himself to a 'father' or 'nurse' (37, 22); but we must guard against any dilution of the sexual content. The higher integration is non-physical, not through any absence of sexual power, but through an abundance and plenitude of sexual accomplishment *within*. Our poet explicitly asserts that he is rendered tongue-tied by his very 'abundance', being 'o'ercharged with burthen of mine own love's might' (23; and see pp. 112, 124–7). The lover is, like the youth, independent; but he nevertheless likes to *see* the image; to see the reflection of, or analogy to, his own soul-state in the objective world. More, he wishes to be one with it; it is more than visual symbolism. He desires, and at choice moments reaches, union; but the union can only be given physical expression through 'eyes'. And here we must turn to the poetry.

The experience recorded is a matter of seeing, of ' imagination' in the exact sense of the word. That is why 'eyes' are so often mentioned.

Eyes are in Shakespeare love's especial intermediaries as in 'I think she means to tangle my eyes too' in *As You Like It* (III, v, 44), or 'they have changed eyes' in *The Tempest* (I, ii, 438). They are important throughout *Cymbeline* (*The Crown of Life*, IV, 200). They are active powers, agents; they do more than reflect. Through sense-perception love awakes:

> I take today a wife, and my election
> Is led on in the conduct of my will;
> My will, enkindled by mine eyes and ears,
> Two traded pilots 'twixt the dangerous shores
> Of will and judgment.
> (*Troilus and Cressida*, II, ii, 61)

That is, dormant desire ('will') is awakened by the senses and made the property of consciousness ('judgment': the passage is analysed in *The Wheel of Fire*, III, 53–4). Eyes are, however, more important than ears; they are 'that most pure spirit of

sense' (*Troilus and Cressida*, III, iii, 106; p. 40). So in the
Sonnets we have, 'To hear with eyes belongs to love's fine wit'
(23). In Biron's great speech on love, they are emphatic:
'From women's eyes this doctrine I derive', 'But love, first
learned in a lady's eyes' (*Love's Labour's Lost*, IV, iii, 302, 327).
Here love is a supreme wisdom and power; and so, too,
Shakespeare 'derives' 'knowledge', or wisdom, from the youth's
eyes shining like 'constant stars' (14). He cannot describe their
beauty (17). They are themselves sources of light, 'gilding'
the object on which their lustre falls (20), like the Sun. The
poet's own eyes cast beams (114). The Sun's light is a 'sovereign eye' (33), and 'that sun, thine eye' (49) comes in naturally.
Eyes may even be 'hungry' (56).

They can, however, be deceptive, and contrasted with more
inward faculties. The song in the Casket scene of *The Merchant
of Venice* contrasts 'fancy' and 'eyes' with 'heart' and 'head' to
indicate a superficiality (III, ii, 64) ; and a similar contrast
is driven home by Hector's lines on the deceiving 'will' in
Troilus and Cressida (II, ii, 51–8). With the Dark Lady the
lover's eyes have 'no correspondence with true sight' (148).
They are 'corrupt'; love has forged 'hooks' of his eyes' false-
hood to hold the 'judgment' of his 'heart', though 'judgment'
may also be said to 'censure falsely' what the 'eyes' had
correctly seen (137, 148; cp. 'eyes', 'will' and 'judgment' in
Troilus' speech above; p. 37). 'Heart' is a usual contrast:
perhaps he does not love her with his 'eyes' at all, since they
observe errors, so it must be his 'heart' that loves (141).

'Eyes' and 'heart' are regularly balanced in addressing the
youth:

> Mine eye and heart are at a mortal war
> How to divide the conquest of thy sight.
>
> (46)

Here 'sight' comes first, but each claims the picture. The eye
holds 'thy outward part', but the heart 'thine inward love of
heart': 'heart' is inward, and there heart speaks direct to
heart (46). It is the problem of Michelangelo's Sonnet 25, and
of Marvell's *Garden*. Which is the truth? The trees and bushes,
or those 'far other', spiritual, realities which are un-individu-
alised, a one-ness only to be defined as 'a green thought in a

green shade'? Is the wondrous thing objective, or is the seen object merely a starting point, a hint? In the next sonnet (47), eye and heart decide to collaborate: in absence 'eyes' invite the 'heart' to the 'painted banquet' of the loved one's image, awaking the inward faculties to enjoyment (as in *Troilus and Cressida*, II, ii, 61–5; p. 37 above). The poet is striving to express a unity of object and subject, of sense and soul; of Apollonian and Dionysian.

The treatment remains primarily Apollonian and visual, with references to the visual arts. It is, perhaps, and despite our earlier argument, rather too Apollonian to last, and if there be any imperfection in the experience, that is where to look for it. We have the 'painted banquet' just noted (47); the youth's beauty is said to be 'with nature's own hand painted' (20); 'painted counterfeit' (16) and 'painted beauty' (21) are used derogatorily, in contrast to the real thing; 'false painting' dishonours him (67; see p. 20 above); 'blazon' is used to fine effect (106), and his 'copy' is to be 'printed' in a son (11).[1] In night-visions the image is more spiritualised:

> Save that my soul's imaginary sight
> Presents thy shadow to my sightless view.
>
> (27)

Here the sight is internal. When parted from his friend, his eyes 'best see' when shut, and, 'darkly bright', visualise in sleep the youth's 'fair imperfect shade' (43). The poet is throughout captured by his 'sweet form' (13), and recognises his presence in every 'blessed shape' (53). The typifying word is 'image' (3, 24, 31, 59, 61). The 'image' of 'this composed wonder of your frame' might be found in some 'antique book' (59): it is an archetypal, eternal, image, a suggestion carried also by 'pattern' in 'beauty's pattern to succeeding men' (19; and see 98). The word 'image' suggests some ultimate authority beyond fancy, or perhaps sense-perception, as in Hector's criticism of any adoration pursued 'without some image of the affected merit' (*Troilus and Cressida*, II, ii, 60; *The Wheel of Fire*, III, 53).

But this mysterious 'image', despite all Hector can tell us, and however eternal, archetypal, or spiritual it may be, has in

[1] A usual Shakespearian metaphor: see *The Wheel of Fire*, 1949, App. B, 333.

fact been experienced only through the miracle of '*this composed wonder of your frame*' (59). The greatness of Shakespeare's poetry matures from his refusal to indulge in vague speculations. He keeps as close as may be to sense-experience, and yet in these terms he attains, at moments, the transparency indicated by Lysander's:

> Transparent Helena! Nature shows art
> That through thy bosom makes me see thy heart.
>
> (*A Midsummer Night's Dream*, II, ii, 104)

Both poetic insight and love reveal, or appear to reveal, the true self, or soul, of the loved one. Or the lover may seem to be drawing the picture of his loved one in his own soul. This experience is expressed in a very difficult sonnet:

> Mine eye hath play'd the painter and hath stell'd
> Thy beauty's form in table of my heart;
> My body is the frame wherein 'tis held,
> And, perspective, it is best painter's art—
> For through the painter must you see his skill,
> To find where your true image pictur'd lies—
> Which in my bosom's shop is hanging still,
> That hath his windows glazed with thine eyes.
> Now see what good turns eyes for eyes have done:
> Mine eyes have drawn thy shape, and thine for me
> Are windows to my breast, where-through the Sun
> Delights to peep, to gaze therein on thee;
> Yet eyes this cunning want to grace their art,
> They draw but what they see, know not the heart.
>
> (24)

This we may compare with Achilles' lines in *Troilus and Cressida*:

> The beauty that is borne here in the face
> The bearer knows not, but commends itself
> To others' eyes; nor doth the eye itself,
> That most pure spirit of sense, behold itself,
> Not going from itself; but eye to eye oppos'd
> Salutes each other with each other's form;
> For speculation turns not to itself,
> Till it hath travell'd, and is mirror'd there
> Where it may see itself.
>
> (III, iii, 103)

Achilles, probably thinking of Patroclus, speaks in the idiom of our sonnet. The speech is analysed in *The Wheel of Fire* (XIII, 263).

What the sonnet says is something like this: My eye has engraved your form in my mind or soul ('heart'), which is enclosed in my bodily 'frame'. People (for the generalised sense of 'you' and 'your' in distinction from 'thy' and 'thee' before and after, see Tucker's notes) must now look through me to see your real self ('true image') represented in my breast's workshop (for 'shop' see Tucker's note), of which your eyes are, paradoxically, the windows, since I can only see the image in me by gazing at you; or perhaps, by being aware of you gazing at me ('thine for me . . .breast'). The Sun itself delights to look, not simply, as Tucker takes it, 'into my breast', but rather 'through these windows, *your* eyes, into *my* breast, where it sees *you*'.

The Sun we may, I think, equate with the mind of God, some greater consciousness enjoying and using human experience; or perhaps the mysterious 'love' to which we refer when we say that two people are 'in love with' each other (*The Christian Renaissance*, XI, 311).[1]

Our sonnet may be compared with Michelangelo's (8) on the boy Cecchino Bracci, addressed to Luigi del Riccio. The boy's eyes are to his lover's eyes 'life and light'. One line makes a neat Shakespearian correspondence: 'If the beloved within the lover shine'. Such thought-mechanisms were, of course, widely used. In Shakespeare's sonnet they are most intricately exploited. It is an excellent example of what might appear merely 'conceits' (Tucker's notes, despite the care of his analysis, regard it as a 'trifling composition' of 'far-fetched conceits'), but which are really working to annihilate the subject-object antinomy in terms of two personalities in love, without losing contact with sense-perception; to assert a transparency and union in terms of eyes (as with Donne's 'our

---

[1] I sometimes wonder if the 'Mr. W. H.' called 'the only begetter' of the Sonnets in Thorpe's dedication might refer to *both* the lovers, one initial taken from each. I am indebted for this thought to Walter Thomson (*The Sonnets of William Shakespeare and Henry Wriothesley*, XI, 80). Mr. Thomson is, however, arguing that the Sonnets were jointly composed by Shakespeare and Southampton. That is unlikely enough; but a more general truth, having nothing to do with Southampton or any joint authorship at all, might conceivably be adumbrated by his suggestion.

eye-beams twisted, and did thread our eyes upon one double string' in *The Ecstasy*). Our sonnet describes an eye-union resembling sexual intercourse, but fully conscious, mental, alert. We find it again in *The Phoenix and the Turtle*:

> So between them love did shine,
> That the Turtle saw his right
> Flaming in the Phoenix' sight;
> Either was the other's mine.

Here the shining 'love' corresponds to our sonnet's 'Sun'. Further analysis would be unprofitable; thought and imagery are strained to the limit. The sonnet's final couplet returns to common-sense, and falls back, with suggestion of an anti-climax, on the inadequacy of 'eyes' and the supremacy of 'heart'. This is a necessary submission: the miraculous perfection cannot be maintained, the mirror in the still pool gets ruffled, and we are forced back on inward, or abstract, categories.

The union, or unity, is elsewhere expressed in more normal terminology. During absence the loved-one is felt to be, though it is admitted that in fact he is not, 'within the gentle closure of my breast' (48). The poet can as easily leave himself as his 'soul' lodged in the other's 'breast' (109). He is 'mine own self' (39), 'my next self' (133); 'thee, myself' is used as an appositional equivalence (62). If his mistress loves his friend, it scarcely matters, since he and his friend are 'one' (42). He is 'all the better part of me' (39). The unity expressed is that of Romeo's, 'It is my soul that calls upon my name' (*Romeo and Juliet*, II, ii, 164); of Viola's 'call upon my soul within the house' (*Twelfth Night*, I, v, 290); or Cathy's words in *Wuthering Heights*, 'I am Heathcliff.' The paradoxes of *The Phoenix and the Turtle* come as near as may be to a satisfactory definition.

The unity is not maintained. As the sequence develops the lovers appear to draw apart. 'Let me confess that we two must be twain', even though 'one' in 'love', occurs early (36), followed by 'even for this let us divided live' (39). The division here is certainly rather obscure; but it becomes more definite. We can detect two main causes: (i) the youth's behaviour, and (ii) Shakespeare's growing self-sufficiency.

The young man had been idealised: he is not exactly the

poet's self, but rather his *higher* self. He is 'all the better part of me' (39), 'my spirit is thine, the better part of me' (74). The test was severe. At first the boy's 'inward worth' was coupled with his 'outward fair' (16). But his chaste reserve, or what Shakespeare took to be that, seems to have, as one might expect, given way to natural instinct. When we hear that the boy is growing old (pp. 10, 14–15, 72), this probably means only that he is losing his youthful, pre-sexual, innocence and grace. But the poet goes further, balancing physical and mental, hinting doubts as to 'the beauty of thy mind', contrasting 'flowers' with 'the rank smell of weeds' and 'canker vice', and saying bitterly that 'Thou dost common grow' (69, 70). For some 'sensual' fault or faults, the youth is called 'lascivious grace, in whom all ill well shows' (35, 40). His looks remain heavenly, though his 'thoughts' or 'heart's workings' suggest 'Eve's apple' (93); 'lilies that fester smell far worse than weeds' (94); his 'sweets' veil 'sins', 'lascivious comments' are being made on his 'sport', 'vices' inhabit the lovely 'mansion' (95); 'wantonness' and 'sport' (i.e. probably sexual indulgence), though some are excusing them as faults of 'youth' and breeding, appear to be gaining him an ill 'report' (96). Shakespeare had apparently found, like Troilus, that 'eye' and 'heart', or 'mind', do not always correspond; he claims to have suffered bitterly through some 'crime', or fault (p. 127), of the young man (120). But we need not assume that the youth was really bad. He had been built into an ideal of Apollonian purity and perfected integration, and failed to live the part. He had fallen to the lower stage of sexuality; in other words, he had grown up. Dionysus, or, remembering the *Hippolytus*, Aphrodite, has come into the picture, and spoilt it.

These aspersions are not continued beyond Sonnet 96, and from then onwards we find another sort, of greater interest, indicating that Shakespeare was being reproached by the youth for his lack of ardour. This theme, which had occurred earlier (e.g. 83–6), now becomes insistent. The young man was, it seems, looking older (pp. 10, 15), and Shakespeare's interest may have suffered, though he still asserts: 'To me, fair friend, you never can be old' (104). When we realise that 'old' may mean merely the loss of adolescent and so bisexual charm, we see the poet's difficulty, since what meant so much to him *is* passing. Youth is here a positive, and high, if not supreme, value, and that is why his friend was called 'most rich in youth' (15). Those riches are going, and the poet's muse has of late been forgetful; he can't write as he used to (100–3); worse, he has been found out giving away one of the young man's presents (122). Shakespeare, as lover, may seem to be cutting a poor figure. To these important sonnets we shall return (pp. 112–36 below).

The Fair Youth, possessing the lower integration of youthful, and therefore in a sense bisexual, charm and grace, has been pointing the poet, through experiences of unity, towards the higher, spiritual, integration. This is the deep meaning within the poet's thought that he cannot be old so long as 'time' spares the boy's beauty, which is the 'seemly' (i.e. appropriate) 'raiment' of his own 'heart' (22). But not only does the boy grow up and indulge in the crude instincts of manhood; the poet himself, driven on by the boy's creative image, begins to enjoy the self-sufficiency, or integration, which he has been attributing to the youth (pp. 34–7). He is accordingly disturbed; he is losing his ideal through possessing it. He appears to have felt this coming as early as Sonnet 56, where he cries, 'Sweet love, renew thy force,' fearing the thought that love should pass like a satiated appetite. Again,

> Sin of self-love possesseth all mine eye
> And all my soul and all my every part;
> And for this sin there is no remedy,
> It is so grounded inward in my heart.
>
> (62)

He is becoming inwardly, or spiritually ('heart'), self-sufficient. The experience, and this happens elsewhere in the Sonnets, is given expression of an almost too naïvely concrete kind. Everything is physically projected; and so here self-love must needs be a matter of admiring oneself in a glass. The poet does so, but finding himself 'beated and chopp'd with tann'd antiquity', he realises that his self-love is a sin, and concludes:

> 'Tis thee, myself, that for myself I praise,
> Painting my age with beauty of thy days.
>
> (62)

He says, in effect: 'I am only growing self-sufficient by attuning my soul to *your* beauty.' We now see why, in terms of the Sonnets' thought-moulds, which preserve a concrete sense-perception almost to absurdity, the poet must call himself old to define the inward worth with outward lack of beauty of the higher integration in contrast to its visual equivalent in the young man. And when, in the later sonnets, he is found apologising for his reluctance to hand out more praise, we may suppose him being gradually forced to suspect that the youth had been a symbol of his own integration quest, and no more. And he is half-ashamed.

But the central experience, however evanescent, had, and has, its rights. We may even hazard the thought that it was something greater, and not less, than an ordinary love. It was certainly far more than an aesthetic indulgence, being throughout entangled with inward and spiritual apprehensions. The attraction was one of 'both truth and beauty' (101). When we are pointed to a 'truth' and 'beauty' born of the boy's 'eyes', which are said to be both 'knowledge' and 'art' (14), we may recall the 'truth' and 'beauty' of *The Phoenix and the Turtle* and Keats' *Ode on a Grecian Urn*. Again, in contrast to the rival poet's learning:

> But thou art all my art, and dost advance
> As high as learning my rude ignorance.
>
> (78)

He is 'truth in beauty dy'd' (101); one of 'the rarities of Nature's truth', one of nature's ideal forms (60); and that is why, in so far as he is himself inconstant, Shakespeare feels himself guilty of having 'look'd on truth askance and strangely' (110).

But what else was possible? 'To be wise and love', we are told in *Troilus and Cressida* (III, ii, 163), 'exceeds man's might', and belongs only to god-hood. The experience of love cannot easily be held in full consciousness. The problem is generally in Shakespeare, as I have elsewhere shown at length (*The Wheel of Fire*, XIII, 261–2; *The Imperial Theme*, IX, 332–3 and note; *The Shakespearian Tempest*, App. A, 308–19), expressed in terms of 'swift thought' and allied images of volatility: the difficult intuitions are too fast for the mind. Thought is miraculous: separation is once welcomed, since it forces the poet to *think* the unity (39). The relation of thought to space is carefully developed in another sonnet of separation:

> For nimble thought can jump both sea and land
> As soon as think the place where he would be.
> But ah, thought kills me that I am not thought . . .
>
> (44)

Any discussion of spirit-nature will converge on this particular mystery for which space is non-existent. Here Shakespeare associates his bodily life with 'earth' and 'water'; but, in the following sonnet (45), thinks of that in himself which is rather 'air' and 'fire' (cp. 'Love is a spirit all compact of fire', in *Venus and Adonis*, 149, and Cleopatra's 'I am fire and air', in contrast to the 'other elements', at *Antony and Cleopatra*, v, ii, 291). This, his thought-self, his spirit-self, with 'thought' and 'desire' corresponding to 'air' and 'fire', is always with his friend. These elements, like Ariel in *The Tempest*, are space-negating as they 'present-absent with swift motion glide' in 'tender embassy of love' (45), for the loved one cannot outdistance his 'thoughts' (47).

Such intuitions are given a more concrete embodiment in two sonnets (50, 51) on the poet's horse. The beast is praised for plodding slowly as he rides from his friend. But on returning, as with Romeo's school-boy from his books (*Romeo and Juliet*, II, ii, 156-7), 'swift extremity can seem but slow':

> Then should I spur though mounted on the wind;
> In winged speed no motion shall I know.
>
> (51)

Love, being of a 'fiery race' (cp. 'a race of heaven' of *Antony and Cleopatra*, I, iii, 37), will run ahead to meet its desire (cp. 'run' at the conclusion to Marvell's *To his Coy Mistress*). Love will replace the horse, or become a super-horse. Horses in Shakespeare often hold aerial and spiritual meaning, as in the Dauphin's speech in *Henry V* and elsewhere (*Henry V*, III, vii, 1-44; *The Shakespearian Tempest*, App. A, 314-15). They conform to the archetype of Pegasus, and Pegasus can be a symbol of poetry.

Poetry is the natural medium for these swift, uncapturable and comprehensive, intuitions. So it is through the poet's verse alone that the perfumed 'truth' of the 'rose' which is his beloved friend can be 'distilled' (54). The rose undistilled cannot for long be possessed, or even, perhaps, endured. To have met an absolute 'best', composed of 'truth' and 'beauty' (101), is embarrassing. The poet has drunk deeply of some supernal excellence to which neither of the lovers as men can permanently adjust themselves. It is too vast:

> For nothing this wide universe I call,
> Save thou, my rose; in it thou art my all.
>
> (109)

He is 'my all the world'; beside him 'all the world' are 'dead' (112). We think of Antony's 'new heaven, new earth', needed for love's reckoning; of Cleopatra's speech at Antony's death, of her dream of the universal Antony (*Antony and Cleopatra*, I, i, 17; v, ii, 76–92). The poet's eyes, indeed, have had to 'wink with fulness', close themselves against too powerful a light (56); he is 'incapable of more' (i.e. 'has no room for anything else'), 'replete with you' (113); at the limit, he calls it, in a sonnet which we shall discuss later (pp. 124–7), a sickness (118).

It is easy to see why Shakespeare's love-poetry became tongue-tied. The love was at once too complete, and perhaps too purely Apollonian, for continued and varied exploitation:

> What's in the brain, that ink may character,
> Which hath not figur'd to thee my true spirit?
> What's new to speak, what new to register,
> That may express my love, or thy dear merit?
> Nothing, sweet boy; but yet, like prayers divine,
> I must each day say o'er the very same . . .
>
> (108)

It is not so easy to keep on doing that, and maintain a standard. After all, poetry is born of unreachable desire, the will to attune oneself to an object. But Shakespeare was now identified, not exactly, I think, with the loved youth, the rose, but rather with the rose 'distill'd' (pp. 47, 88, 181), the vision, the image, the archetypal and eternal form seen through him; and whether this be the boy, or the boy's greater soul-self, or Shakespeare's soul, or a reality beyond which one or both of these reflect, we need not decide. This poetic distillation had become a lasting possession, a vast, expanding, inspiration, which was both the youth (as, beauty, truth, and muse; pp. 45, 107) and the feminine principle in Shakespeare's soul (pp. 30–3); both Phoenix and Turtle, Ariel and Miranda (pp. 55–6). But what was left for either of them, as lovers stretched out in temporal existence? The boy was growing, and Shakespeare more and more dominated by a demanding vision, got from the boy in his period of youthful integration. After being thus distilled, it seems that the young man, who cannot be expected to have understood the forces at play, rather pathetically, and not unnaturally, complained of neglect, and perhaps eventually handed the Sonnets to Thorpe; and that is all we know of him. As for Shakespeare, with what may appear the callousness of genius, he proceeded—a second-best, no doubt, but what else was he to do?—to compose, or continue composing, the works of Shakespeare. The love-story was at an end, as in *The Phoenix and the Turtle*:

> To this urn let those repair
> That are either true or fair;
> For these dead birds sigh a prayer.

Such may, perhaps, be one meaning of this strangely wonderful poem.[1]

We have now given a brief outline of the progress to integration shadowed by the Sonnets. We are not claiming any particular status for Shakespeare as a man, but only for his poetry, or for the man in the creative act. There is evidence that Shakespeare was indulging in 'public manners' late in the sequence (111). The perfectly integrated, beyond-sex, man would not be primarily an artist; and yet art is the only language of integration. That art Shakespeare attained, and the Sonnets help us to understand its origins.

Whether the more vicious elements in our story are necessary to the result, we need not pause to enquire. According to Nietzsche, it seems that chastity can be maintained on the path (*Thus Spake Zarathustra*, 1, 13; or, if the Introductory Discourse be numbered, 1, 14); and the Christian tradition supports him, as well as Plato. Saints and philosophers tend to

---

[1] The relation of *The Phoenix and the Turtle* to the Sonnets is not, of course, new: see Kenneth Muir and Sean O'Loughlin, *The Voyage to Illyria*, v; also my reference to Charles Downing on p. 193.

emphasise chastity, while the biographies of poets (e.g. Dante, Shakespeare, Goethe, Burns, Byron) record a fair amount of free love. For Shakespeare we have few details. But once at least he appears to assert some kind of beyond-good-and-evil claim:

> 'Tis better to be vile than vile esteemed,
> When not to be receives reproach of being,
> And the just pleasure lost, which is so deemed
> Not by our feeling, but by others' seeing:
> For why should others' false adulterate eyes
> Give salutation to my sportive blood,
> Or on my frailties why are frailer spies,
> Which in their wills count bad what I think good?
> No, I am that I am, and they that level
> At my abuses reckon up their own:
> I may be straight, though they themselves be bevel;
> By their rank thoughts my deeds must not be shown;
>   Unless this general evil they maintain:
>   All men are bad and in their badness reign.
>
> (121)

This is a crucial and a difficult sonnet.

Tucker's paraphrase of lines 1–8 runs:

It is better to *be* vicious than to be *thought* vicious, when, though one is *not* so, one is reproached as *being* so, and when (meanwhile) there is not obtained (as some compensation) the *pleasure* (from the vice) which (in the circumstances) would only be fair, (though in point of fact it would not be real pleasure, but only pleasure) which is *deemed* so by others' way of *looking* at it, and not by any such *feeling* on our *own* part: (not felt as such, I say), for why should any wantonness in *my* blood be aroused by what *others*, misled by their lewdness, choose to see (in a certain connection), or why are frailer men on the watch for frailties in me, choosing at their own good pleasure to find badness where I find nothing but innocence?

He continues by rendering 'I am that I am' by what appears to be a simple statement of rectitude: 'No base thinking on their part will make me anything else.' For 'my abuses' we have 'errors and lapses *ascribed* to me'; for line 12, 'What is *done* by *me* is not to be judged by what is *thought* by *them*'; and for the last couplet, 'Unless they assert this (following) general rule as to evil, that *all* men are bad, and are prevailingly so in *their* particular form of badness' (Tucker, pp. 198–9).

The paraphrase, which reduces the sonnet to a statement of uncompromising innocence, is not beyond criticism. 'So deemed', though it follows 'pleasure', is clearer if it refers back to 'vile', the rhyme of 'esteeméd' and 'deeméd' *as dissyllables* (Quarto) assisting. Tucker's reading cramps too much un-assimilated thought into a single line; what we want is a meaning that is better supported by the sonnet as a whole. The 'eyes' giving 'salutation' Tucker calls 'a condensed expression', and translates it: 'Lewd men find their own blood "saluted" when they look at a certain object, but why should *I* find the same salutation because of what *they* see?' That is, surely, to expand it beyond all reason. 'Give salutation to' he reads, in effect, as 'arouse sexual excitement in', and quotes Ann Boleyn in *Henry VIII* (ii, iii, 102), 'Would I had no being if this salute my blood a jot.' There 'blood' is not specifically sexual; and it is doubtful if 'salute' can mean exactly 'arouse'. We have recently (p. 40) quoted Achilles' words:

> . . . but eye to eye oppos'd
> Salutes each other with each other's form.
> (*Troilus and Cressida*, iii, iii, 107)

Here the act of seeing is in question, and so it is, with 'eyes', in our sonnet. Some sort of *recognition* is implied by the word; perhaps visual recognition, and perhaps, too, a pleasure in the recognition. Ann Boleyn, who has just heard of the King's favour to her, may mean: 'Would I had no being if this news and my instincts recognise each other'; that is, if I am responsive to it. Or there may be a suggestion of flattery: 'if I am flattered by it'. Tucker's meaning may here be reached, but only as a derivative. I would accordingly render 'give salutation to my sportive blood' as 'enjoy prying into and recognising the secrets of my sexual life'.

The contrast of 'frailties' and 'frailer' is killed by Tucker's rendering, which does not admit any real content to 'frailties' at all; 'in their wills' is better rendered—he admits a possible overtone—'from their lustful viewpoint'. 'I am that I am' loses all force if it means no more than 'I am good.' His rendering of 'abuses' (as with 'frailties' before) as *imaginary* abuses only weakens what is otherwise a strong line. 'I *may* be straight' asserts a triumphant revelation, with the implication 'after all', not merely a reiteration of 'I am good'; and 'though they themselves be bevel' contains the thought, 'even though their wrongheadedness seems at first to be the correct thing'; otherwise 'may' and 'though' are pointless. Tucker's conclusion, instead of raising great issues of good and evil, becomes merely a trite statement that such men apparently think everyone as bad as themselves. His reading of the phrase 'their badness' as referring to the critics' own particular form of licentious badness is surely a straining of syntax.

Here is my alternative: 'Since I am being unjustly slandered, I might as well be thoroughly vicious. As it is, I merely lose the corresponding pleasure, which anyway only appears evil from an objective and impersonal viewpoint, and would not necessarily be felt as such, inwardly, by me. Why should the lustful and falsifying eyes of other people enjoy recognising and prying into the secrets of my sexual indulgence? Why should my own weakness be scrutinised by those far worse, if the truth were known, than myself; people who, by reason of their own lustful propensities, consider evil something which I consider good? I refuse to submit to their judgments. I am being true to my own nature, and those who criticise my faults are in reality recording their own limitations by so doing. The truth may well be that I am running straight after all, even though their wrong-headedness cannot see it; it is they who are crooked. I will not have my actions assessed and labelled by moralists whose thoughts are thoroughly unclean: it is their thoughts that are evil, not my actions. The only way to make sense of their attitude would be to suppose that man is by nature a wicked creature, human instinct vitiated at its source, and that evil rules the world; which would be a strange conclusion when we consider the greatness of mankind.'

The poet's use of 'reign' is difficult. I have split its content into 'rules the world' and 'the greatness of mankind'. Tucker's translation in terms of 'an overwhelming majority' does slight justice to its dominating position. His whole paraphrase reduces to little more than a statement that the poet is being slandered. He is made to say: 'People speak ill of me. The pleasures they think me guilty of would not be real pleasures to me. My sexual instincts are not aroused so easily as they think. No. I have always been a moral man, and still am so. They are lying.' There are occasions when we all have to speak like this, but it seldom, for some reason, makes great literature, and is usually best done in simple prose. Surely our sonnet is a little more exciting? After all, Shakespeare elsewhere confesses to 'lust', 'public manners' and so on (pp. 15–16, 117), and 'deeds' is a recurring word for such faults (p. 17).

I am not, however, advancing any arguments about Shakespeare's actions. Certainly, we must not refer this piece to his relations with the Fair Youth, since it comes within a series where he is apparently defending himself against the young man's complaints as to his general behaviour as reported by scandal-mongers. We can deduce no specific actions from it; nor, in view of the word 'deeds', can we easily suppose that there were none. Shakespeare may, with the sensitiveness of a Byron, have been ready enough to malign himself. He once, in exactly Byronic style (*Lord Byron: Christian Virtues*, Index A, IV, 'Self-Accusations'), claims to know more about his own 'weakness' than anyone, is willing to fight 'against' himself, and offers a whole 'story' of 'faults concealed' (88). He is fighting much the same battle as Byron. Shakespeare could be a stern self-critic: we know how readily lust raised his revulsions. But he knew that there was much to be said on the other side too, and we find this sonnet saying it. Our concern is with something more subtle and less easily definable than any specific action; with something deep within the human psyche, entwined with sexual stimulus, which is, or may be, at once less than action and more than morality (*Christ and Nietzsche*, IV, 135–8; V, 214–15); and it is with this core of the personality that our sonnet is primarily concerned. Read so, its relation to Pope's *Essay on Man*, the thought of Blake, Byron's life, Nietzsche's philosophy, Bridges' *Testament of Beauty*, and much else in Renaissance literature, will be clear. It is all one statement.

It is only because Shakespeare had, in certain moods, the mood of this sonnet, penetrated beyond good and evil, that he could deploy their interaction with so impersonal a clarity;[1]

[1] I would here draw attention to Mr. T. S. Eliot's words in his introduction to my *Wheel of Fire*: 'For the very Catholic philosophy of Dante, with its stern judgment of morals, leads us to the same point beyond good and evil as the pattern of Shakespeare' (xx).

just as he was the better able to create men and women in their normal relationships by reason of his own, abnormal, bi-sexuality, or integration. Beside 'I am that I am' we can surely place Gloucester's remark in *3 Henry VI* (v, vi, 83), 'I am myself alone.' Whatever the dark, or seemingly dark, thing behind our sonnet, it held the germ of *Richard III*, Iago, *Macbeth*. Evil must be assimilated; and in our story, with all its various suggestions of lust and vice, it is certainly contained. We gladly recognise (pp. 24–5, 30, 34) that even Shakespeare's love for the Fair Youth does not appear immaculate.

The main themes of the Sonnets are reflected in Shake-speare's other work. *A Lover's Complaint*, which was published with them, turns on what looks like a rather bitter study of the same young man; *Venus and Adonis* and *The Rape of Lucrece*, taken together, balance love for a young man against lust for a lady, as do the Sonnets; and *The Phoenix and the Turtle* condenses their central statement of spiritual union in a series of tight paradoxes. All Shakespeare's poems inter-relate.

His drama necessarily shows variations. We shall speak of it in general later on (pp. 109–11, 139). From the conflict of love's idealism and lust's revulsion much of Shakespeare's greater work matures; while *Antony and Cleopatra* fascinatingly fuses into a single splendour a sublimated love in terms of 'lips' 'eyes' and 'brows' (I, iii, 35–6) and a harshly criticised lust, thus compacting—and herein lies its peculiar supremity—the two main themes of the Sonnets.[1] I would here point to three strange works as especially revealing: *Troilus and Cressida*, *Timon of Athens*, and *All's Well that Ends Well*.

The first narrates a closely similar love-experience to that of the Sonnets and indulges in the same kind of metaphysical discussion, some passages of which we have quoted (pp. 37–41). That an edition was published with the claim that it had never been staged and 'clapper-claw'd' by the 'vulgar' might suggest a peculiarly personal reason for its composition, while reminding us of the aspersions on the stage to be found in Sonnets 110 and 111 (pp. 9, 116–17), and probably also intended

[1] My remarks here on *Antony and Cleopatra* may be compared with those of Muir and O'Loughlin in *The Voyage to Illyria*, VIII, 209–10.

by the 'worthless song' and 'base subjects' of Sonnet 100
(pp. 112–13).

Our next, *Timon of Athens*, which I have elsewhere (*The
Wheel of Fire*, x, 211) compared in point of passionate friendship with the Sonnets, and which might conceivably have been
prompted by their publication in 1609, if that be not too late
a dating for the play, is Shakespeare's grandest expression of a
universal love for men and the most violent exposition of his
recurring theme of ingratitude. The feminine interest falls here
to the semi-masculine Amazons of the dance, the two pros-
titutes, Phrynia and Timandra, and Timon's denunciatory
speeches loaded with sexual disgust. Clearly, this strange play
repeats what many would call the unhealthy balance of the
Sonnets. Unhealthy it may be, and certainly abnormal; but if
there were no divagations from normality, we should have no
Shakespeares.

Our third, *All's Well that Ends Well*, registers an extreme
development of the poet's tendency to express his love-instincts
through a woman. Helena is a spiritualised version of Venus
and Bertram remarkably like the men, or man, of the Sonnets
and *A Lover's Complaint*. *All's Well that Ends Well* contains
more than this; very much more. It is, I think, a more deeply
important play than has as yet been recognised, and this I hope
to show in a considered analysis at not too distant a date.
Meanwhile, I am content to indicate its relation to the Sonnets
and suggest that it was written, or at least revised, later than
is usually supposed.

These three difficult and rather exceptionally personal-
seeming plays are, within our present context, highly significant.[1] And there is one more. Once only did Shakespeare
succeed in expressing his own integration-pattern in terms of
an acceptable stage-piece for an average audience; and this was
done through a highly symbolical work which can be accepted
on the lower plane as a fantasy. *The Tempest*, as I have shown
in *The Crown of Life*, may be called the dramatist's 'artistic
autobiography'. It also makes a perfect introduction to Shakespeare's work, and perhaps that is why it was placed first in the
Folio. The main persons are Prospero as controlling and

---

[1] From the start, I have myself tended to group *Troilus and Cressida* and *Timon of
Athens* together as peculiarly philosophic works: see *The Wheel of Fire*, XII, 252.

directing power; Ariel, Caliban, and Miranda as coadjutors, all three being part of Prospero's own, intimate, world; and a varied, but typical, assortment, of mankind. For brevity, I give my correspondences crudely.

Prospero is, from this view, Shakespeare, or Shakespeare's controlling 'judgment' (the correct Shakespearian word: see pp. 15, 37–8). Ariel, with his two female disguises, has something in common with the Fair Youth, being a-sexual or, like Shelley's very similar Hermaphrodite (*The Starlit Dome*, III, 228) in *The Witch of Atlas*, bisexual; and also coldly unemotional (compare 'Mine would, sir, were I human' at v, i, 20 with 'unmoved, cold and to temptation slow' in Sonnet 94). His symbolic function as the spirit of poetry, corresponding to Goethe's 'boy-charioteer' in the second part of *Faust* (I) and Shelley's Hermaphrodite, may be related to the youth's emphasised function, which we shall study later (pp. 104–13), as inspiration, or 'muse'. He is, like that part of Shakespeare which loves the youth (pp. 45–6; also 28, 89), a creature of air and fire. For a more exact study of these significances, I must point to my considered analysis in *The Crown of Life*.[1] Caliban, and his mother Sycorax, correspond to the lust-prepossession so strong in Shakespeare from his Sonnets on the Dark Lady onwards, represented here also by Prospero's severe moral doctrine (IV, i, 13–23). Caliban is part of Prospero: 'This thing of darkness I acknowledge mine' (*The Tempest*, v, i, 275). Miranda is less easy to place. She it is who is given back to mankind, and greets them, with all their faults, as 'beauteous' creatures of some 'brave new world' (*The Tempest*, v, i, 183). She is the distilled essence (pp. 47, 88, 181) of the poet's love springing from that feminine aspect of his personality, which, as we have seen (pp. 30–3), inspires his human sympathies and creative work; she represents a refined love, or soul-contact, which, though drawn from an actual romance—and her union with Ferdinand may itself be allowed to reflect it—yet becomes the spiritual and creative principle behind, or within, the great works that followed. As for the shadowy, yet representative, other persons, they are the world of men as Shakespeare knew and dramatised them; it is to them that Miranda is given in

[1] For similar views on Ariel, expressed by John Masefield, and by Kenneth Muir in collaboration with Sean O'Loughlin, see p. 106 below.

union, and it is for this union that the action has been developed. They are, as persons, less vital: the real drama is made of Prospero, Ariel, Caliban and Miranda, the rest being important rather in the mass, as the alien community that must nevertheless be mastered, forgiven, and served.

The Tempest is a fully matured and indeed supreme working-out of the integration pattern, and may accordingly be directly compared, as I have elsewhere (*Christ and Nietzsche*, v, 204; vi, 226) compared it, with Nietzsche's *Thus Spake Zarathustra*, Prospero, Ariel and Caliban corresponding respectively to Zarathustra, his Eagle and his Serpent. Nietzsche's great work is helpful in our study of the Sonnets. Both develop less through sharp conflicts than through a succession of interchanging and discontinuous moods, like those hinted in Keats' *Ode on Melancholy*. In this, they have much in common with the variations, the undulating swell and subsidence of mood or thought, that I have discussed at length as being a dominating characteristic of *Antony and Cleopatra* (*The Imperial Theme*, viii, 263–6; 274; 288–9, etc.), our one Shakespearian work where the lust and reason of Sonnet 147 are, as it were, for once allied, fused, mingled, blended, without stark opposition; and in this poetic action lies the play's claim to a certain supremacy unmatched elsewhere. This varying, undulatory, movement appears to characterise works where poetry is philosophic, in its own way doctrinal, but with a doctrine that aims at a full integration of essences, without any too-rigid exclusions or taboos: such are, variously, the poetry of Pope throughout, with its peculiarly beautiful use of an undulatory, paragraphic technique; Byron's *Don Juan*; Tennyson's *In Memoriam*; Bridges' *Testament of Beauty*; and T. S. Eliot's *Four Quartets*.

Eliot's poem labours towards the fusion of 'fire' and 'rose', of spiritual quest with incarnate beauty; and in Nietzsche's integration-pattern, Zarathustra loves two symbolical ladies, called Wisdom and Life, corresponding to Eliot's two symbols, and also to Swift's significantly named Stella and Vanessa. The first, directly related to Zarathustra's 'friends' (ii, i), has clear analogies with Shakespeare's friend as source of 'truth' and poetry (pp. 45, 104–13); the other, on the sexual plane, though without the Shakespearian aspersions, corresponds to the Dark Lady. But there is a third lady, who alone receives the seer's final devotion and marriage-song, Eternity (III, 16; *Christ and Nietzsche*, v, 187). This supreme conception points on to the next stages of our study, for the Sonnets likewise converge on it. Our integration-quest, with its perversions and sexual horrors, its unnatural lusts and its compelling idealisms, and all its attendant loneliness and insecurities, would really be little better than a mad-house were it not for that supreme reward which tempts and torments one great genius after another.

III

SYMBOLISM

O, Love, you be a King. A King.
The Tragedy of Nan

WE have seen how certain supposed 'conceits' or 'fancies' may be in reality attempts to grapple with some super-thought which baffles expression. The most usual medium for such intuitions is poetic symbolism, and the Sonnets show a rich use of it. Indeed, the weighty realisation of these imaginative solidities sets them apart from the poetry of Donne and Marvell. True, both Donne and Marvell have their imagery and symbols, and some of Donne's recall Shakespeare's. But with the more metaphysical poets the symbol is, as it were, subdued to—in Donne it is often there to be mocked by—the thinking; it grows from a matrix of metaphysical speculation and intellectual gymnastics. In the best Sonnets the thinking is put at the service of the symbol, and sometimes appears, as we shall see, to lag behind it. The result is that whatever 'eternity' Shakespeare succeeds in establishing is far more than a concept, or web of concepts: it flowers from close physical perception, and holds all the colour and perfume of spring.[1]

One feels that it is only with the greatest reluctance, and perhaps even a sense of guilt, that the poet is forced to admit, if he ever does admit, that it is the distilled truth of the boy, the eternal 'idea', in Plato's sense, that he loves rather than the boy himself; and in so far as he writes of the 'idea' rather than of the thing itself, his writing becomes philosophic rather than strictly poetic; at the best, 'metaphysical poetry', as with Donne and Marvell. Those are concerned with, and brilliantly transmit, their own experience of love, but they have nothing much to say of the loved-one: in Marvell's *Definition of Love* we cannot even be sure of his or her sex. Since they never realise a person-

[1] For a similar judgment see G. K. Hunter's *Dramatic Technique of Shakespeare's Sonnets*; *Essays in Criticism*, III, ii; April, 1953.

ality outside themselves, we are not forced to join with them in adoration. But when in Shakespeare we read:

> Why should poor beauty indirectly seek
> Roses of shadow, since his rose is true?
>
> (67)

we cannot avoid being half-in-love with the youth ourselves. There is a more vivid realisation of the loved person in that one little word 'his', which might well be italicised, than in all Donne's love-poetry. Nor does Shakespeare confine himself, as, on the whole, you might say that Michelangelo does, to a few archetypal thoughts. Such thoughts he has, but they are part only of a closely realised drama, showing all the variety, and hinting the physical detail, of an actual experience. Sense-perception is vivid. We enjoy a rich physical apprehension, the flush and bloom of a young life, with all the perfumes of spring in company, rather as when we read Chaucer's description of his young Squire. We are aware of nature before we proceed to metaphysics: if 'this composed wonder of your frame' (59) is a miracle, it is a miracle born less from our minds than from the 'great creating Nature' of *The Winter's Tale* (IV, iii, 88). At their greatest moments the Sonnets are really less love-poetry than an almost religious adoration before one of 'the rarities of Nature's truth' (60); that is, one of the splendours of human creation. So, though nothing but poetry can meet his problem, yet Shakespeare's move from love to the great poetry of the plays might yet be called, paradoxically, a fall, a second-best: 'for these dead birds sigh a prayer'.

We shall now list the main associations used by the poet to establish verbal contact with the miracle which is his theme. About these there is nothing very abstruse or learned. They are, on the natural plane, flowers, especially the rose; on the human plane, kingship, with gold; on the universal, the Sun, with gold; on the spiritual, jewels. Rose, King, Sun, Gold, Jewels. Our examination need pay slight regard to the Sonnets' order: we shall use our usual practice of 'spatial' analysis, seeing the symbols as existent powers in their own right irrespective of, though of course never contradicting, their particular contexts.

Our first sonnet has 'beauty's rose' (1). One of our finest
end-couplets runs:

> For nothing this wide universe I call
> Save thou, my rose; in it thou art my all.
>   (109)

The rose as truth is contrasted with shams and vices. The
youth's 'true' rose of beauty, in the exquisite passage recently
(p. 59) quoted, is contrasted with the false beautifyings of
society (67). If faults be present in him, 'roses have thorns, and
silver fountains mud' (35). His beauty encloses 'sins' as the rose
contains a 'canker' (95). But 'canker' may also mean wild roses,
as when 'canker-blooms' are said to have colour without 'the
perfumed tincture' of 'sweet roses', which survive death in
distillation, even as the inmost truth of the boy's beauty is distilled by poetry (54). With the rose we may group the lily:
'Lilies that fester smell far worse than weeds' (94). The youth
is the 'pattern' of both 'the lily's white' and 'the deep vermilion
in the rose' (98). In one sonnet the poet relates, point by point,
violet, lily, marjoram and roses, red and white, together with
the 'vengeful canker' of destruction, to the separate excellences
of his love's beauty (99). In contrast his mistress' cheeks have
nothing of 'roses damask'd, red and white' in them (130). It is
easy to understand the intense poetic appeal made by the Wars
of the Roses to Shakespeare in the three parts of *Henry VI*, so
rich in impressions of human loveliness and pathos caught in the
shambles of meaningless destruction, all summed by the line,
'The red rose and the white are on his face' (*3 Henry VI*, II, v, 97).

Next, kingship. Royal images recur, as in the love-poetry
of Donne, some of them holding similar connotations. The poet
addresses the youth as 'lord of my love', to whom he sends a
'written ambassage' (26); he is 'my sovereign' and the poet his
'servant' or 'slave' (57). Love-passages in the dramas offer
parallels. There is Bassanio's

> There is such confusion in my powers,
> As, after some oration fairly spoke
> By a beloved prince, there doth appear
> Among the buzzing pleased multitude . . .
>   (*The Merchant of Venice*, III, ii, 178)

and Troilus'

My heart beats thicker than a fev'rous pulse;
And all my powers do their bestowing lose,
Like vassalage at unawares encountering
The eye of majesty.

(*Troilus and Cressida*, III, ii, 36)

The lover is abased before a blazing power.

The loved one is royal, and so compared to 'a throned queen' (96). He is 'crowned' with various gifts of nature and fortune (37), especially 'all those beauties whereof now he's king' (63). Like a sovereign, he radiates worth, his eyes lending 'a double majesty' to the rival poets' 'grace' (78); if it were not for certain suspicions, he would be owning 'kingdoms of hearts' (70). This royalty is somehow shared by the lover; having found his own king, he regards all other, more commonplace, grandeurs as poor stuff in comparison. His astronomy, learned from those 'constant stars', his love's eyes, cannot, and clearly has no desire to, busy itself with the fortunes of 'princes'; it is a different 'art', prophesying 'truth and beauty' (14). After all, 'great princes' favourites' enjoy an insecure glory in comparison (25); time changes the 'decrees of kings', but his love is lasting (115); it is in no sense 'the child of state', and is independent of 'smiling pomp' (124); bearing 'the canopy' means nothing to him, nor does any such external 'honouring' (125). The result is that the poet, through accepted love, becomes himself royal. His mind is 'crown'd' with the wondrous youth, and is accordingly 'kingly' (114); when he is sure of him, he is a 'king', but when disillusioned, 'no such matter' (87). However depressed he may be in other ways, in so far as his love is assured, it brings such wealth, well-being and power, 'that then I scorn to change my state with kings' (29).

Such symbols act variously as contrasts or comparisons, and apply to either partner of the love-association. Our final impression is of love itself as king, of some super-personality, the Sun of Sonnet 24 (pp. 40–2), made of, or liberated by, the love of two human beings, as when Donne in *The Ecstasy* writes 'else a great Prince in prison lies'. Love liberates this mysterious sovereign, allows him to realise himself in human terms. This sovereign reality it is which is indicated by the word 'love' of our phrase 'in love with', Nerissa's 'lord love' of *The Merchant of Venice* (II, ix, 101). It is something, or someone, experienced

immediately, 'crowning the present' (115); either that, or
known beyond death, as in Romeo's 'I reviv'd and was an
emperor' in *Romeo and Juliet* (v, i, 9), and Cleopatra's 'I
dream'd there was an emperor Antony', in *Antony and Cleopatra*
(v, ii, 76). The associations are just, since the king, properly
understood, holds within society precisely this super-personal
and supernal function. In more obviously religious terms we
have Henry VI's:

> My crown is in my heart, not on my head;
> Not deck'd with diamonds and Indian stones,
> Nor to be seen.
>
> (*3 Henry VI*, iii, i, 62)

But the Sonnets never engage too far in mysticism, and perhaps
our finest example of all, warm with meanings both physical
and heraldic, is the line, 'Then in the blazon of sweet beauty's
best' (106), where kings are not specifically mentioned at all.

Kingship is naturally golden, and golden impressions recur
with similar variations in use. 'Gilded honour' may be 'shame-
fully misplac'd' (66); poets flatter the youth with 'golden quill'
(85); his hair is contrasted with false 'golden tresses' (68);
Shakespeare's poetry can make him outlive 'a gilded tomb'
(101). More important is his eye 'gilding' the object on which
it gazes (20)—eyes in Shakespeare's are active powers, not just
passive reflections (p. 37)—and the lovely phrase characterising
youth as 'this thy golden time' (3). Stars are 'gold candles' (21).

The Sun is nature's king, and also pre-eminently golden.
Throughout Shakespeare king and sun are compared. The
Dark Lady's eyes are 'nothing like the Sun' (130); they are
'mourning', because dark, eyes, and may at the best be compared to the 'morning sun' in a grey dawn, or the evening star
(132). With the Fair Youth, the association 'that sun, thine eye'
(49) comes easily enough. The successful lover compares himself to the morning 'lark' singing 'hymns at Heaven's gate'
(29), though, when things go wrong, 'basest clouds' obscure the
Sun, who now rides 'with ugly rack on his celestial face', and
steals to the west disfigured (33); for 'clouds and eclipses
stain both Moon and Sun' (35). In our 'transparency' sonnet
(24) the Sun functions as the supernal love corresponding to
Donne's prince (p. 61). The Sun, 'daily new and old' (76), is

visualised in all positions of his diurnal course, with close reference to age. Youth is a 'day' ready to decline (15), and the poet's
age just such an hour 'as after sunset fadeth in the west' (73).

We have various clusters of king, gold, and sun. King and
gold come together in 'the gilded monuments of princes' (55);
and sun and gold, when the Sun's 'gold complexion' is dimmed
in the sonnet, 'Shall I compare thee to a summer's day?' (18),
or the young man graces 'the day' and 'gilds' the evening in
place of stars (28). We may have all three. So 'great princes'
favourites' are compared to the mari*gold* opening to the Sun's
'eye' (25). Man's life resembles the diurnal progress of the
Sun, who first 'lifts up his burning head' from the orient,
everything beneath him doing 'homage' to his 'sacred majesty'
as he makes his 'golden pilgrimage', till finally he 'reeleth' to
his setting (7). Love resembles a 'glorious morning' seen to
'flatter the mountain tops with sovereign eye', kissing meadows
with his 'golden face', and 'gilding' streams with his 'heavenly
alchemy' (33).

These impressions are not just decoration. They are
attempts to realize in 'black ink' (65) the wonder of youthful
beauty at 'this thy golden time' (3); and beyond that, to make
real and visible, without relying on abstract terms, that supernal
and authoritative Love of which lovers are part only, expres-
sions, voices.

Nor is all this so simple and obvious as it sounds. The Sun
is not a necessary, nor even a natural, accompaniment to
Shakespearian romance: the Moon is more usual. Shakespeare's
heterosexual love-themes are usually moonlit, as with the
Balcony scene of *Romeo and Juliet*, the central scenes of *A Midsummer Night's Dream*, and the fifth act of *The Merchant of
Venice*, though Portia has 'sunny' locks (I, i, 170). Much of *As
You Like It* shows us a shadowed, dappled, world, and in
Twelfth Night the Sun never dominates until Sebastian's, 'This
is the air, that is the glorious sun' (IV, iii, 1). *Antony and Cleopatra* has 'gaudy' *nights* (III, xi, 182) and Enobarbus' moonlit
death, the Sun itself acting rather as a background power than
as a present witness, until Cleopatra's dream. Certainly in *Love's
Labour's Lost* the Sun is lyrically vivid as a love-accompaniment.
But this early play is made on a pattern of its own; it ends with
winter; it is full of sonnet-material; and it is exactly this sort of

love-poetry that is not repeated. Our first really convincingly
sun-impregnated love-scene is the sheep-shearing festival of
The Winter's Tale.[1]

The Sun is male, the Moon female; the one suggests the
intellectual consciousness, the other emotion, the twilit world
of romance. When Shelley's Hermaphrodite (= poetry) in *The
Witch of Atlas* is fully *awakened*, then we may expect the Sun.[2]
When sensual love, whose natural medium, as D. H. Lawrence
insisted, is the dark world below consciousness, is our theme,
the Sun may, as in Donne's *The Sun Rising*, be an intruder,
though, in so far as such a love is vividly and directly lived by
day, with a strong physical awareness fully accepted, as in *The
Winter's Tale*, it may be in place. Normally, we can say that it
is far from easy to blend it with a heterosexual love. As an
extreme example of a natural tendency, we have the 'woman
wailing for her demon-lover' under a 'waning moon' in *Kubla
Khan*; and we must remember Lorenzo's and Jessica's list of
famous moonlit love-incidents in their 'In such a night . . .'
duet (*The Merchant of Venice*, v, i, 1–22). That last act is, in its
way, a recovery and a retreat—yet how wonderful a retreat—
from the stern compulsions of the greater action.

But it is precisely among those 'stern compulsions' that the
Sun is likely to assume poetic centrality. So Theseus, man
of power, efficiency, chivalrous courtesy and common-sense,
enters with the dawn on the moonstruck world of *A Midsummer
Night's Dream*; the heroic idealism of *Julius Caesar* is marked
by important passages of sunrise and sunset, before and after
the assassination (ii, i, 101–11; v, iii, 60–3); and in *Cymbeline*
the royal boys are sun-worshippers (iii, iii, 1–9) and Cymbeline
himself 'radiant' (v, v, 476). Shakespeare's kings, in so far as
they carry, or claim, true, that is magical, royalty, are regularly
given sun-correspondences, as with Richard's comparison of
himself to a rising sun:

> But when, from under this terrestrial ball,
> He fires the proud tops of the eastern pines,
> And darts his light through every guilty hole. . .
>   (*Richard II*, iii, ii, 41)

---

[1] For an amplification of these judgments, see *The Crown of Life*, iii, 102.
[2] For the awakening of Shelley's Hermaphrodite, see *The Starlit Dome*, iii, 229; also
p. 220 below.

Henry VIII is a 'sun' (III, ii, 416), and so on. All this is fairly
clear. But, with the waning of the royalistic and aristocratic
valuations, there is less of it in English poetry than you might
expect. Milton's Samson-like figure of power-with-virtue at the
close of the *Areopagitica* is as a sun-gazing eagle; Keats offers
some notable splendours in *Hyperion*, and Coleridge's *Zapolya*,
with its youthful hero Andreas, is a complete work constructed
from this particular area of the imagination (*The Starlit Dome*,
IV, 284–7; II, 160–78). Byron, perhaps our subtlest sun-poet
of all, offers many variations, serious and amusing (*The Burning Oracle*, VI, 256–9, 284). The sombre Tennyson is happiest
with the setting sun: you have to be empowered with an innate,
virile, humanistic faith to use the sun-symbol with power.
Wordsworth once crashed badly (*The Excursion*, IV, 232; *The
Starlit Dome*, I, 55).

The Sun tends to assume poetic centrality when our concern is: (i) any fully-*conscious*, or victorious, love, as defined in
Biron's great speech in *Love's Labour's Lost* (IV, iii, 290–365);
with love-as-power, love virile and victorious; or, (ii) royal
power felt magically, almost, we might say, erotically. We may
say, more generally, that it fits any strong conviction of power
or sexual virility fused with virtue, and it is true that in the
Renaissance period it can accompany any love in so far as that
love is, as in Spenser's *Hymns*, felt as a sovereign power. But it
is clear that a male love lends itself most readily to the symbol,
and indeed we cannot always be sure how far our Renaissance
love-lyrists are using heterosexual terms for a homosexual
engagement. In such engagements, being as they are denied
sexual consummation, sex is forced into consciousness, so that it
becomes, as we have seen (pp. 37–9), a matter of 'eyes', of burning, over-flooding, apprehension; all is strongly idealistic; while
the loved object, being male, inevitably assumes the power-
properties of male action, aristocracy, and royalty. In his adoration for the loved youth, the two main positive directions of
Shakespeare's work are accordingly implicit.[1]

The various natural and cosmic symbolisms of the Sonnets
grow from a soil of normal Shakespearian imagery: flowers,
crops, and seasons; moon and stars; effects of winter, cloud,

---

[1] For my general placing of the Sun within the integration-pattern, see *Christ and
Nietzsche*, IV, 139–46; also pp. 219–20 below.

storm and tempests; inundation (64); and wrecks (80). The
love-quest is a sea-voyage (80, 86), as in *Troilus and Cressida*
(p. 37; and see *The Shakespearian Tempest*, ii, 72; iv, 172–4).
Stars may be important, sometimes holding astrological significance (14, 15, 26, 116); they may be more directly
descriptive or symbolic (21, 132); they are symbols of
constancy (14, 116).

We have already reviewed certain impressions of 'gold'.
'Gold' naturally accompanies 'sun' and 'king'; the king's crown,
and indeed gold in general, might be called 'solid sunlight'.
Gold has for centuries exerted magical radiations and its value,
worth and power, its 'virtue' in the old sense, need no emphasis.
These properties make it an apt symbol for any high value, or
worth.

Love is such a value, and it is regularly in Shakespeare compared to rich metals or merchandise (*The Shakespearian Tempest*, ii, 65–9). Throughout poetry precious stones symbolise
what may be called 'spiritual value' (*Christ and Nietzsche*, v,
193–5; and see below pp. 137, 141, 159). All this is powerful
in the Sonnets.

The 'rich gems' of 'earth and sea' are regarded as a natural
love-comparison (21); though cruel, the Dark Lady is 'the
fairest and most precious jewel' (131); and the youth's image
by night hangs 'like a jewel' before the poet's soul (27), recalling Romeo's 'It seems she hangs upon the cheek of night like
a rich jewel in an Ethiop's ear' (*Romeo and Juliet*, i, v, 49).
Compared with 'a prize so dear', the poet's 'jewels' are as
'trifles' (48); even the youth's faults are to be prized as a poor
'jewel' may be on the figure of 'a throned queen' (96); his tears
are as 'pearl', and called 'rich' (34); he is himself costly, a matter
of 'riches' (87). One sonnet is packed with suggestions of 'rich',
'treasure', 'stones of worth', 'chest', and 'robe', and contains the
grand line, 'captain jewels in the carcanet' (52). Most striking
of all is:

> Where, alack,
> Shall Time's best jewel from Time's chest lie hid?
>   (65)

As elsewhere throughout Shakespeare, such symbols blend
with rich merchandise and sea-voyages. Love, it is true, is too

rich to be 'merchandis'd' (102), but symbolically the thought
may act serenely enough:

> Was it the proud full sail of his great verse
> Bound for the prize of all too precious you . . .
>
> (86)

Poetry is itself a quest. Apart from all flattery and advantage,
it is a spiritual penetration and achievement, in some deep sense
a possession, of the mysterious splendour. But the poet is, of
course, jealous in a human fashion too: he is like a 'miser' so
intent on 'the prize of you', that he varies between pride of
possession and horrible doubts lest 'the filching age' may 'steal
his treasure' (75).

Shakespeare's bitter comments on the youth's risking 'infection' from a sinful society (67), with the cutting conclusion
'thou dost common grow' (69), may in fact arise from a
questionable jealousy and possessiveness. We need not assume
that the young man, who is once specifically said to have survived the temptations of youth victoriously (70), was naturally
vicious. In certain moods Shakespeare would, clearly, regard all
society as too base for a youth of so infinite and mysterious a
worth. His love was to him the inmost centre and furthest aim
of all things, its value lying beyond human assessment:

> It is the star to every wandering bark,
> Whose worth's unknown although his height be taken.
>
> (116)

It was the crowning glory of creation, and more than that.
'Jewels', as we have said, suggest spiritual values, and this love
is also religious.

Our theme (31) is 'dear, religious, love' ('dear' meaning 'of
highest value'). It is not 'idolatry' (105)—compare Hector's
aspersions on idolatry at *Troilus and Cressida*, II, ii 56—
because it and its object are constant (105). Even though
faults be found, even though there be no objective 'image', to
quote Hector, 'of the affected merit' (*Troilus and Cressida*, II, ii,
60), 'Heaven' has somehow decreed in the youth's 'creation'
that only 'sweet love' can dwell in his 'face'; he cannot *look*
faithless or bad (93). Such beauty, with its 'heavenly touches'
(17), exists in its own right; it is itself 'sacred' (115); and the

poet complains that, since artifice became the fashion, 'sweet beauty' has no 'holy bower' (127). As it is, the youth's presence is said to 'grace impiety' when he mixes with sinful people (67). Shakespeare's love-poetry, his own 'better part', is 'consecrate to thee' (74); he has 'hallow'd' his 'fair name' in verses which are as 'prayers divine' (108); and his own love is offered as an 'oblation' (125). The idealised boy is even called 'a god in love', and 'next my heaven the best' (110). He is the poet's 'better angel' (p. 28). Adoration can go no further.

Such is the experience, or phenomenon, straining the sweetest and grandest symbols, natural, human, and divine, to do justice to 'this composed wonder of your frame' (59). It is pre-eminently an incarnate mystery or miracle, not unlike that symbolised by Dante's Gryphon in the *Purgatorio* (xxxi). The poetry gives us a close-up of the thing itself, not merely, as does Donne, of the supervening and enclosing experience. It is a marvel here and now, 'crowning the present', even though leaving us 'doubting of the rest' (115). For there can be no permanence. That is our problem: the problem of *Troilus and Cressida, Hamlet, Othello, Timon of Athens, Antony and Cleopatra*. And yet, somehow, we feel that it should, indeed must, be permanent. The poet must say, and we applaud him for saying it, 'Love's not Time's fool' (116), but he fears, and so do we, that it may be. He starts a sonnet with 'To me, fair friend, you never can be old', but continues:

> Ah, yet doth beauty, like a dial-hand,
> Steal from his figure and no pace perceiv'd.
>
> (104)

Can both be true? One way or another, we shall surely come up against the agony of Troilus: 'This is, and is not, Cressid' (*Troilus and Cressida*, v, ii, 143). On this torturing antithesis, the greatest passages of the Sonnets converge.

IV

TIME AND ETERNITY

Oh! how should I not burn for Eternity, and for the marriage ring of rings—the Ring of Recurrence?

Never yet found I the woman by whom I would have children, save it be by this Woman that I love: for I love thee, O Eternity!

Thus Spake Zarathustra

WE now approach the three great issues: Time, Death, and Eternity. So strangely idealistic and esoteric a love as that of Shakespeare's Sonnets is, in essence, not only poetic, but also tragic, if only because, countering the biological order, it remains, to quote again from Marvell's *Definition of Love,* 'begotten by despair upon impossibility'. It is easily associated with tragic meditation. That is why elegies are so regularly composed, following the ancient pastoral tradition, to a male friend: in *The Phoenix' Nest* (see pp. 150, 152, 205), *Lycidas, Adonais, Thyrsis, In Memoriam.* But there is more in it than negation. Poetic elegy and poetic tragedy mark no defeat; they are rather penetrations, or attempted penetrations, of some higher dimension. Love of this kind may often appear, as in some of Michelangelo's sonnets (e.g. 55, 58, 59; see p. 192), more at ease with death than with life. Writing in *The Arrow and the Sword* on what he calls the prevailing 'Uranian' temper of the greatest ages of Greece, Rome, England and France, Hugh Ross Williamson (p. 24), after agreeing that the biological protest against such sexual or romantic tendencies is inevitable if the race is to continue on the plane of procreation, insists that its safeguarding is nevertheless vital 'if civilization is to continue on any other plane' (v, 81). Such supposedly 'unnatural' tendencies have an intimate relation to genius, and what we call 'genius' is, exactly, the awareness, and expression, of planes, or dimensions, beyond the biological and the temporal. That is why Shakespeare's Sonnets are so deeply

69

concerned with the problems of time, death and eternity. These we shall now discuss.

Our study will not be easy, and in the course of it we shall incur the risk of regarding certain thought-moulds as conventional, and attributing to certain great passages of poetry a higher degree of significance than their place in the chain of logical reasoning strictly warrants. This is an admission new to my interpretative work, and I would warn the reader to be on his guard against a subjective interpretation.

The Sonnets offer no easy assurances. They never forget that

> Golden lads and girls all must,
> As chimney sweepers, come to dust.
> (*Cymbeline*, iv, ii, 262)

Their drama is set within contexts of diurnal and seasonal change. We see the Sun in glory of his rise and splendid in mid-career, but also reeling to his end so tragically that eyes are averted (7). Seasonal change is continually before us. We are not allowed to forget how

> never-resting Time leads summer on
> To hideous winter, and confounds him there.
> (5)

We watch 'summer's green all girded up in sheaves', borne on the bier 'with white and bristly beard' (12). The future promises 'winter' storms, and the 'barren rage of death's eternal cold' (13). Such is our setting.

Summer is wholly desirable, but winter is 'full of care' (56). The loved youth is like 'the spring and foison of the year' (53), sweet and perfect as 'a summer's day' (18). In his absence 'teeming autumn', with all its 'increase', is a mockery:

> For summer and his pleasures wait on thee,
> And, thou away, the very birds are mute.
> (97)

Either that, or their songs forbode 'winter'. The youth's absence makes it all a period of 'freezings' and 'December's bareness' (97). The thought is next elaborated: even 'proud-pied April', who injects youth into all nature, is now no better

than winter (98). Thinking of their three years' acquaintance,
the poet writes:

> Three winters cold
> Have from the forests shook three summers' pride,
> Three beauteous springs to yellow autumn turn'd
> In process of the seasons have I seen,
> Three April perfumes in three hot Junes burn'd,
> Since first I saw you fresh, which yet are green.
> Ah, yet doth beauty, like a dial-hand,
> Steal from his figure and no pace perceiv'd . . .
>
> (104)

There is a contrast between 'fresh' and 'green'. The sonnet
started with, 'To me, fair friend, you never can be old', but the
doubt is clearly underlined. However miraculous his youth,
the boy is part of nature and subject to her laws.

To establish his poetic statement, the poet plays tricks with
age. He, on the road to the higher integration, is not particularly good-looking, and even if he were, he would not have the
supreme good looks of youth. He accordingly drives home the
contrast:

> That time of year thou may'st in me behold
> When yellow leaves, or none, or few, do hang
> Upon those boughs which shake against the cold,
> Bare ruin'd choirs where late the sweet birds sang . . .
>
> (73)

Shakespeare could not, whatever the date of composition, have
been so old as that, but he finds it poetically worth the sacrifice
in accuracy to pretend that he is. So he next compares himself
to 'twilight' after 'sunset', nearing 'death's second self' or
'night' (73). The comparison of human life to seasonal or
diurnal change is emphatic throughout. However transcendent
the experience, it is locked in nature. It is not, as you feel in
Donne, an experience all-dominating and existent in its own
right: we may call it an experience pointing rather to drama
than to theology.

All depends on the youth *as* a youth, and his youth is
subject to nature:

> When I consider every thing that grows
> Holds in perfection but a little moment . . .
>
> (15)

The 'perfection' cannot last. Men grow 'as plants', 'cheer'd and check'd even by the self-same sky', and their 'youthful sap' and 'brave state' are shortlived as a flower (15). This 'perfection' is part of a natural time-order which *both* makes and unmakes men: the very hours which 'did frame' the wondrous boy, work to 'unfair' that 'which fairly doth excel' (5). Now this 'perfection', this 'excelling', though transitory, is somehow an absolute; and it is a perfection and an absolute precisely because it is at youth. That is why the boy is called 'most *rich* in youth' (15). In semi-eternal terms we can talk of the lower, bisexual, integration; that is, wholeness, and so 'perfection'.[1] But in temporal terms its appeal lies rather in its promise, like a bud. The boy is compared to a bud (1); and elsewhere we have 'the sweetest buds' (70), and 'the darling buds of May' (18). He is as one of 'April's first-born flowers' (21). He possesses the attraction of a rose-bud, more perfectly compacted than the splayed flower. He is a momentary personification of the creative miracle.

But he is also, like the rose-bud, fragile and short-lived. In a world of hostile forces, mortality and decay,

> How with this rage shall beauty hold a plea
> Whose action is no stronger than a flower?
>
> (65)

'Beauty' means 'youthful beauty', and so to imagine the boy at forty years old is equivalent to admitting the powers of age and mortality. The 'proud livery' of youth will, in this comparison, be then merely 'a tatter'd weed' (2). The poet fears any suggestion of lines or 'wrinkles' on his love's face (2, 19, 22, 60, 100). They and 'mouthed graves' are waiting (77). If Shakespeare did, as it seems, lose interest in his loved one, this was not exactly unfaithfulness, since it was less a growing person that he had ever loved than that person 'most rich in youth', enjoying 'your day of youth' (15), as a rose-bud, compacting not merely his own future, but, somehow, in his precarious and evanescent integration as one of 'the rarities of nature's truth' (60), symbolising the inmost secret and most expansive meaning of human creation. It was a splendour and

---

[1] For the word 'perfection' applied, for a similar reason, to the Phoenix, see pp. 182–4 below.

a meaning 'crowning the present' (115); no more, but no less. For further understanding we may turn to the 'boy eternal', and related, passages of *The Winter's Tale* (*The Crown of Life*, III, 77–8, 107); and also to various poems, which we shall discuss later, on the Phoenix.

This state of being cannot for long be isolated and held. It is tugged, stretched out, dissolved into a nothingness, by time:

> Time doth transfix the flourish set on youth,
> And delves the parallels in beauty's brow.
>
> (60)

The Sonnets approach time in the manner of *Troilus and Cressida*, where, as I have already shown (*The Wheel of Fire*, III, 65–8), it is a recurring concept. Throughout Shakespeare's later work, as I have emphasised in my own commentaries from *Myth and Miracle* onwards, 'time' and 'death' are central problems, pushing towards solution in *Antony and Cleopatra* and the Final Plays. This whole progress is adumbrated in the Sonnets.

Time's action is subtle and silent:

> Ah, yet doth beauty, like a dial-hand,
> Steal from his figure and no pace perceiv'd.
>
> (104)

'Figure' is precisely used for both the youth and the dial's numberings. So the dial shows 'how thy precious minutes waste' (77). The poet is said to 'count the clock that tells the time' (12), ruminating on time like Henry VI and Richard II (3 *Henry VI*, II, v, 21–40; *Richard II*, v, v, 42–60). Time is a mysterious continuum within which all nature is contained and limited:

> Like as the waves make towards the pebbled shore,
> So do our minutes hasten to their end;
> Each changing place with that which goes before,
> In sequent toil all forwards do contend.
>
> (60)

In these passages time's paradox has been conveyed by suggestions of both slowness, as in 'steal', 'no pace', and 'toil'; and speed, as in 'hasten'; and elsewhere we find such phrases as 'swift-footed Time' (19), 'his swift foot' (65), Time's 'continual haste' (123). Slow or fast, one thing is certain: Time is 'never-resting' (5).

It also appears to be all-embracing. Significant passages emphasise how it brings to birth as well as destroys (p. 72; also p. 92). The word 'time' may accordingly be used for the immediate, and in one sense timeless, excellence whose transience raises all our problems. So the youth is said to be at 'this thy golden time' (3), and standing 'on the top of happy hours' (16). But this glory, so vividly 'crowning the present', leaves one 'doubting of the rest' (115). The contrast is between the 'now'—Shakespeare's thought does not call it, though it may suggest, an 'eternal now'—and the temporal sequence. He is concerned with the simple actuality of 'all those beauties whereof *now* he's king' (63), as against the inevitable future; with time as now, and time as sequence. Normally 'time' means 'sequential time'.[1]

Sequential time is destructive. The poet will not easily submit. Fearing 'Time's furrows' in his love (22), he takes up the challenge and is 'all at war with Time for love of you' (15). The words are apt. The Sonnets are exactly this: a poetic war with Time. Time, with its 'wrackful siege of battering days' (65), is a besieging force, and would pierce, as with a weapon, beauty's heraldic crest: 'Time doth transfix the flourish set on youth' (60). It is a powerful foe, since 'nothing 'gainst Time's scythe can make defence' (12); 'Time's fell hand', which can 'deface' the proudest monuments, is out for the 'spoil' of 'beauty', and nothing of nature or human fabrication appears able to withstand the onset (64, 65). But it is scarcely an honourable foe. The youth is urged to 'make war upon this bloody tyrant, Time' (16); its very hours are 'tyrants' (5); 'Time's tyranny' has no more respect for 'sacred beauty' than —we may suggest—a ruthless conqueror desecrating the holy places of religion (115). It engages in a haphazard and general laying waste, indicated by the phrases 'wastes of Time' (12) and 'wasteful Time' (15); 'Time's injurious hand' and 'age's cruel knife' suggest the degree of its stony-hearted ruthlessness (63);

[1] For time in relation to birth see also *The Wheel of Fire*, XIII, 265, note. Time can also mean, as so often in the plays, what Tucker (202) calls 'the vogue of the contemporary world'. Such a use he notes in Sonnets 70, 76, 123, and 124.

'devouring Time' is as a beast with insatiable hunger, or, if at all human, is just criminal, and in destroying the loved one's beauty will be guilty of a 'most heinous crime' (19). More, there is something intrinsically wrong, perverted, twisted, about Time's behaviour, as it 'wastes' life with its 'crooked knife' (100). As in *Troilus and Cressida*, Time is essentially underhand, mean, like a thief by night, the dial's 'shady stealth' always witnessing his 'thievish progress to eternity' (77). To sum up, Time is just 'sluttish' (55); worse, he fools you (124, 116). It is a thoroughly degrading business.[1]

And it makes nonsense of our existence. It cannot be right. Time and Death are brutal allies. 'Mortality' acts as in a 'rage' (64, 65); it is both brutal and stupid, and its easy conquest of fine things appalling. The thought is an extension of Romeo's on his lady's conquest by 'the lean, abhorred monster', Death:

> Thou art not conquer'd; beauty's ensign yet
> Is crimson in thy lips and in thy cheeks,
> And Death's pale flag is not advanced there.
> (*Romeo and Juliet*, v, iii, 94)

So in the Sonnets, the poet's love is called 'much too fair' to be 'Death's conquest' (6). Somehow he must be preserved

> Against the stormy gusts of winter's day
> And barren rage of Death's eternal cold.
> (13)

'That churl, Death', like Time, is a despicable thing (32). He must not be allowed to 'brag' of this conquest (18). When the poet shall have fallen under his 'fell arrest' (cp. *Hamlet*, 'as this fell sergeant, Death, is strict in his arrest'; v, ii, 350), his love, which is his 'spirit' and 'better part', now housed in poetry, shall not remain 'the coward conquest of a wretch's knife' (74).

It is all-important that the poet should somehow be able to say, 'Death to me subscribes' (107). Somehow he must find a way and a reason to say it, since Time and Death are clearly usurpers. In contrast to our Rose, King, Crown, Sun and Gold impressions, these are ragamuffins, churls, deformed things,

---

[1] These aspersions should be carefully compared with the long passage on Time as 'Eater of youth' and spoiler of 'antiquities' in *The Rape of Lucrece* (925-94).

nonentities, usurping power—like Richard III, only worse—to which they have no proper right. This is the poet's insistence. He *wills* to conquer Time, insisting: 'No, Time, thou shalt not boast that I do change'. One suspects that, as the youth grows up, he *is* changing. Nevertheless, he continues, 'Thy registers and thee I both defy', and concludes:

> This I do vow, and this shall ever be,
> I will be true, despite thy scythe and thee.
>   (123)

That is, 'I *will* be true despite Time's action on my love's appearance'. The asseveration marks both a failing in love and a will towards an attainment greater than his failure. He can even assume authority greater than death's:

> But I forbid thee one most heinous crime:
> O carve not with thy hours my love's fair brow.
>   (19)

Is this just rant? Or do we respond to anything deeper? Is there any point at all in talking like this? That is our problem.

Here we must allow ourselves a short critical excursion. We have already shown how certain thought-processes usually written off as 'conceits' may hold precise and important meanings. But there are also passages that do not convince us. Consider this, in a sonnet analysing the poet's reaction to the Dark Lady:

> If that be fair whereon my false eyes dote,
> What means the world to say it is not so?
> If it be not, then love doth well denote
> Love's eye is not so true as all men's 'No'.[1]
> How can it? O, how can love's eye be true,
> That is so vex'd with watching and with tears?
>   (148)

The reasoning is purely fanciful, and no depth can be found in it. But the two statements which it links up are valid enough in separation: the poet undoubtedly *is* confused by the fascination exerted by a person whose appearance he does not admire,

---

[1] Tucker gives good reason for supporting the Globe pun on 'aye'; but the Quarto text with a stop after 'men's' and grouping 'No' with 'How can it?' certainly makes better reading today. Peter Alexander follows the Quarto.

and he *is* very sorry for himself in his sufferings. Moreover, he wants, and has every right, to say these things. We can see how the fanciful transition is here acting as a link, as a concession to the habitual logic of writing; a concession, we may say, to time.

But poetry need not always subscribe, to use Shakespeare's word (107), to such disciplines. Modern poetry does not even pretend to do so, and in this refusal it constitutes an attack on logic rather as Shakespeare's Sonnets constitute an attack on time. That is, of course, why, in studying the deeper meanings of poetry, we may be forced back on what I call a 'spatial', as opposed to a 'temporal', or sequential, approach. This comes from a recognition that poetic composition is made from various stabs of insight, each existent, like the Fair Youth himself, in its own right: we see, or feel, them 'crowning the present', however we may be doubting 'of the rest'; that is, in our transposition, doubting the final validity of the logical links. True, it may be more satisfactory if the poet can arrange his pieces in logical order. A poem such as Eliot's *The Waste Land* is, as it stands, too chaotic, and its interpreters cannot always be blamed for their errors, serious though these may be. You could in this regard call Shakespearian drama more satisfying than Webster's, in that the links are clearer, and Byron's more satisfying than Shakespeare's. Yet few would agree with this last statement: surely we rather like the occasional hiatus, the mysterious depths and crevices, of Shakespearian drama. Developing the thought of Nietzsche's *Birth of Tragedy*, we may say that the Dionysian, which is the dramatic, essence, jets up from below, moment by moment, and that it is the Apollonian partner who arranges, as best he may, the Dionysian stuff into a rational coherence. A surface too lucid, logical and Apollonian may even appear to be a disadvantage to drama, since the audience have to attend too sharply with their logical reason. Dramatic thought is made of a succession of almost independent, transfixing, moments, vertically motivated from the unseen. Such, too, was the nature of the dithyramb on which Nietzsche lays so heavy an emphasis, those religious rhapsodies whose passion-impregnated song-music developed into the Dionysian chorus of Attic drama, and has left its imprint ever since on dramatic composition. But really these

rough distinctions apply to all poetry; the logic is not everything; and with the Sonnets especially the logic is, if not
exactly misleading, often subsidiary. I agree with Mark van
Doren that what we have to ask is: 'What was he writing about
when his deepest imagination was engaged? What are the
best sonnets, or the best parts of them, actually saying to
the reader?' (*Shakespeare*, New York, 1939; 11). That is the
question we shall try to answer. In his all-too-short treatment
Mark van Doren finds their essential statement tragic, and
many will agree with him. But here we shall nevertheless
diverge, and attempt to show how, at their 'best' moments,
they are announcing, instead, a *victory* over tragedy. In so doing
we must be allowed, in so far as certain recurring emphases
are emotionally powerful, dithyrambic, rhapsodic—indeed, in
contrast to the poet's rational thinking, inspired—to isolate
them for inspection, whilst giving no more than secondary
attention to the overlay of Apollonian thought; and even, on
occasion, to read within them significances that might be said
to contradict that thought.

Such a deliberate technique, which goes well beyond my
usual methods of interpretation, has its dangers, and must be
used with caution. So warned, we shall now proceed to analyse
the poet's various attempts to master the problem of time.
Some of these we shall, whilst remaining conscious of the risks
involved by the use of such terms, conclude to be 'conventional', specious, and finally unsatisfying; some as adumbrating
certain mysterious, poetic, powers which leave us in a state of
half-satisfied expectation; and some, through their rhapsodic,
dithyrambic, virtue, their inspirational quality, as all but
directly stating a solution for which Shakespeare's own con-
ceptual logic is inadequate. We shall study his apparent solutions under three main headings: (i) biological; (ii) artistic;
and (iii) religious.

In the early sonnets the poet urges the young man to
perpetuate his beauty by the begetting of a son in marriage.
This is one very obvious answer to death on the biological
plane, which we can all recognise. All Shakespeare's thought
is rooted deep in nature, in the biological order, the thought-
world of 'common-sense', and from this he will not depart
except under poetic pressure. It is accordingly right that his

sequence should start with this solution, stated and reiterated from Sonnets 1 to 17.

But it is somehow unsatisfying. For one thing, we gather from the later sonnets that when the originally chaste youth is found mixing in what appears to be a gay society, the poet grows very angry. True, this is not marriage, but it might well lead to marriage, and certainly might produce a son. That may seem an irrelevant criticism, but the poet's affection was clearly both idealistic and possessive, and it is likely enough that he would have set so high a standard for the young man that any one individual applicant would be almost certain to fall below it. This is merest speculation, but, in terms of the account as we have it, it appears to be justified.

Poetically, the thought never really carries conviction. Continually the final couplet drives home the one point in such a way that we feel it to be a weak conclusion to a good poem. Here is an example:

> This were to be new made when thou art old,
> And see thy blood warm when thou feel'st it cold.
>
> (2)

And here another:

> Thy unus'd beauty must be tomb'd with thee,
> Which, used, lives th' executor to be.
>
> (4)

And a third:

> So thou, thyself outgoing in thy noon,
> Unlook'd on diest unless thou get a son.
>
> (7)

These, and there is one worse, are not good enough for their contexts, the last coming as an unworthy conclusion to the noble sonnet about the Sun on his 'golden pilgrimage' from east to west (p. 63).

Yet why, we may ask, does Shakespeare do this? The answer is: first, that it was a convention, to hand, and second, that it served his purpose. That it was a convention does not, by itself, detract one *iota* from its meaning or value; conventions exist to express meaning and value. Besides, when we hear that 'breed' alone withstands 'time' (12), we recognise that this is, as we have just seen, one, and the most obvious,

answer to death, and, since answers to death are not so easy
to come by, should certainly be surveyed. Nevertheless, it falls
poetically flat, with a flatness witnessing the poet's instinct for
a better answer, and we are forced to conclude that its primary
office is to serve as an excuse for the main body of a poem
whose significance is not to be limited by its conclusion. The poet
uses it as a thought-mould into which to pour his exquisite
apprehensions of the boy's loveliness, his horror at thought of
its passing, and his *will* to save him from the worst 'death' can
'do'; to save him from 'death's conquest' (6). The very form
of the sonnet, with its final relaxation of tension, enables him
to end with a glib couplet; the reader accepts the weakness as
organic to the form, though it is far more than that, being
really a fault intrinsic to the triviality of the thought. But the
thoughts that build up to it are not trivial: here the building
is nothing, the scaffolding everything.

Our next proposed solution, corresponding to Socrates'
contrast of ideal as opposed to biological propagation in *The
Symposium* (pp. 216–19 below), though it has much in common
with the first, lands us in greater complexities. The last marriage
sonnet concludes:

> But were some child of yours alive that time,
> You should live twice—in it, and in my rhyme.
>
> (17)

From then on, the thought of a literary immortality is reiterated.
As before, we can hint an insincerity. When the prospects of
successful immortalisation are improved by the praises of
another poet of greater learning and repute, Shakespeare does
not welcome him, any more than he welcomed the youth's first
sexual engagements. Moreover, it is often supposed, as Butler
supposes, that the publication of even his own sonnets would
have caused Shakespeare suffering and it has generally been
supposed that he had nothing to do with it. But we forget to
ask: what, then, did he mean by all this emphasis on the
immortalisation of the loved youth? If he sincerely desired that,
you would expect him to have done his part to assure it. All
that we know of Shakespeare suggests that he took little enough
interest in literary immortality, for himself or anyone else.

As before, the poetic statements lack cogency. There is,

certainly, an attraction in literary survival, and most writers know it; it is an extension of the parental instinct already discussed. But neither instinct enjoys more than a chance expectation of some moderately long period of time, and there is something poetically unsatisfactory about any too-great an emphasis on such speculations. True, when Pope in *The Rape of the Lock* promises a poetic immortality to Belinda's lock, we feel an engaging pleasure in recognising how the crippled poet, who must have felt deeply his severance from society, has indeed, up to our time, made Miss Fermor's lock a thing of splendour, though she is long forgotten. But is this of much use to her? Besides, Pope at least did his best to secure his work for posterity.

With Shakespeare, you certainly again feel like using the dangerous word 'convention' in its more derogatory sense of a, to him, *dead* convention, though this will not cover the whole field of our enquiry. We find sonnets building up to a strong third quatrain with a drop, not only in tension, since this is expected, but in quality of thought too, in the last couplet. Examples are thickly sprinkled, occurring among many of the later pieces. This is typical:

> Yet do thy worst, old Time: despite thy wrong
> My love shall in my verse ever live young.
>
> (19)

The splendid sonnet containing

> Time doth transfix the flourish set on youth,
> And delves the parallels in beauty's brow

concludes:

> And yet to times in hope my verse shall stand
> Praising thy worth, despite his cruel hand.
>
> (60)

This is at once slack poetry and cold comfort. The even greater Sonnet 65 ends with a couplet only slightly more convincing.[1]

Yet there is more to say. When we are told that the poetry will make the youth 'to be praised of ages yet to be' (101) so

[1] In discussion of these weak couplets, Edward Hubler (25-6) concludes that they are 'poetically, but not intellectually, false'; that the weakness has nothing to do with what the couplet 'says'. My own finding is different, but I hope that the two arguments will be compared. Mark van Doren (*Shakespeare*, 7-10) finds a similar weakness in the couplets of *Venus and Adonis* and *The Rape of Lucrece*.

that his worth stands 'even in the eyes of all posterity' (55), the conception of futurity as an infinite extension holds, in itself, a certain grandeur despite the dubious quality of the underlying thought. When the underlying thought itself is weighty, as with the 'olives of endless age' of the national Sonnet (107), there is no doubt of it, though even here the logic may have to be forgotten. For, though the poet had no good reason to expect an everlasting peace, the phrase reverberates; and in the reverberation, the echoing response in our minds, lies its real meaning.

We have noticed examples associating love, poetry, and long future time; but there is an even more interesting association of love, poetry, and long past time. Here especially, long time is saturated with feeling and felt almost mystically, as in Prospero's 'dark backward and abysm of time' in *The Tempest* (i, ii, 50). A whole sonnet is given to the poet's summoning up 'remembrance of things past' (30). But we also meet a deeper, racial, past with the peculiar aura, or mystique, of such conceptions, and this, too, recalling the well-known thought that 'memory is the mother of the muses', is regularly associated with literature. Our key-word is 'antique'.

This 'old time' is regarded as intrinsically good in contrast to modern corruption, after the manner of Orlando's words to Adam:

> O good old man! How well in thee appears
> The constant service of the antique world
> When service sweat for duty, not for meed.
> (*As You Like It*, ii, iii, 56)

So here the beauteous boy is, in comparison with the showy flamboyance and false decoration of contemporary society in 'these' days 'so bad' (67), a symbol of old time:

> In him those holy antique hours are seen,
> Without all ornament, itself and true . . .
> (68) [1]

He is a living contradiction of 'false art'. He, as a person, corresponds to Shakespeare's own poetry which refuses 'new

[1] The original text, which reads, 'it selfe and true', Tucker regards as impossible, and substitutes 'but self and true'. I do not see why 'it selfe' should not apply vaguely to a composite of 'beauty', 'him' and 'antique hours', all rolled into one. Elsewhere the syntax appears careless of singular and plural: see 55, l. 12; 106, l. 7. See also the *New Variorum* note. Peter Alexander follows the Quarto.

pride', 'variation' and 'quick change', and will not conform itself to 'the time', to fashion, eschewing all 'new-found methods' and 'compounds strange', precisely because 'I always write of you' (76). For truth and sincerity, old things are best. The youth's very youth thus holds the honour and integrity of 'holy antique hours'.

These old-time passages generally involve literature. So the poet imagines his pages of adoration, all 'yellow'd with their age', being called 'the stretched metre of an antique song' (17). Even when the word 'antique' accompanies the thought of time's destructiveness, it supports a literary, or near-literary, association, Time being told to draw no lines on the youth 'with thine antique pen' (19). Elsewhere the poet wonders if there be in truth 'nothing new', if all which exists 'hath been before'. If so, our brains are 'beguil'd', deceived, as they labour to deliver in poetry 'the second burthen of a former child'. He wishes that literary records would

> Show me your image in some antique book
> Since mind at first in character was done,
> That I might see what the old world could say
> To this composed wonder of your frame.
>
> (59)

The 'image' is not only to be perpetuated for future generations; it has pre-existed, and so might be found in ancient writings sinking back to the origins ('since mind at first in character was done') of literary composition. In one important example, Sonnet 123, literature is not involved, the 'registers' and 'records' being instead architectural. In this sonnet, to be discussed later (pp. 95-6), the poet reasserts the thought that nothing is new, with phrases ('former sight', 'we before have heard them told') that almost suggest a background theory of reincarnation or recurrence, such as Nietzsche's, or that of Shelley's 'The world's great age begins anew' in *Hellas*, or Rossetti's *Sudden Light*. Elsewhere, our natural medium for spanning the centuries is literature. We often seem to be thinking as much about poetry as about love, but the living and present reality of the beloved boy in whose service and honour these vast time-periods are imagined, remains central. When the poet reads 'in the chronicle of wasted time' descriptions of 'fairest wights' wherein 'beauty' is found 'making beautiful old rhyme', the poetry being born of the beauty, in praise of wondrous persons now 'dead', he finds his own, present, love therein depicted:

> I see their antique pen would have express'd
> Even such a beauty as you master now.
> So all their praises are but prophecies
> Of this our time, all you prefiguring;
> And, for they look'd but with divining eyes,
> They had not skill enough your worth to sing . . .
>
> (106)

They were really writing of Shakespeare's friend without knowing it. He either is, or reflects, a reality—the word here is 'image' (p. 39)—that was already apprehended by generations long dead, and this process is to be continued by Shakespeare's verse for generations unborn. So thought of long time, past and future, together with poetry, may be our entrance to possession of the truth. As far as poetry is concerned, it is the present that is at fault:

> For we, which now behold these present days,
> Have eyes to wonder, but lack tongues to praise.
>
> (106)

This couplet we need not call perfunctory, but our main interest is in the preceding build-up, wherein we feel the loved excellence to be, in some sense, *at home* with vast time-periods. In Sonnet 108, apologising for the falling off of his love-poetry, the poet's thoughts take a strange progress, as follows: 'I have already said it all. There is no more to say. But yet I go on saying it, "counting no old thing old".' What appears a trivial thought brings us up against a statement more interesting in its own right than in its context. In love age does not exist: it is beyond time. So, the thought burgeoning, igniting, he continues:

> So that eternal love in love's fresh case
> Weighs not the dust and injury of age,
> Nor gives to necessary wrinkles place,
> But makes antiquity for aye his page . . .
>
> (108)

'Antiquity' again, with literature present in 'page'. The quatrain asserts that love now and for ever masters age and *revivifies* antiquity, the word 'aye' covering the future as well as the past and tending to generalise the statement. More is meant, or at least said, than the superficial logic, concerned here with the youth's increasing age (see p. 115 below), might justify.

The youth is an archetype of all that is best in legend and literature, and he will exist in poetry for ages to come, as he existed in ages past; almost, we may add, irrespective of whether Shakespeare's poetry survives or not, since there will be other poets at work, and the theme is immortal. But again, literature is only a poor reflection (p. 20). The young man, through poetry, will live, we are told, 'in lovers' eyes' (55); 'eyes' are our most potent implements of love-intercourse (pp. 37–42); and what has this to do with *reading*? Is it not rather that the poetry awakens us to a knowledge of his universal significance? Of some indefinable Love beating through love-sight generation after generation? But Shakespeare will not so dissolve his subject into abstractions. He keeps close to the incarnate miracle 'crowning the present' (115); and it is, we may suggest, this *present moment* that must be supposed to have existed long ago, and is somehow to exist in some sort of futurity, temporal or super-temporal, in association, either way, with literature, if only because there is no other way to talk about it. It again seems that we are being forced towards some such conception as Nietzsche's doctrine of an *eternal*, which is not the same as a *temporal* (*Christ and Nietzsche*, v, 191), recurrence.

There are two primary *objective* realities (the mystery of complete union has already, on pp. 35–42, been handled): (i) the beauteous youth, and (ii) the poetry created by Shakespeare, or by others. The first exists in the immediate, the now, 'crowning the present' (115), and only there. The second, literature, is to be associated with long time, either past or future, but is definitely inadequate, dwarfed, within the immediate experience (83; pp. 20, 84). We may call this long time, for want of a term, 'poetic time', and add to our references 'the prophetic soul of the wide world, dreaming on things to come' and 'olives of endless age' of Sonnet 107.[1]

[1] With this 'prophetic soul' compare Hamlet's 'O, my prophetic soul' (*Hamlet*, I, v, 40) and the Queen's long metaphysical passage of foreboding (*Richard II*, II, ii, 1–66), analysed in *The Wheel of Fire*, XIII, 257–8.

Within 'poetic time' the youth is felt to be immortal, present equally in antiquity and for posterity. But much depends on the poetry. What is its relation to the real thing? The poet knows well that getting a son is a more effective way of self-perpetuation than 'barren rhyme' (16); that the youth's 'eyes' hold more life than 'both' his admiring poets can possibly devise (83); and that in the last resort he can only himself avoid falsification by repeating 'you alone are you' and 'you are you' (84), like Antony in his cups describing the crocodile (*Antony and Cleopatra*, II, vii, 47–57; *The Imperial Theme*, VII, 232). Poetry appears to be the only means of possessing the reality in temporal terms and yet written poetry is surely inadequate, and the inadequacy is driven home in two final literary-immortality couplets promising in one that the boy will remain 'green' in these 'black lines' (63), and in the other showing a specific doubt:

> O none, unless this miracle have might,
> That in black ink my love may still shine bright.
>
> (65)

In both the word 'black' deliberately underlines an important contrast. It is a term natural to a poet who was careless of, and perhaps scorned, publication. And yet he is certainly aware of some *miraculous* possibility. The truth is, that there is indeed a poetic 'miracle', but it is not just a matter of publication and perpetuity. Rather the poet knows that through his poetry, or the poetic consciousness, he establishes, or focusses, a supernal reality, or truth, what we may call a 'poetic dimension', that cannot otherwise be attained; and of this the written poetry ('black ink'), though it be necessary, is really subsidiary, the carrot to the donkey, but not the journey's purpose.

In Pope's *Temple of Fame* we have an intricate pattern of lasting renown, virtue, judgment, and a goddess who might almost be called 'eternity', much of it directly associated with poetry, either as a perpetuating medium, or as a cause, of fame. The poet is careful to distinguish just from unjust fame, and gets into some confusion in so doing. But his confusions are themselves salutary and point us, exactly as do the Sonnets, and Socrates' very similar reference to fame in *The Symposium* (p. 217 below), to some greater reality, evident throughout the poem, of which poetry, fame, and long time are derivatives. And it is to this greater reality alone that Pope finally subscribes: 'Oh, grant an honest fame, or grant me none.' So in the Sonnets, what the poetry is trying to say in all long-time passages, past or future, might run like this: 'The poetic consciousness is in some way related to a dimension that may be inadequately expressed as aeons of time (e.g. the 'olives of endless age' of Sonnet 107) within which dimension I believe that the beauteous youth enjoys some mysterious existence'. He does not actually say this, but what the poetry is getting at is obviously very like it: in one of Michelangelo's sonnets (62) the poetic immortality is directly associated with the soul's heavenly existence, and we may suppose that the Shakespearian meaning is not so very different. We are, of course, deliberately trying to penetrate below the surface into possibilities which Shakespeare need not be supposed to have formulated. But they are nevertheless thoughts which, as we shall see, speak again and again through the greatest passages, provided that we do not let the superficial reasoning cloud them.

There is some direct evidence that the poetry is, more or less, fulfilling the function indicated. It is shown as not merely a perpetuating instrument, but a way of making contact with, of mentally entering, or possessing, the wondrous thing. There is a reciprocity between the object and the poetry, and it may be hard to say which is most indebted to the other. Shakespeare often writes proudly as though his poetry is making something of the youth that would not otherwise exist (e.g. 'I engraft you new', 15). But he can also admit, as we have just seen (pp. 85–6), that poetry is nothing in comparison. So, too, the rival poet only 'invents' for the youth what he has stolen *from* the youth; he lends the 'virtue' and 'beauty' which he first 'stole' (79). This is the paradox of all art, adequately discussed in Perdita's flower-dialogue in *The Winter's Tale* (IV, iii, 79–108; see *The Crown of Life*, III, 105). Nature is above art, but without art you cannot realise that in nature which is above art. The art is a fusing medium, and Shakespeare's relation with the Fair Youth could be exactly defined as a 'poetic marriage'; but by that phrase we mean very much more than a 'literary' marriage. The distinction is subtle.

This poetic marriage takes the place of the real marriage

urged in the opening sonnets. In both we have some interesting thoughts on *distillation*. A son would act as a distilled essence:

> Then, were not summer's distillation left,
> A liquid prisoner pent in walls of glass,
> Beauty's effect with beauty were bereft,
> Nor it, nor no remembrance what it was:
>> But flowers distill'd, though they with winter meet,
>> Leese but their show; their substance still lives sweet.
>
> (5)

The material 'show' is felt as refined. Notice the lovely line 'A liquid prisoner pent in walls of glass', recalling 'Leading him prisoner in a red-rose chain' in *Venus and Adonis* (110). There is no defeat in it; the real 'substance', a word heavy with medieval respect, is maintained; and it is precisely this 'no defeat' which the poet regularly strives to establish. Here it is, superficially, a matter of getting a son, but precisely the same thought recurs with the next, literary-immortality, mechanism, and this repetition itself does something to suggest—we shall meet the process again (pp. 91–3)—that it is *the core of the thought*, not its conventional trappings, that has the poet, as Keats puts it, 'in thrall'. In our next example (54), the boy is compared to a rose in contrast to a 'canker-bloom', or wild rose. The latter's colour is as good, but its 'virtue' (i.e. spiritual validity, magical radiations, power) is only a 'show', and so such blossoms 'die to themselves'. But 'sweet roses do not so', for 'of their sweet deaths are sweetest odours made'; their deaths are, as in great tragedy, for the line compresses volumes, creative. Death *is* their poetic immortality:

> And so of you, beauteous and lovely youth,
> When that shall fade, my verse distills your truth.[1]
>
> (54)

This is not a weak conclusion. Why? Simply because the poet has found a metaphoric expression which does not commit him to a platitude; and once we see this, we may be prepared to feel the same drive behind the platitudes themselves, or at least to

---

[1] The emendation of 'vade, by' to 'fade, my' makes better reading today, but 'vade' (= decay) may be correct. Butler points to 'fade' in l. 10. In support of 'my', we can adduce the passive 'distill'd' of Sonnet 5; and see p. 181.

do justice to the great lines without allowing the platitudes to
smother them.

The poet knows well that his poetry is more than his
ordinary self. It is 'the very part was consecrate to thee', his
own 'spirit', 'the better part of me', to be contrasted with the
element of 'earth' which is 'the dregs of life', bound for death
(74). This 'better part' is the 'air' and 'fire' elsewhere stated to
be *always with his loved one* (45; pp. 45–6). It is a refined state of
being, like the refinement of distilled essences, like, to use a
phrase from Donne's *A Valediction*, 'gold to airy thinness beat'.

Self-supported by such arguments, let us once more risk
finding a profundity within a platitude. The youth, says the
poet, will live in the life-breath of poetry as nowhere else:

> You still shall live—such virtue hath my pen—
> Where breath most breathes, even in the mouths of men.
>
> (81)

The superficial thought is nothing, but the words used, the
quiet security of 'still', placed as it is, meaning 'perpetually';
the 'virtue', meaning magical power, of the poetry; the emphatic
'breath' and 'breathes' insisting on a living, not an abstract,
reality; the humanism of 'men'; all these may well point us
on to Hermione's resurrection in *The Winter's Tale*, 'warm' as
in life, raised by a magic 'lawful as eating' (*The Winter's Tale*,
v, iii, 109–11; for a similar use of 'still' in 'move still, still so'
at IV, iii, 142, see *The Crown of Life*, III, 107). My suggestion
is that a not dissimilar miracle is, if not hinted, at least deep-
buried, as a bulb in the soil, in these lines.[1]

In such passages a reality outspacing, or eluding, definition is being apprehended through poetry. Why? For the very
reason which we are analysing, and indeed using: because
under poetic, or as Nietzsche would say, Dionysian, control,
the rhythm, rhyme-scheme, and sonnet-form performing the
function of the Dionysian music and inspiration, things are
continually being suggested beyond the superficial thought-
moulds that contain them. We must beware of reading the

---

[1] On l. 14 George Wyndham comments: 'In Shakespeare's day the *breath* was all but
identified with the spirit, and the *mouth*, consequently, is held in special honour by
Platonic writers. In Hoby's *Courtyer*, iv. (1561), kissing is defended on the ground of
the sanctity attaching to the mouth as the gateway of the soul'. See also below pp. 163–4,
178, 199.

letter and missing the spirit; that is, the experience prompting
and behind the poetry, springing from what we have called the
'poetic dimension', something at least not too dissimilar from
those wondrous powers defined in Biron's speech on 'love' in
Love's Labour's Lost (IV, iii, 290–365, *The Shakespearian
Tempest*, App. A, 312–13). That is why the poet asserts that
the youth will, through his poetry, 'live' in men's 'breath' or
'eyes' (18, 55): he does all he can to preserve physical vitality.
The poetry in such passages must always be felt not only as
living thought, but also as thought about what is living. It
depends on the reader whether or not it remains, in any given
instance, merely 'black ink' (p. 86). We are trying to assure
that it does not.

Poetry we can define as 'virtue' in the old sense, or 'power'
in our own, Keats' 'might half-slumbering on its own right arm'
in *Sleep and Poetry*. Such a definition will make sense of our
response to that great opening:

> Was it the proud full sail of his great verse
> Bound for the prize of all too precious you . . .
>   (86)

Superficially this refers to a learned poet with a reputation trying to win the youth's favour. Read otherwise, it speaks of a fine
poet, with majestic powers, trying to *capture the reality which is
the miraculous youth*. This, admittedly, will not fit the sustained
argument that follows, without some forcing. But it has justification in terms of Shakespeare's symbolism in general and the
Sonnets in particular (p. 66; and see p. 94). Even if we be un-
duly expanding the thought, the result, provided that we realise
what we may be doing, may be worth the price: as that 'proud
full sail' is bellied out, enlarged, by the breath of Heaven to
drive the great ship to its prize, so does poetry, impelled by
rhythms, by spirit-powers, enlarge the mind to drive the soul to
its desire.

Shakespeare's meaning outdistances his concepts. He keeps
close to actual experience and normal, even platitudinous,
thought-moulds. He relies comparatively little on metaphysical
paradox, and not at all on any esoteric symbolism. In so far as
an explicit transcendence is spoken of, it is done through the
orthodox religious conception of 'doom', or Doomsday. The

term held a precision and detonation far in excess of our abstract term 'eternity'; it was known as a conclusion to time, as in *Macbeth* (IV, i, 117); but, though closely related to arithmetical time, it had, as may be seen from its use in a certain fine passage of *2 Henry VI* (v, ii, 40–5), the strongest emotional overtones. People believed in it, or thought that they did, without question, but it was also as mysterious as could be.

It appears in the Sonnets. The youth, through poetry, shall be known to 'all posterity, that wear this world out to the ending Doom' (55). Comparing love's steadfastness with Time, the poet assures himself that:

> Love alters not with his brief hours and weeks
> But bears it out even to the edge of Doom.
>
> (116)

A more than personal life-span is included: love lasts till Doomsday. Notice, too, how time itself ('hours and weeks') is, as a numerical sequence, trivial ('brief')—a thought found elsewhere in contrast of love's strength with 'short-number'd hours' (124)—in comparison with the greater reality, or dimension, shadowed by 'doom', or, as we should say, though with less impact, 'eternity'. It is, of course, difficult to respond simultaneously to such a long-time passage as 'olives of endless age' in Sonnet 107, where the word 'doom' is actually used as a *confining* term, and to the time-annihilating Doomsday. But, though rationally incompatible, they are both used as adversaries to time as we know it: a greater reality is adumbrated in contrast to time's triviality.

The poet plays every variation known to him on time and its antagonists. Time may be ruthless and villainous, but it may also hold an aura of almost religious grandeur and mystery, as aeons, past or future, swing into our view, with thoughts of 'antiquity' (pp. 82–5), 'posterity' (55), and 'the prophetic soul of the wide world dreaming on things to come' (107). The use of 'soul' brings in religious associations; and such associations are even stronger in 'doom', the great act of God annihilating Time. Rival and incompatible conceptions jostle each other, but that matters little, since the reality is behind, and indefinable.

The exact interrelation of our various attempts may be best seen from noticing the recurring and highly significant thought of loss and gain as mutually dependent on each other, as when we are told that 'Time that gave doth now his gift confound' (60). The boy's beauty, destroyed, or hidden, by Time, is itself 'Time's best jewel' (65). The gain and loss may be conceived as all but simultaneous, as aspects of a single activity. As we have seen (p. 72), the same hours which 'did frame' the boy work to 'unfair' that 'which fairly doth excell' (5). These paradoxes suggest a universal law. There is gain as well as loss. That the sun should be daily 'new and old' (76) is obvious enough, but we have a more interesting thought concerning the continual contests of ocean and land, 'increasing store with loss and loss with store' (64). Not only is all life 'consum'd with that which it was nourish'd by' (73): we are almost tempted to put it the other way round, and the poet sometimes does so. This is done in terms of both (i) marriage-advice and (ii) literary-immortality. In the first, we have, 'As fast as thou shalt wane, so fast thou grow'st' (11); that is, by getting a son. In the second we find, 'As he takes from you, I engraft you new' (15); that is, in verse. Observe the nature-metaphors; a natural process is hinted; and that each mechanism should use this same thought suggests an underlying universal below the semi-conventional and often trite statements. We are accordingly not surprised to find the paradox once firmly stated in religious terms in a famous and valuable sonnet. The poet contrasts his 'soul' with his 'sinful earth' (cp. the elemental sonnets, 44, 45, and 74; pp. 46, 89), and the one is said to grow as the other wanes:

> Then, soul, live thou upon thy servant's loss,
> And let that pine to aggravate thy store:
> Buy terms divine in selling hours of dross;
> Within be fed, without be rich no more:
>> So shalt thou feed on Death, that feeds on men,
>> And Death once dead, there's no more dying then.
>
> (146)

Time ('hours') is sold in exchange for the 'terms divine,' but 'fed' preserves contact with the natural order; it is a natural law.

Here we have a clear statement of what is elsewhere shadowy. It repeats, and interprets for us, our other thoughts on the universal principle of interaction and balance, loss and gain. These, and we shall later on (p. 97) observe yet another example, we have listed in relation to the temporal process, as a

natural phenomenon; in terms of the marriage, biological, process; and in the literary-immortality thought-pattern. Clearly,
we are to feel it as a universal principle of which all these are
aspects, and it is the principle that matters. Here, in our
religious sonnet, the great thing is firmly said, because an
adequate thought-mould, in terms of a religious tradition, is
being used.

The precision however derives again from reliance on a
'convention', or 'tradition', and by the use of such, in our present context, question-begging terms as 'soul', 'divine', 'within'.
On these the poet normally refuses, as Donne does not, to place
any final emphasis. He prefers to use more human implements.
The marriage-mechanism is, it is true, soon thrown over, and
never re-introduced. But it is not so with the poetic-immortality
thought-pattern: this he will not let rest. He keeps worrying at
it. Our religious pieces at least show that the truth at which he
is driving has strong religious affinities; it is a truth most easily,
if not quite satisfactorily, expressed in terms of religious
phraseology.

Such terms, for Shakespeare, had lost authority. They were
somehow believed in, and yet not all-sufficient. To his more
humanistic imagination, romantic love and beauty were not
honoured, as he wished to honour them, by the orthodox tradition. Failing a complete submission to a religious dogmatism as
precise and as firmly accepted by the whole community as that
of the medieval church, this was bound to happen; and not only
with themes of love and beauty. The poet's instinct tells him
that the wanted key is somehow in his own poetry: so poetic
thought-patterns, images, symbols, must be found.

Later English poets have used various mechanisms and
symbols. We have all the various tricks and penetrations, with
use of orthodox, scientific, homely and humorous associations,
of the Metaphysicals. The central problem is always some sort
of 'eternity'. Various symbols may be used. There is the 'ring
of light' in Vaughan's *The World*; Pope's 'wheel' (*Essay on Man*,
I, 59); the mountains, domes, and urns of romantic poetry to
which I give a study in *The Starlit Dome* (summarised in
Laureate of Peace); the circular symbolisms of Browning, the
best occurring in *Abt Vogler* and *An Epistle of Karshish*; Nietzsche's doctrine of the eternal recurrence and his 'ring' of

'eternity' (pp. 57, 69, 83–5); the dome and other packed symbols in Yeats' two *Byzantium* poems; and Eliot's 'vase', 'dance' and other circular intuitions in *The Four Quartets*. We may on occasion find it helpful to suppose some sort of vertical time to represent a kinetic eternity, as used by J. W. Dunne in his *Experiment with Time* and my own discussions in *The Christian Renaissance* (x, 260–1) and *Christ and Nietzsche* (v, 189–93). The choice lies between that and the circle. Both can be helpful.

Shakespeare's visual imagination, being so eminently humanistic, is mainly limited to the horizontal; he has few architectural symbols, and no mountains of importance outside *Cymbeline*. In the plays, as I have shown in *The Shakespearian Tempest*, transcendence is generally suggested through music or infinity-symbols of vast ocean. Music is important in Sonnets 8 and 128; and the sea is an infinitude when the youth's 'worth' is called 'wide as the ocean' and the poet's 'saucy bark', though 'inferior' to that of his poetic rival, is to be kept 'afloat' by his friend's 'help', whilst the other, presumably risking disaster, 'upon your soundless deep doth ride' (80). Both expanse and depth are involved. But our ruling eternity-symbol here, and it is a clearly ruling symbol throughout Shakespeare's plays, is the crown itself, the king, so repeatedly used (pp. 60–3). The Crown, in both its rondure and its height, is a symbol of the eternal dimension, while its gold symbolises the value, or 'worth' (80, 116), of our theme. We remember Donne's 'great Prince' in *The Ecstasy*, love there giving the superhuman experience, or being, the Deity, whatever deity he be, his, or its, freedom; as though, when two people are 'in love with' each other, a great presence is liberated. Or something quite outside the natural order may be created, born, as with the 'naked seraph' of Shelley's additional lines to *Epipsychidion*, a poem explicitly compared by Shelley to Shakespeare's Sonnets. To this poem we shall return (pp. 210–15) in discussion of the Phoenix. The Phoenix is an obvious symbol of immortality, but, though it appears once in the Sonnets (19), is not there very important, since they rely little on an esoteric symbolism.

They do, however, offer some interesting vertical eternity-symbols of a traditional and obvious kind in terms of those 'monuments' impregnated with dramatic power in the last act of *Romeo and Juliet*, in the poetry of *Pericles* (v, i, 140; p. 102), and occasionally elsewhere. Architecture itself derives from sacred structures, kings' tombs, and temples, aiming simultaneously at permanence and vertical emphasis to counter the horizontal qualities of nature and time. Such impressions are used in the Sonnets to excellent, though negative, effect. Their great powers are introduced to be shown as less than those of poetic-immortality, or immortality-within-the-poetic-dimension. So 'marble', 'gilded monuments', statues, all shall pass whilst the other remains indestructible (55); so shall 'lofty towers' and 'brass eternal' (64); 'gilded' tombs, 'tombs of brass' (101, 107); indeed, 'brass', 'stone', 'earth' and 'boundless sea', all shall bow their 'power' to 'mortality', while 'beauty' may survive within the 'miracle' of poetry (65). Every hint is given that somehow there *is* a 'miracle', like, yet unlike, 'black ink', in which the excelling thing outlasts nature ('earth' and 'boundless sea'). These obvious, material, grandeurs, the 'cloud-capp'd towers', 'gorgeous palaces', 'solemn temples' and 'great globe' of *The Tempest* (IV, i, 152), the poet deliberately rejects as inadequate; but even so, their presence here, as in Prospero's speech, lends mass and weight to the massive quality of the otherness adumbrated. The poet specifically scorns all state ceremonies and 'great bases' laid 'for eternity' (125). He refuses to submit, possessing a reality nobler and more enduring than the greatest monuments that have survived from the antiquity which he elsewhere (pp. 82–5) so deeply honours:

No, Time, thou shalt not boast that I do change:
Thy pyramids built up with newer might
To me are nothing novel, nothing strange;
They are but dressings of a former sight.
Our dates are brief, and therefore we admire
What thou dost foist upon us that is old,
And rather make them born to our desire
Than think that we before have heard them told.
Thy registers and thee I both defy,
Not wondering at the present nor the past,
For thy records and what we see doth lie,
Made more or less by thy continual haste.
  This I do vow, and this shall ever be,
  I will be true, despite thy scythe and thee.

(123)

An uneasy sonnet, to which we shall return, written by a man who knows that his love *is* changing, but who refuses to believe that the essence of it is lost. And more than simple personal loyalty is concerned. What the poetry says is: 'Fine new edifices are merely copies of antiquity, which we, creatures of an hour, mistakenly admire as new. But for my part, I refuse to abase myself before either old or new, since the mightiest symbols of lastingness are nothing to the lastingness I feel within my own experience, and to that feeling I will stand true, and give it my faith'.[1]

We should explain it all—and yet how can a word be an explanation?—by use of the word 'eternal'. Shakespeare uses the word too, with various shades of meaning, sad and happy. We have the 'barren rage of Death's eternal cold' (13); 'thy eternal summer shall not fade' and the 'eternal lines' of poetry's perpetuating (18); 'eternal numbers' (38); 'brass eternal' (64); 'Time's thievish progress to eternity' (77); 'eternal love' (108), and the 'great bases' laid 'for eternity' recently quoted (125). There is, too, a strange sonnet in which the poet apologises for having given away a gift, urging that a keepsake is unneeded since his friend's memory is already graven on his mind 'beyond all date, even to eternity'; or at least, he adds, with a typical return to realism, so long as 'brain' and 'heart' last in 'nature' (122). Here eternity probably means 'Doomsday', so that the line means 'beyond time up to the day of judgment', when 'time' will be destroyed. However, most of our eternity-references appear to mean roughly what they would mean today. They suggest a state-of-being, or dimension, which can be thought of variously as infinite time or as timelessness. We may think of vertical time in the eternal dimension, or of time circling back on itself, recalling our antiquity passages (pp. 82–85). Anything will do, provided that it is not subject to ending. Once, after apologising for a temporary disloyalty, the poet reasserts his love with: 'Now all is done, have what shall have no end' (110). The sonnets are in fact so powerfully charged with this battering insistence that the insistence alone goes far towards establishing a generalised statement.

[1] In his notes on this sonnet Tucker, as sometimes elsewhere (p. 131), appears to me to dissolve the symbolism too far into a secondary sort of metaphor. Wyndham reads 'dressings of a former sight' as 'repetitions of antenatal experience'.

The last sonnet of the main series to the Fair Youth is a farewell in twelve lines, in which many past themes are interwoven. It runs:

> O thou, my lovely boy, who in thy power
> Dost hold Time's fickle glass his fickle hour;
> Who hast by waning grown, and therein show'st
> Thy lovers withering as thy sweet self grow'st;
> If Nature, sovereign mistress over wrack,
> As thou goest onwards, still will pluck thee back,
> She keeps thee to this purpose, that her skill
> May Time disgrace, and wretched minutes kill.
> Yet fear her, O thou minion of her pleasure!
> She may detain, but not still keep, her treasure:
> Her audit, though delay'd, answered must be,
> And her quietus is to render thee.
>
> (126)

The poet writes without bitterness, admitting that the boy must grow up, whatever the loss ('waning'). There is the give-and-take process at work which we have already met in various forms (pp. 91–2), and somehow the 'sweet self', the eternal self or soul as we may call it, is *within the growing*. Nature, always at work recreating what is dissolving, is herself in sovereign control over any destruction within her own domain. We have already (pp. 72, 92) found nature and time responsible for the making of the thing which they appear to kill. Here elucidation is gained by contrasting nature as responsible for the whole with time as destroyer. The youth must go onward in time, but nature continually ('still') preserves him, holding him 'back', as in 'Or what strong hand can hold his swift foot back' (65). Nature's hand, the 'great creating Nature' of *The Winter's Tale* (iv, iii, 88), *is* strong enough, up to a point. But she cannot do it for ever. She must finally 'render' him up, to death.

The sonnet comes near to establishing nature as itself a safeguard controlling destruction. We are near to reading into it the significance we have a right to find in the Witch's

> Though his bark cannot be lost
> Yet it shall be tempest-toss'd

in *Macbeth* (I, iii, 24). We cannot quite do so. But the words 'sovereign mistress over wrack' and 'may time disgrace', which are true enough of nature if a wide view be taken, remain too powerful for our paraphrase; 'quietus', though a legal term, also suggests peace; and 'render' surely indicates 'render up safe'. If nature be greater and more good than time, may there not also be some power greater and more good than nature? If so, and perhaps only if so, the use of 'render' is felicitous.

In reading the Sonnets we are continually treading the brink of Abt Vogler's 'There shall never be one lost good' in Browning's remarkable poem. Shakespeare does not quite say that, either because the thought was in his day impossible, or because he considered that it was not worth saying. But it must be remembered that for these shattering assurances Browning chose a musician improvising on the organ. They are *what the musician knew whilst living in the music*. Such was the Dionysian experience celebrated by Nietzsche throughout *The Birth of Tragedy*, whereby, through music, your inmost self, to be distinguished from the superficial 'ego', your deepest *I am*, sounds from 'the abyss of being' and becomes one with the 'Primordial Being' in wisdom and power (*The Birth of Tragedy*; v; xvii). You then *know*, subjectively, what cannot be proved, or known, or even thought, through the objective intelligence. Such a subjective wisdom is accorded by Nietzsche to the impassioned lyrist, the dithyrambist; and to reach any final judgment as to what the Sonnets, as poetry, mean, we must give exact attention to their more impassioned, emotionally authoritative, dithyrambic, moments; when, to borrow a metaphor from Shelley's *Defence of Poetry*, the poetry becomes 'a sword of lightning' which 'consumes the scabbard that would contain it'.

We must therefore not remain content with Apollonian logic, or even with the Apollonian image; we must feel the kinetic, energic, Dionysian movement; the heave of its ocean, its swell and crests. In many of the Sonnets the power tends to rise at the second or third quatrain, and falls at the conclusion. In this they point to Shakespeare's dramatic technique, where every long speech advances in waves, two or three; flowers, burgeons out, from within, like a fountain. Power increases; but the conclusion is quiet. It is the same with his wider structures: his plays gather momentum and power, taking a new lease of life in the third act, as though a surface was burst open to reveal imaginative splendour; and here, too, there is a quiet conclusion, a fall to commentary and ritual. The same is true of Shakespeare's work as a whole, from the Histories and the Romantic Comedies, to the violence of the Tragedies, the wonder of the Final Plays, and the ritualistic conclusion in *Henry VIII*. In matters small and vast alike, this is the typifying Shakespearian form; and we have it already within the Sonnets.

The third quatrain of the sonnet 'Shall I compare thee to a summer's day?' rises to:

> But thy eternal summer shall not fade,
> Nor lose possession of that fair thou ow'st,
> Nor shall Death brag thou wander'st in his shade . . .
>
>   (18)

This crests and breaks as a wave of assurance, with a sense of victory for which the opening lines had scarcely prepared us. Next we have:

> When in eternal lines to time thou grow'st.
>   (18)

Starting by saying something large, the poet ends by saying something small: the great claim 'eternal' is subdued beneath 'time', the thought directly contradicting the definition of Time in *The Rape of Lucrece* (967) as 'thou ceaseless lackey to eternity'. The poetry promises, in a way *is*, eternity, as again in the line 'eternal numbers to outlive long date' (38), since it is the language of the eternal dimension; but the poet has only actually said that it offers a considerable time-period of memory. The conclusion

> So long as men can breathe or eyes can see,
> So long lives this, and this gives life to thee
>   (18)

is only worthy of the earlier assurance in so far as we allow 'breathe', 'eyes', 'lives' and 'life' to carry such meanings (p. 89) that we are left with the thought that poetry actually gives, and not merely records, life; and it needs more than *written* poetry to do that.

The crest may come in the second quatrain, as with the daring alliteration and conquering impact of:

> Then, in the blazon of sweet beauty's best,
> Of hand, of foot, of lip, of eye, of brow,
> I see their antique pen would have express'd
> Even such a beauty as you master now.
>
> (106)

Here the conquest is of past time; the excellence is so great that all past excellences are offered in vassalage to it; it is lord of antiquity as well as of the future. This is a fine example of the strong physical adoration lying at the heart of the poet's meanings. It is also a fine example of cresting, rising, movement. It is only in so far as we respond to these victorious, compelling, dithyrambic, assurances, or rather to the victorious*ness* and rhetorical compulsions *of* these assurances, that the greater meanings break through, the meaning I will not say *of*, but resounding *within*, such pieces as:

> Love's not Time's fool, though rosy lips and cheeks
> Within his bending sickle's compass come;
> Love alters not with his brief hours and weeks
> But bears it out even to the edge of Doom.
>
> (116)

Beauty fades; love, and he *wants* to say beauty too, does not. As we have observed (p. 91), time here is 'brief', a nothing, to the conjured vastness of 'doom'.

Sometimes a single word assume a largeness of thought that is not otherwise explicit, as when, in one of our marriage-advice pieces, we start:

> But wherefore do not you a mightier way
> Make war upon this bloody tyrant, Time?
>
> (16)

'Mightier' is too strong for its context. The same is true of 'pace' in this, one of the greatest sonnets of all, powerful though the context itself be:

> Not marble, nor the gilded monuments
> Of princes, shall outlive this powerful rhyme;
> But you shall shine more bright in these contents
> Than unswept stone, besmear'd with sluttish time.

> When wasteful war shall statues overturn,
> And broils root out the work of masonry,
> Nor Mars his sword nor war's quick fire shall burn
> The living record of your memory.
> 'Gainst death and all-oblivious enmity
> Shall you pace forth; your praise shall still find room
> Even in the eyes of all posterity
> That wear this world out to the ending doom.
>   So, till the judgment that yourself arise,
>   You live in this, and dwell in lovers' eyes.
>
>   (55)

See how clear is the thought in the final couplet: the young man's immortality is not questioned. He will rise, presumably in good repair, at the day of judgment. But if so, what is all the fuss about? What does it matter whether he be known to readers of poetry during the few intervening centuries?

Clearly, there is more in the sonnet than this. It is throughout filled to overflowing with the elixir, the ecstasy, the dithyrambic certainties. Observe that the main emphasis is on, not love, but the powers of poetry. We have already (pp.84–6) seen how poetry is in the Sonnets felt as a medium for supernal intuitions. Here every image piles up to suggest that the poetry enjoys an authority, or exists from a dimension, to which all temporal fabrications and engagements are as nothing; and the weightiest and most serious are chosen for the purpose. This poetic authority creates a 'living record'. The phrase recalls the living God of the Gospels and St. Paul; like that god, it is conqueror over death. Read so, there need be no worry about the incompatibility introduced by 'doom' and 'judgment' day, since a context has been generated of sufficient power to absorb them, with all their awful associations, into the main assertion. The two ways of eternal understanding, religion and poetry, are happily balanced in our final juxtaposition of 'judgment' and 'lovers' eyes'.

The truth present within the noble music of this sonnet is underlined by the simple word 'pace':

> 'Gainst death and all-oblivious enmity
> Shall you *pace* forth . . .

Tucker's comment is: 'Keep steadily on; but "forth" implies conspicuousness before the world's eyes.' But it also, I think, means, 'Come forward,' 'come out of obscurity to be seen' as in the Friar's

> Romeo, come forth! Come forth, thou fearful man!

in *Romeo and Juliet* (III, iii, I). 'Pace' suggests a great numinous presence, recalling, once again, Donne's 'great Prince' (p. 61), or Wordsworth's

> . . . huge and mighty forms, that do not live
> Like living men

in *The Prelude* (I, 398). Such was the presence hinted by our conception of the youth as an eternal archetype (p. 85); it is both ghostly and royal, like the Ghost in *Hamlet*, but without his sepulchral and purgatorial connotations. It moves with authority. It is something, or somebody, to which 'death' clearly 'subscribes' (107).

This is, indeed, an intuition which Shakespeare laboured to possess or define in drama after drama. It is in the great speeches of eternal recognition in *Hamlet*, *Macbeth*, *King Lear*, *Timon of Athens*, and *The Tempest* (v, ii, 232–8; v, v, 19–28; v, iii, 8–19; v, i, 191–3, 219–24; IV, i, 151–8). It is in Romeo's dream of love beyond death:

> I dreamt my lady came and found me dead—
> Strange dream, that gives a dead man leave to think—
> And breath'd such life with kisses in my lips,
> That I reviv'd, and was an emperor.
>
> *(Romeo and Juliet, v, i. 6)*

It is in Cleopatra's 'I dream'd there was an Emperor Antony . . .' (*Antony and Cleopatra*, v, ii, 76); in Pericles' vision of Marina as 'a palace for the crown'd Truth to dwell in' (v, i, 123), and

> Like Patience gazing on kings' graves and smiling
> Extremity out of act.
>
> *(Pericles, v, i, 140)*

It is finally dramatised in the awakening of Hermione's statue in *The Winter's Tale*.

We cannot argue that Shakespeare ought to have expressed it more clearly, more rationally. What rationality is there in the dogma of the resurrection of the body? Or in Nietzsche's doctrine of eternal recurrence? What religion, what philosophy, what poetic symbols, ever have made immortality a simple thing? But again, what religion of highest worth, what philosophy of weight, what poet of calibre, have not levelled all their powers against Death? To take an example from an at-first-sight very different poet, Dante:

> The celestial love, that spurns
> All envying in its bounty, in itself
> With such effulgence blazeth, as sends forth
> All beauteous things eternal. What distils
> Immediate thence, no end of being knows;
> Bearing its seal immutably impressed.
> Whatever thence immediate falls, is free,
> Free wholly, uncontrollable by power
> Of each thing new . . .
>
> (*Paradiso*, trans. Cary, VII, 60)

This is, too, what Shakespeare is saying. But the saying of it is, of course, in itself of slight value. What is wanted is its realisation. At the greatest moments of the Sonnets the realisation, both emotional and perceptual, is superb. Shakespeare's peculiar importance lies in his reluctance to part with flesh and blood, with actual dramatic experience, with the thing seen and known. He keeps as close as he can to nature, and to common-sense, though he does not stop there. We may even hazard the thought that his very reliance on conventional thought-moulds is an aspect of his strength: you cannot easily separate the one from the other.

V

THE EXPANSION

The reborn soul is as the eye which, having gazed into the
Sun, thenceforward sees the Sun in everything.
MEISTER ECKHART

WE shall now discuss more precisely the relation of the
Sonnets to Shakespeare's dramatic work. The Sonnets
record a progress through the bisexual adoration and integration to an eternal insight, or intuition. And from such an
intuition, creation inevitably proceeds; nor can it come from
anything less. On the biological plane, sexual intercourse is
prompted by sense of some mysterious fascination, by, pre-
eminently, a certain recognition, which, under a final analysis,
may be called a recognition of eternal significance. This is the
tree's blossom, and the fruit of it is procreation. It is the same
with artistic creation. Dante's life-work was prompted by love:

> Count of me but as one,
> Who am the scribe of love; that, when he breathes,
> Take up my pen, and, as he dictates, write.
> (*Purgatorio*, trans. Cary, XXIV, 52)

In Dante all creation descends from the eternal divinity, or
'triune love', which impresses variously lower and higher forms
with its 'ideal stamp':

> Were the wax
> Moulded with nice exactness, and the Heaven
> In its disposing influence supreme,
> The brightness of the seal should be complete:
> But nature renders it imperfect ever,
> Resembling thus the artist, in her work,
> Whose faltering hand is faithless to his skill.
> (*Paradiso*, XIII, 67)

To Michelangelo his love is as an angel descended to lighten
'this prison-house' our world; things high and rare, wrought in

ture', reflect the 'blessings' of their divine origin; ...nage, and this image it is which the poet loves (... ...h insight penetrates the truth of the created w... ...r some equivalent, must always be felt behind cre... ...an never be properly understood on the horizont ...,ane alone.

Nietzsche's thinking follows this law. In *The Birth of Tragedy* the Apollonian surface is sustained in its evanescent appearance by the Dionysian powers of the primordial, creative, being, or deity, searching always for more and more self-expression. That expression is to be found pre-eminently in drama, or in life dramatically conceived and understood.

Eternity cannot be easily defined, nor can these Dionysian forces; and for this there is a good enough reason. What the eternal powers crave is not definition, but creation. They *will* creation. The only thing to do about eternal insight is to create from it. Had Shakespeare been able to define, to his own satisfaction, exactly how his loved one would conquer time, he would never have composed his greatest dramas. There would have been no need for them.

Nietzsche's other great imaginative work, *Thus Spake Zarathustra*, emphasises love, creation and eternity. Zarathustra is the great lover, the heart of his wisdom is eternity, and his primary concern is to create, to remake human-kind (III, 14, and IV, 15; III, 16; II, 20; *Christ and Nietzsche*, v, 211; v, 187; v, 158). His book records the integration, the internal love-intercourse, of these powers. The integration matured, the prophet goes out at 'the great noon' to deliver his message. We are shown the integration, but not the message. In Shakespeare's Sonnets we watch the integration and we can also study its flowering and promulgation in works that have reverberated across the world.

In *The Portrait of Mr. W. H.* Oscar Wilde argues through his fictional spokesman that 'the young man to whom Shakespeare addressed these strangely passionate poems must have been somebody who was really a vital factor in the development of his dramatic art' (1). Here is the problem as he saw it:

Who was that young man of Shakespeare's day who, without being of noble birth or even of noble nature, was addressed by him in terms of such passionate adoration that we can but wonder at the strange worship, and are almost afraid to turn the key that unlocks the mystery of the poet's heart? Who was he whose physical beauty was such that it became the very corner-stone of Shakespeare's art; the very source of Shakespeare's inspiration; the very incarnation of Shakespeare's dreams? To look upon him as simply the object of certain love-poems is to miss the whole meaning of the poems: for the art of which Shakespeare talks in the Sonnets is not the art of the Sonnets themselves, which indeed were to him but slight and secret things—it is the art of the dramatist to which he is always alluding.

(1)

We need not agree with all Wilde's conclusions to recognise a certain value in these suggestions, dependent, as he himself, through the person of his spokesman, puts it, 'not so much on demonstrable proof or formal evidence, but on a kind of spiritual and artistic sense, by which alone he claimed could the true meaning of the poems be discerned' (1).

Masefield, as we have seen (pp. 7, 55), comes to a not dissimilar conclusion, supposing the existence of some remarkable boy actor who did not grow up; saying that 'when Shakespeare considered his own genius, he thought of it as an attendant boy-spirit'; that in *The Tempest* he thought of his own genius as Ariel; and that it was this same boy-spirit who is addressed as 'my lovely boy' in Sonnet 126. 'No doubt', he concludes, 'the "lovely boy", Ariel, was a real presence in Shakespeare's mind' (*Shakespeare and Spiritual Life*, 13–14, 27).

Both Wilde and Masefield suppose an actor as the incarnation, as it were, of Shakespeare's ideal, though for Wilde he was the performer of Viola, Imogen, Juliet, Rosalind, Portia, Desdemona, and even Cleopatra, and for Masefield Moth, Puck, Falstaff's Page, Maria, the Player Queen, Mamilius and Ariel (and he might have added Arthur in *King John*).

Even though such exact identifications be called fanciful, there remains a substratum of truth, if not within, at least behind, them. Muir and O'Loughlin regard Ariel as 'a reincarnation of the Indian boy, the Southampton of the early days, the lovely boy of the Sonnets, the dynamic inspiration of Shakespeare's poetry' (*The Voyage to Illyria*, VIII, 225). The youth's function was, from the start, one of poetic inspiration. The recurring word is 'muse'. The poet's muse wants no subject

whilst he is its 'sweet argument'. Indeed he *is*, in a sonnet
quoted by Wilde, the poet's main muse:

> Be thou the tenth muse, ten times more in worth,
> Than those old nine which rhymers invocate.
>
> (38)

Once we start with

> So oft have I invok'd thee for my Muse,
> And found such fair assistance in my verse
>
> (78)

and end with 'but thou art all my art' and thought of how he
infuses 'learning' into the poet's own 'rude ignorance' (78).
That is precisely what was to happen; the seed of love and
beauty, of grace and courtliness, of breeding—for here, without
subscribing to the orthodox theories, we must, I think, part
company with Wilde and Butler (pp. 8–9)—were all there,
awaiting expression in drama. When the rival poet gains favour,
the poet writes how formerly 'my verse alone had all thy gentle
grace' ('gentle' meaning 'refined'), but that now his muse is
'sick' (79). Later, as we shall see, he appears to have deserted
poetic adoration for other sorts of writing, and fights out his
problem with himself in terms of his 'forgetful' and 'truant'
'muse' (100, 101). He is gradually being forced to expand his
subject-matter; he is becoming more and more of a dramatist.
But the youth still functions as inspiration.

That Shakespeare's total work does actually present a vast
expansion of substances already treated in the Sonnets, is
reasonably clear. We have already shown how not only his three
poems, but also *Troilus and Cressida, All's Well that Ends Well,
Timon of Athens* and *The Tempest*, isolate, amplify and variously
develop some of their leading themes. And we need not remain
content with these. We find the same influence at work in the
more obviously objective and dramatically normal compositions.

But are we then to follow Butler and Hotson in dating
the Sonnets earlier than all the dramas? That would be, in
the present state of our knowledge, a too hazardous basis
for literary interpretation. Nevertheless a relation does exist
between the Sonnets and Shakespeare's early work. We have
already (p. 53) observed how *Venus and Adonis* and *The Rape*

of Lucrece may be called fictional developments of the Sonnets' two main themes of love and lust. We can always say that the instincts which prompted his early choice of poetical subjects were precisely those which later involved him with the Fair Youth and the Dark Lady. Or the events handled by the Sonnets may be early, and the poetry late, 'recollected in tranquillity'. Or again, the Sonnets may be a composite and condensation of various love-affairs. Even if we date both them and the experiences they record somewhere late in the 90's, we can hardly suppose that Shakespeare had lived in London for ten years or so without any previous experiences of the kind. *A Lover's Complaint*, which Thorpe published with the Sonnets in 1609, is composed round a young man very similar to the young man of the Sonnets, and one would naturally suppose the two studies to have a single origin. But they may not. Even so, the earlier study may be poetically constituent to the later. So may others; in Sonnet 31 the poet refers to a number of past loves. The Sonnets may be a deliberate working out, for his own satisfaction, of certain recurring sexual and artistic problems of the poet's life, with what might be called an essential rather than causal relationship. We may, indeed, enlist Wilde himself against his own theory. Speaking in general of the art of the poet in his fascinating dialogue *The Critic as Artist*, his fictional critic says: 'A real passion would ruin him. Whatever actually occurs is spoiled for art. All bad poetry springs from genuine feeling. To be natural is to be obvious, and to be obvious is to be inartistic' (*The Critic as Artist*, 11).[1] The paradox holds a truth: poetry exists in a dimension vaster than factual reporting. But it is something greater, something more and not less inclusive, than such reporting. In the Sonnets, Shakespeare may be supposed to be telling us truths as to his life more, and not less, valid and substantial than what usually passes for autobiography, though this is not to say that exact biographical facts may not be included too.

Is there then no way of discussing with any kind of exactitude the relation of Shakespeare's Sonnets to his drama?

---

[1] Compare Byron's: 'To write so as to bring home to the heart, the heart must have been tried—but, perhaps, ceased to be so. While you are under the influence of passions, you only feel, but cannot describe them . . . When all is over—all, all, and irrevocable —trust to memory—she is then but too faithful' (*Journal*, 20 Feb., 1814).

On the contrary, we can do it with the utmost freedom, provided that we lay no exclusive emphasis on any one causal connection. As so often in the discussion of poetry, we must adopt a spatial, rather than a temporal, approach. We must see the Sonnets not as *antedating* Shakespeare's drama, but rather as *central* to it. We shall presently be analysing a sequence of sonnets suggesting the move from personal love to dramatic art; but that 'from' and 'to' must be regarded as an expansion from a centre outwards, that was, or may have been, going on continually during Shakespeare's literary life, from start to close. The nature of this process was, at some period or periods, defined and crystallised in the Sonnets. Looked at in this fashion, we may say that, even were the Sonnets' final version complete just before their publication in 1609 they, or all that they stand for and mean to us, may yet be supposed behind the composition of *Henry VI*.

Henry VI shows some vivid correspondences to the Sonnets. We have a delicately handled story of the youthful and saintly king, so religiously withdrawn and, as the Sonnets have it, so 'unmoved, cold and to temptation slow' (94) that, when urged for state reasons to take a wife, he remarks that marital 'sport' (i.e. intercourse) has little attraction for him (*I Henry VI*, v, i, 21–3; v, v, 80–2). However, he marries Margaret of Anjou, a terrifying woman who, as surely as Vergil's Allecto or Ibsen's *half-feminine* Bishop Nicholas in *The Pretenders*, stirs up dissension. In the dramatic inter-relation of our two main persons we already have a complication like the seduction of Fair Youth by Dark Lady. The resulting action, showing the sweet king's holy simplicity utterly at a loss within the dissentious rivalries and policies of his subjects, may be naturally compared with the poet's fears lest his idealised boy become contaminated by a decadent society (pp. 43, 79). But perhaps most important of all is the blend of passionately maternal and tinglingly erotic feeling in description of brutally slaughtered youth: young Talbot, Rutland, Prince Edward. Such impressions attain to a formal emphasis in the Father who has killed his Son and the Son who has killed his Father (*3 Henry VI*, ii, v), and are given perfected expression in the King's exquisite simile, recalling the Sonnets' recurring pain, of the mother cow lowing for her 'darling' (*2 Henry VI*, iii, i, 216). The King is, in fact, our

chief spokesman, and the blood-stained action seen through his
eyes. He may be related to—1 do *not* say 'copied from'—the
Fair Youth, and also to Shakespeare's fears for him. He is, like
Richard II, at once pathetic, lovable, and royal. He finally
attains spiritual and eternal insight: 'My crown is in my heart,
not on my head' (*3 Henry VI*, III, 1, 62). Both he and Richard II
under tragic destiny meditate, after a fashion recalling the Sonnets, on time (*3 Henry VI*, II, v, 24–40; *Richard II*, v, v, 42–60).

The slaughtered lovely ones of these passionate plays rise
again from the poetry of *Richard III*. It matters not at all
whether they be of Lancaster or York. Richard himself both
remembers how he 'cropp'd the golden prime of this sweet
prince', Edward (I, ii, 249), and dwells bitterly on 'the faultless
blood of pretty Rutland' (I, iii, 178). This note, once struck,
recurs throughout Shakespeare; but it is most obvious, most
erotically alive, in these early works.

That is one link with the Sonnets. But indeed, they suggest
correspondence of all sorts. All typical Shakespearian themes
of love, jealousy, and ingratitude [1] are hinted, the poet seeing
himself, though his love be no woman, 'like a deceived husband'
(93). The Iago-spirit, the 'suborn'd informer' of Sonnet 125
(p. 135 below), is at work, with all its cogent arguments, to ruin
a romantic faith: romance and cynicism, love and hate, are at
their tussle. All feminine love and feminine evil are, as we have
seen (pp. 31–3, 26), contained in embryo. So is all masculine
friendship, as in the relationship of Mercutio to Romeo and his
love, throughout *Julius Caesar*, and in *Hamlet*. Much of *Hamlet*
is forecast by the recurring meditations on death, and the rest
of it implicit in Sonnet 66. All melancholia is in Sonnet 29; all

---

[1] In *The Voyage to Illyria*, Muir and O'Loughlin, rather in the manner of Middleton
Murry in 'Shakespeare's Dedication' (*Countries of the Mind*, II), relate the bitterness
apparent in Shakespeare's work from *2 Henry IV* onwards to Shakespeare's 'betrayal'
by Southampton. They use, aptly for their purpose, Falstaff's rejection by Prince Hal
and the murder of Caesar by Brutus, called his 'angel' (*Julius Caesar*, III, ii, 186;
Sonnet 144); and the strong emphasis on *ingratitude* from this period on (VI, 144–8).
That these stresses derive from events in Shakespeare's experience is possible, and
they can be referred back to certain sonnets in particular. But I cannot myself find
sufficient evidence within the Sonnets to throw any great suspicion of baseness on the
Fair Youth, since the poet is finally shown as the less ardent of the two (pp. 112–36
below). The theme of ingratitude may have derived mainly from the natural grumblings
of a genius at what he regards as lack of appreciation by his contemporaries; though this
can, of course, be allowed to cover everything else.

horror of lust, so recurring a dramatic emphasis, in Sonnet 129. All tragedy is in the thought of time's destructive power, and the 'monumental mockery' (*Troilus and Cressida*, III, iii, 153) of the Sonnets' weightier symbols; and all dreams and themes of immortality in their conquering convictions of beauty's eternal heritage. We even have Shakespeare's aspersions on black magic (as in *1* and *2 Henry VI*, *Macbeth*, and Sycorax in *The Tempest*) suggested in the 'affable familiar ghost' who 'gulls' the rival poet (86).

Verbal parallels are too many to record here, and though many are parallels with early work, there are others too, as with the 'eye of scorn' of Sonnet 88, parallelled by Othello's

> fixed figure for the time of scorn
> To point his slow and moving finger at.
> (*Othello*, IV, ii, 53)

Imagery and symbolism we have already discussed: the cosmic, natural, and human settings are the same.

But what of world-affairs? Well, one great sonnet 'Not mine own fears, nor the prophetic soul . . .' (107) is as great a small piece as one could wish for on a nation's destiny. True, no one knows what it means, but in that very vagueness lies much of its appeal, the sense we receive of great issues, rather as with the mysterious 'two-handed engine at the door' in *Lycidas*, which would lose half its potency if we knew what it was; and we may, in passing, record a hope that the conflicts of scholars may continue to load both that phrase of Milton's and this noble sonnet with a salutary obscurity.

That the poet of the Sonnets was deeply concerned with such themes is clear from the many comparisons of his love to kings and state-affairs. His very love is felt as royal and stately. The Sonnets are the heart of Shakespeare's royal poetry. Like them, the dramas are both pastoral and kingly. Their kings are men, not just political symbols; and also their men, all of them, are, each in his own way, kings; and in this interplay of state royalty and spiritual royalty lies the essence of Shakespeare's greatness (pp. 112, 139). For the royal self is, as may be understood from Donne's love-poetry, the greater, cosmic, eternal self. Under it, nature, individual and society, all meet; here eternity is at peace with time. And it is because Shakespeare, through love, has penetrated to this greater, eternal, soul-reality of nature, men, and affairs, that he can handle men and affairs, dramatically, with such royal authority and control.

Within it all burns the love of Shakespeare's Sonnets. What is the distinguishing quality of that love? What I have called (pp. 35–7) the glassing of unity in unity, the recognition in his adored boy of a bisexual strength-with-grace, such as Tennyson found in Hallam (p. 35). And what is the ultimate end of Shakespeare's more weightily conceived work? The blend of masculine action and feminine pathos, of power and love; of justice and mercy, as in *The Merchant of Venice* and *Measure for Measure* (iv, i, 184–197; ii, ii, 58–63); of soldiership with chivalry, most perfectly shown in the marvellous thumb-nail sketch of Theseus in *A Midsummer Night's Dream*; of State and Church, as in *Henry VIII*; of, once again, 'strength-with-grace', allowing 'grace' to hold, as it must, religious overtones. The one principle, as a golden thread, runs through it all.

Such a relationship granted, we can listen in to a record of the expansion as it is set down in the later sonnets. These, at the risk of repetition of certain points already made, we shall now discuss in their original order.

It would, clearly, make our task easier could we follow Samuel Butler and Leslie Hotson in supposing that the Sonnets were composed at the start of Shakespeare's literary career. But the evidence from style is too strong for that. So, without confining ourselves to any one period of Shakespeare's career, we shall now read these sonnets as reflecting a general principle which may be defined as the expansion of love to integration, and of integration to art. The bowl of love becomes full, love-poetry is now the less easy to compose, the elixir overflows, must overflow, into other themes. It is a process of *overflowing*: that is the easiest way to picture it.

Already in Sonnets 83 to 85 Shakespeare was found apologising for his 'tongue-tied Muse'. Now he returns to the theme:

> Where art thou, Muse, that thou forget'st so long
> To speak of that which gives thee all thy might?
> Spend'st thou thy fury on some worthless song,
> Dark'ning thy power to lend base subjects light?
>   (100)

Whatever the work involved, the 'might' still comes from the youth as inspiration. The worthless song may be some poem, or, more probably, in view of 'base subjects', a play. Such are 'idle' pursuits. Again he calls, 'Return, forgetful Muse', and:

> Rise, resty Muse, my love's sweet face survey,
> If Time have any wrinkle graven there;
> If any, be a satire to decay,
> And make Time's spoils despised every where.
> (100)

The use of 'satire' marks a cold objectivity towards the formerly passionate themes. The perfunctory 'if any' is almost an insult. The lines seem to say: 'I suppose this means going over all the same old ground once again.' Even so, the poet half fears that the real thing is being lost: he cannot understand himself.

The next piece, 101, again invokes his 'truant Muse', which he accuses of neglecting the 'truth' and 'beauty' which is the source of its own strength. He is baffled at his own coldness: 'Make answer, Muse.' It is no excuse that 'Truth needs no colour with his colour fix'd,' that 'best is best' when not blended with alien matter; that is, with poetry. That is no excuse for silence; and yet, though love-sonnets cannot well be repeated *ad infinitum*, anything else is worthless in comparison: that is the crux. 'Then, do thy office, Muse': the Muse does, and he concludes with a couplet of literary-immortality platitude of the weakest kind. But how can this be worth more than the great themes that are tempting him away from these continual repetitions? It is hard to believe it. And yet, why must poetry descend to fiction? Why must his love be expressed *indirectly*?

The poet next insists:

> My love is strengthen'd, though more weak in seeming;
> I love not less, though less the show appear.
> (102)

It is true: it *is* 'strengthen'd', a greater and more potent reality than before. In comparison, more sonnets would be poor things. He insists now that the love is 'merchandiz'd' (i.e. cheapened) if its praise be 'publish'd everywhere': those sonnets were right enough, like the early songs of the nightingale, in their love's 'spring', but the year moves on to 'riper days'; now everyone is singing; 'that wild music burthens every bough', and what is common is no compliment (102). There may be a reference to the growth of sonneteering; or simply to the expanding universe of Shakespeare's poetry. Anyway, his friend should now recognise that 'the argument all bare' is really of far 'more worth' than anything he can say: 'O blame me not', he pleads, 'if I no more can write' (103). It is three years now since they first met. He insists that 'to me, fair friend, you never can be old', since he still sees him as he *was at 'first'*. But—'Ah, yet doth beauty, like a dial-hand . . .' And yet his hue *seems* to 'stand' safe (104). What does this mean? The boy is losing his first youthful charm, but in Shakespeare's mind that charm is fixed, eternally, as it had been, and it is this image that acts still as an inspiration, though only for the less obviously personal works. Therefore, when he reiterates the constancy of himself and his friend, saying that his songs are 'to one, of one, still such, and ever so', all 'constant in a wondrous excellence' (105), it *is*, in the depths, true enough, though the young man, whose complaints appear to have prompted these pieces, can hardly have been expected to understand that he was more interesting to the world in dramatic guise than as the object of yet another sonnet. Shakespeare is attracted by vaster themes.

Suddenly the poet revives and proves his love poetically by producing the magnificent 'When in the chronicle of wasted time' (106). This is followed by the famous 'Not mine own fears', significantly fusing the love-theme with what is here the far more impressive and poetically charged theme of national recovery. Middleton Murry has rightly insisted that it must be read as part of a sequence within which it registers a renewal of love's certainty after doubt (*Countries of the Mind*, II; Notes, 201–6). But even so, the balance tilts the other way; personal 'fears' are overweighted by 'the prophetic soul of the wide world dreaming on things to come'. This I take to refer either directly or through some sort of analogy to world-affairs. In his *Literary Genetics* (XI, 309–11) T. W. Baldwin regards it as no more than an answer to earlier sonnets (e.g., 65, 104, etc.; see pp. 3–5 above). But surely the sonnet describes a relationship of two orders of thought, personal and communal, which are tied together in 'Now with the drops of this most balmy time': some sort of a distinction is clearly implied by 'with', 'time' holding, in Shakespeare's usual manner, a reference at once communal and contemporary. It may be worth noting that the poet is here primarily interested in *his own* literary immortality, saying, with a touch of pride, and even egotism, 'Death to me subscribes', and contrasting his own good fortune with all who are 'dull and speechless'. The young man is given a share in this immortality as an afterthought: 'and thou in this shalt find thy monument' (107). Directly after, we are back at our apologies:

> What's in the brain, that ink may character,
> Which hath not figur'd to thee my true spirit?
> What's new to speak, what new to register,
> That may express my love or thy dear merit?
> Nothing, sweet boy; but yet, like prayers divine,
> I must each day say o'er the very same,
> Counting no old thing old, 'thou mine, I thine',
> Even as when first I hallow'd thy fair name . . .
>
> (108)

I follow Tucker's use of quotation marks in line 7, the phrase referring back to 'the very same' and 'thing'. The boy is still his ideal, a semi-divine inspiration, but a stream of sonnets as good as 106 cannot reasonably be expected. It is not just that the youth is growing old: 'eternal love' is next said to pay no regard to 'wrinkles' and 'age', since it 'makes antiquity for aye its page'; revivifying the image *as it had been* when 'first' it gave birth to the 'conceit' of 'love', and which, though now outwardly 'dead', exists still, despite all change, as an eternal reality.

Through his love Shakespeare had touched a universal which now demands more and more universal expression. The Fair Youth is still in his heart:

> O, never say that I was false of heart,
> Though absence seem'd my flame to qualify.
> As easy might I from myself depart
> As from my soul, which in thy breast doth lie . . .
>
> (109)

The unity is accomplished, and that is precisely why the youth can no longer be an object. Shakespeare is still certain that he could not err 'so preposterously' as 'to leave for nothing all thy

sum of good'; but this very totality constitutes an embarrassment. The youth *is* now the universe, but without any loss of
personality, or of the old fragrance:

> For nothing this wide universe I call,
> Save thou, my Rose; in it thou art my all.
>
> (109)

He is not only identified with Shakespeare's mind: he is the
universe, and as such must be given universal expression.

But what is this 'absence'? What has Shakespeare been
doing? Clearly, we must suppose him to have been acting and
composing plays. So we follow on with:

> Alas, 'tis true I have gone here and there
> And made myself a motley to the view,
> Gor'd mine own thoughts, sold cheap what is most dear,
> Made old offences of affections new;
> Most true it is that I have look'd on truth
> Askance and strangely . . .
>
> (110)

Tucker and Hotson (*Shakespeare's Motley*, 1952) deny that
'motley' refers to the stage. Hubler, having regard to the next
two sonnets, considers that it has. The implications may,
however, be wide: 'motley' suggests variegated colours and a
diversity of interests and guises, and may cover social activity
as well as stage composition and stage performances. All these
have replaced the one central purity and devotion.

The public stage was certainly considered disreputable.
Hubler adduces the analogy in our time of film work: 'Many
a dramatist working in Hollywood feels as Shakespeare felt
during his early days in London' (*The Sense of Shakespeare's
Sonnets*, 118). In using his own most intimate experiences for
dramatic material, Shakespeare had 'gor'd' his 'own thoughts',
opened up old wounds, and been guilty of selling 'cheap' something of infinite worth. His new enthusiasms, personal relationships, lusts and ambitions (any or all may be carried by 'affections') are indeed offences against the past ('old'; but the word
also holds an intensifying meaning as in the Porter's 'old
turning the key' in *Macbeth*, II, iii, 2). He has been looking on
and using 'truth' (i.e. his friend, the all-but-divine 'image';

pp. 39, 45) *indirectly*, obliquely ('askance'), in the way of art,
expressing the central experience through various masks. Byron
regularly regarded his life's work as a fall from youthful purity.
Shakespeare is incurring the guilt symbolised in Ibsen's *When
We Dead Awaken*, where the sculptor, Rubek, is shown as
having spoilt the youthful purity of his statue of *The Resurrection* by grouping round it a number of satiric and bestial figures.
But he now swears that he will no longer 'grind' his 'appetite'
on such 'newer proof' (i.e. new experiments, which may, of
course, include amatory experiments), but return to his 'god in
love' (i.e. 'god through love'), to whom he will be henceforth
'confin'd', as 'next my heaven the best', and 'pure'; unadulter-
ated with alien matter, as dramatic art is not (110).

He is utterly abased, referring next to his 'harmful deeds'
and regretting that his state of life has forced him to fall back
on 'public means' which have led to 'public manners', and to
his name receiving a 'brand'. He appears to be guilty of some
disreputable behaviour related to the disreputable society in
which he is moving:

> And almost thence my nature is subdu'd
> To what it works in, like the dyer's hand.
>
> (111)

But he trusts to his friend's 'love and pity' to remove the 'vulgar
scandal' (which might mean only 'the scandal of being associated with common entertainers'). And yet there is more in it
than disgrace. He is doing pretty well in the profession, but
scorns, or tries to scorn, his success:

> For what care I who calls me well or ill,
> So you o'er-green my bad, my good allow?
> You are my all the world, and I must strive
> To know my shames and praises from your tongue.
>
> (112)

'Well', 'good', 'praises': the account has not been all negative.
Here Shakespeare tries ('I must strive') to remain unaffected
by his *successes*. He will be 'alive' to nothing and no one but
his friend; his 'senses' will be 'steel'd' against all 'right or
wrong' (i.e. good or bad) in other directions. He will disregard

'other's voices', and be deaf 'to critic and to flatterer' alike. He concludes, recalling Sonnet 109:

> You are so strongly in my purpose bred
> That all the world besides methinks are dead.
>   (112)

His quandary is clear. He cannot, and in the depths does not wish to, give up his work. As T. W. Baldwin puts it, 'Shakespeare was becoming too busy with acting, writing, and business affairs to continue dancing attendance in sonneteering' (*Literary Genetics*, XI, 313). And yet things are not quite so simple as that, since it is only because the youth is so deep-bedded in his main 'purpose', or life-direction, that his instinct forces him away. All else is, in comparison, dead; and yet the principle of life itself forces the expansion.

The poet's experience resembles that of Cleopatra following Antony's death, when, after 'the odds is gone and there is nothing left remarkable beneath the visiting moon', Antony himself next becomes the universe (*Antony and Cleopatra*, IV, xiii, 66; v, ii, 79–92). So now the Fair Youth is 'all the world'. This thought is quickly developed. We have already heard Shakespeare asserting that all his dead friends are now seen, living, in the Fair Youth; he *is* all of them (31). We have known him as the pattern of all things lovely:

> What is your substance, whereof are you made,
> That millions of strange shadows on you tend?
> Since every one hath, every one, one shade,
> And you, but one, can every shadow lend.   (53)

Other beauteous forms are *aspects* of him: he is within Adonis and Helen, in Grecian 'tires'; within the 'spring and foison of the year'; indeed, to be recognised in 'every blessed shape we know', having 'some part' in 'all external grace', though his 'constant heart' remains all his own (53). Again, the sweetest fruits of spring are all

> but figures of delight
> Drawn after you, you pattern of all those.
>   (98)

About such thoughts there was nothing very remarkable. But now, in the next sonnet of our present sequence, we have a most important extension of them.

It is not merely now a question of *similarity*; of, say, the Fair Youth in relation to Adonis, the slaughtered youths in *Henry VI*, or whatever other similarities from later plays we may hit on. The universal 'all' of Sonnets 109 and 112 is really *meant*. Now everything and everybody, good *or* bad, is an expression of him:

> Since I left you mine eye is in my mind,
> And that which governs me to go about
> Doth part his function and is partly blind,
> Seems seeing, but effectually is out;
> For it no form delivers to the heart
> Of bird, of flower, or shape which it doth latch,
> Of his quick objects hath the mind no part,
> Nor his own vision holds what it doth catch;
> For if it see the rud'st or gentlest sight,
> The most sweet favour or deformed'st creature,
> The mountain or the sea, the day or night,
> The crow or dove, it shapes them to your feature:
>   Incapable of more, replete with you,
>   My most true mind thus maketh mine untrue.
>   (113)

His ordinary eye is blind; his mental eye sees splendours (cp. Marvell's 'Here blinded with an eye' in his *Dialogue between the Soul and the Body*). Whatever natural 'form' the eye sees ('latch'), 'the mind' disregards, does not hold it. This, he thinks, *must* be what is happening, since whatever the poet sees *is* the loved youth. Since he is now full ('replete') of 'you', there is no room for anything else; and so 'my most true mind' (i.e. 'my mind being true to you', also 'my mind in touch with the great truth—pp. 45, 116–17—which is you') makes his ordinary mind (or 'eye', if we emend) appear false.

Here we touch the secret of Shakespeare's extraordinary creative power, maturing as it does from love-sight into the eternal self of each creature, good or bad. We begin to realise how this power was learned or inspired by the love *and the eternal insight born of that love* witnessed throughout the Sonnets. As Biron puts it:

> Never durst poet touch a pen to write
> Until his ink were temper'd with Love's sighs.
>   (*Love's Labour's Lost*, IV, iii, 346)

The Fair Youth has already been praised as lending dignity, or worth, to poetic creation:

> But he that writes of you, if he can tell
> That you are you, so dignifies his story.
> Let him but copy what in you is writ,
> Not making worse what nature made so clear,
> And such a counterpart shall fame his wit,
> Making his style admired everywhere.
>
> (84)

But more than nature is involved. He acted on Shakespeare as Beatrice did on Dante. In him Shakespeare recognised not merely *a* miracle *of* creation, but *the* miracle *behind* creation, and, having seen it there, he sees it everywhere. That is why every person or thing in Shakespeare is expressed as a being of eternal rights: the soul-life of each is touched, and the rest follows.

True, Sonnet 113 does not quite say that. It says 'I see you *instead of* other forms'; it does not quite say 'I see you *in* other forms'. But in practice there is little enough distinction, and anyway we proceed at once to a sonnet that drives home the point more strongly, and even critically. Shakespeare always keeps one foot—we may be thankful that it was only one—within the world of Johnsonian common-sense that repudiated Berkeley's philosophy by kicking a stone. He is accordingly doubtful, with the kind of doubt to be later expressed through Iago, Thersites and Apemantus, whether this highly romantic and abundantly creative vision can be true:

> Or whether doth my mind, being crown'd with you,
> Drink up the monarch's plague, this flattery?
> Or whether shall I say, mine eye saith true,
> And that your love taught it this alchemy,
> To make of monsters and things indigest
> Such cherubins as your sweet self resemble,
> Creating every bad a perfect best
> As fast as objects to his beams assemble?
> O, 'tis the first; 'tis flattery in my seeing,
> And my great mind most kingly drinks it up:
> Mine eye well knows what with his gust is 'greeing,
> And to his palate doth prepare the cup:
>   If it be poison'd, 'tis the lesser sin
>   That mine eye loves it and doth first begin.
>
> (114)

His mind is 'crown'd with you': he enjoys a royal consciousness, a consciousness of eternal things, and the eternity within
things, the concept 'king' corresponding to the greater, eternal,
self. The result is a kind of 'flattery': all creation, whatever its
evils, appears graceful and harmonious, like those courtiers 'as
free, as debonair', as 'bending angels' in *Troilus and Cressida*
(I, iii, 235). The experience recorded corresponds exactly to
the lucid patterns announced at the conclusion to the first
epistle of Pope's *Essay on Man*, and also to Shelley's theory of
poetry as a revelation of harmony in place of distortion in his
Defence of Poetry.[1] We have an exactly opposite process when
Bertram's 'contempt' in *All's Well that Ends Well* is shown as
having led to a 'scornful perspective' which so 'warp'd the line
of every other favour' that all human 'proportions' were reduced
'to a most hideous object' (v, iii, 45–55).

But which is true? That is our sonnet's problem. Can he
say that 'love' transmuting, like 'alchemy', base things to gold,
has given him an insight into the truth of creation? 'Things
indigest' suggest variously Richard III, Thersites, Parolles,
Iago, Caliban; but it is just here that Shakespeare's creation
is so wonderful. Are they not fine acting parts, precisely because
each has his own perfection? 'Creating every bad a perfect
best': what more perfect description could you find to characterise Shakespeare's human delineation, surveying, as it does,
both good and evil with inhuman clarity and charity, as though
from a consciousness itself looking down on them from some
eternal dimension? Shakespeare never appears to *aim* at the
good, the beautiful, the romantic. It comes. He does not even
aim at proving its validity here: his words are really the more
convincing for their Johnsonian standpoint. It must, he thinks,
be 'flattery', and yet the very action of the line 'my great mind
most kingly drinks it up' counters the aspersion with suggestion of such amplitude that we can scarcely agree. Whatever
the truth, we have a fine description of the royal consciousness
that composed the great dramas, through insight into what
Lysander calls the 'heart' (p. 40); the 'true image' of Sonnet

---

[1] See *Christ and Nietzsche*, I, 18–27. We might also compare Walt Whitman's
apprehension of God 'in every object', and 'in the faces of men and women', including
his own (*Song of Myself*, 48); and Nietzsche's 'creative friend' with 'a perfect world in
his gift' (*Thus Spake Zarathustra*, I, 16; or 17—see p. 48 above).

24; the consciousness of harmony whose loss is deplored in Hamlet's, 'What a piece of work is a man!' (*Hamlet*, 11, ii, 323), and which lies behind Miranda's exclamation, 'Oh brave new world that has such people in it!' (*The Tempest*, v, i, 183). The sonnet's conclusion is less important: the 'eye' is the king's taster, and only serves up this miraculous poison because it has first in all 'good faith' (Tucker) loved it.

Having gone so far in self-analysis, the poet can now claim to be loving his friend more truly than ever before:

> Those lines that I before have writ do lie,
> Even those that said I could not love you dearer:
> Yet then my judgment knew no reason why
> My most full flame should afterwards burn clearer.
>
> (115)

It cannot, indeed, be more *full* (most 'full flame') than it was at love's unmediated impact, nor perhaps ever again *so* full, but it can, and now does, 'burn clearer'. He could not then see how, the youth's beauty failing and his own adoration being unable to maintain its first intensity, his love could be expected to gain in steadfastness and light. But that is what has happened. In the past, he says, he had feared time,

> whose million'd accidents
> Creep in 'twixt vows, and change decrees of kings,
> Tan sacred beauty, blunt the sharp'st intents,
> Divert strong minds to th' course of alt'ring things . . .
>
> (115)

Notice the contrast of 'million'd', with its numerical, arithmetical, emphasis, against the more weighty, because spiritualised, values housed in 'vows' and 'decrees'. He had feared that the numerical would conquer the nobler realities, that the boy's 'sacred beauty' would fade, and his own 'intents' waver, since even 'strong minds' must alter with changed conditions. And in fact this, exactly this, *has* happened. Shakespeare wants to compose dramas—kingly dramas; he cannot go on repeating himself in love-poems. But that is not the whole truth. In those days, he says, fear was natural enough:

> Alas, why, fearing of Time's tyranny,
> Might I not then say, 'Now I love you best',

> When I was certain o'er incertainty,
> Crowning the present, doubting of the rest?
>
> (115)

But he was wrong. The 'flame' now somehow burns 'clearer'.
The couplet sums up:

> Love is a babe; then might I not say so
> To give full growth to that which still doth grow.
>
> (115)

From the new viewpoint, the first great love was only a child:
he could not see it then, could not understand how it could
expand, but it did, and is 'still' growing.[1] Whether the original
experience or its creative result is, in the last resort, the finer,
is perhaps a profitless enquiry. All we can say is, that the
supernal experience cannot be perpetuated on our plane of
consciousness except through creation. Of other planes, we
cannot judge, though we may recall that Dante meets the love
of his youth, Beatrice, and Goethe's Faust Gretchen, but not
Helen, in Paradise.

Having established this principle of growing love at least
to his own satisfaction, the poet now comes forward in full
confidence with the great sonnet, 'Let me not to the marriage
of true minds' (116). Now he can truly claim in a general
way, rather as did Michelangelo (in Sonnet 60), not to 'alter'
with 'alteration'; his love is indestructible, and no longer,
whatever may become of 'rosy lips and cheeks'—the prettiness
underlining a fragility, almost a triviality—'Time's fool'. It is
now less an immediate experience than a reality to be 'recollected', as Wordsworth says, 'in tranquillity'. It is rather
distantly conceived as a divine principle, 'the star to every
wandering bark'. Its precise validity, 'worth', may, as in the
critical questionings of Sonnet 114, be 'unknown', but its
'height' is self-evident. It is conceived as a trust to hold fast
to as you plunge into the trackless wastes. These assurances
conclude with:

> If this be error, and upon me prov'd
> I never writ, nor no man ever lov'd.
>
> (116)

---

[1] For an exactly similar record of the creative process composed before ever I had
given exact attention to this Sonnet, see my own experience as recorded in *Atlantic
Crossing*, IX, 301-2.

His writing, which comes first, is to prove that love is a sure guide, the love following on, but rather as a universal involving love-in-general ('no man') than as an intimate conception.

It appears that his friend was less easily convinced. Shakespeare, itching for new fields to conquer, must have felt rather like Goethe's Faust after the betrayal of Gretchen, with Part II, and all that it means, opening before him. Our next piece is an admission, as by a cornered man, that he has incurred a just accusation:

> Accuse me thus: that I have scanted all
> Wherein I should your great deserts repay,
> Forgot upon your dearest love to call,
> Whereto all bonds do tie me, day by day;
> That I have frequent been with unknown minds,
> And given to time your own dear-purchas'd right;
> That I have hoisted sail to all the winds
> Which should transport me farthest from your sight.
> Book both my wilfulness and errors down,
> And on just proof surmise accumulate;
> Bring me within the level of your frown,
> But shoot not at me in your waken'd hate.
>
> (117)

The ship-metaphor throws back to the previous sonnet. 'Unknown minds' may refer to literary people, patrons perhaps; 'hoisting sail' suggests a welcoming and skilful use of various means to establish his success, as author or actor. The 'proof' is admitted to be, logically, 'just'; and yet the word 'surmise' perhaps indicates a reservation, since the facts could be read, as we are reading them, more sympathetically. The piece rings with a bitter honesty, rising to: 'But shoot not at me in your waken'd hate.' The clash of emotions appears to have been strong.[1] The final couplet, asserting that he had merely been testing his friend, is the lamest of lame expedients, and might almost be ironical.

Our next is profoundly important. In it the poet elaborates his defence. What he says is: 'We sometimes take medicine that makes us ill in order to prevent sickness. My love was so

---

[1] In human relationships nothing is impossible, but it appears to me almost inconceivable that a man in Southampton's position should have been pestering a man in Shakespeare's for attention. See Bradley's *Oxford Lectures*, 332.

perfect that it became a kind of sickness, and I was forced to descend to certain dubious engagements. This seemed a good thing to do in order to avoid danger (e.g., perhaps, madness). However, it may all have been unnecessary; bad led to worse; and I find that my particular disease of love had nothing in common with, and cannot be remedied by, such poisons'. Here it is, with the crucial phrases italicised:

> Like as, to make our appetites more keen,
> With eager compounds we our palate urge;
> As, to prevent our maladies unseen,
> We sicken to shun sickness when we purge;
> Even so, *being full of your ne'er-cloying sweetness*,
> To bitter sauces did I frame my feeding,
> And, *sick of welfare*, found a kind of meetness
> To be diseas'd, ere that there was true needing.
> Thus policy in love, to anticipate
> The ills that were not, grew to faults assur'd,
> And brought to medicine *a healthful state*
> Which, *rank of goodness*, would by ill be cur'd:
> But then I learn, and find the lesson true,
> Drugs poison him that so fell *sick of you*.
>
> (118)

Here we have Shakespeare's most exact defence, and it is one of considerable interest.

Why does he call his supreme experience a 'sickness'? We may profitably compare Shelley's view of Byron's genius as 'a bright blot upon this gloomy scene' in his sonnet 'Lift not the painted veil'; and also Teresa Guiccioli's recognition of so supreme a virtue as a positive 'defect' within the context of a decadent society (*Lord Byron: Christian Virtues*, v, 254; 281). The higher, supersexual, integration is likely enough on occasion to appear, and perhaps even feel like, an illness. Nietzsche's Zarathustra suffers pain from his own plenitude. I quote from my own analysis of the Night Song (*Thus Spake Zarathustra*, 11, 9):

All but complete, he cannot quite accept his completeness; he has no object, and, being himself light, cannot 'suck at the breasts of light'. Living in his own hard brilliance, drinking the flames that break from himself, he cannot know the 'happiness of the taker' . . . He thirsts not for drink, but for thirst itself: he is chaste through his own plenitude . . .

It is a testing moment at which he, replete with virtue, tired of giving, hungers for its opposite, for 'wickedness', in order to make contact, to 'touch' the 'souls', of others.

(Christ and Nietzsche, v, 178)

The analogy is close. In an earlier sonnet Shakespeare had compared himself, at a time when his love was tongue-tied, with

> some fierce thing replete with too much rage,
> Whose strength's abundance weakens his own heart.

(23)

He was 'o'ercharged with burthen of mine own love's might' (23). His eyes had had to 'wink with fulness', close themselves against too powerful a light (56). This is an experience normal enough to the highest genius. So Shelley writes of Byron:

> The sense that he was greater than his kind
> Had struck, methinks, his eagle spirit blind
> By gazing on its own exceeding light.

(Julian and Maddalo, 50)

We may recall Shakespeare's explanation of love's silence in terms of summer's 'riper days' and a superabundance of music (102; pp. 113–14 above), and also such phrases as 'my most full flame' (115), and 'replete with you' (113). A similar experience is described by Troilus who, after an ecstasy of imaginative expectation, fears that love's 'thrice-repured nectar' may mean 'death', 'swooning destruction',

> or some joy too fine,
> Too subtle-potent, tun'd too sharp in sweetness,
> For the capacity of my ruder powers . . .

(Troilus and Cressida, iii, ii, 17–24)

Such, too, is the problem of Shakespeare's Sonnets, and also of Michelangelo's, where (26) the 'rapture' of love's 'light' 'threatens' his life more than any 'agony', and he fears 'lest joy so poignant slay a soul so weak'.

Shakespeare had, through what we have called the super-sexual, or bi-sexual, integration, come very near to full *conscious* possession of the experience of which Troilus speaks. As we have already (p. 37) suggested, such a state must be supposed to enjoy its wholeness and purity not through any absence of sexuality, but rather through a plethora of sexual attainment within. A man cannot, however, be expected to live continually on that height. It may be necessary to descend, like Byron's Manfred—'I plunged amidst mankind' (ii, ii; and see *Lord Byron: Christian Virtues*, v, 256)—if only to preserve one's sanity; which Nietzsche failed to do.

Our sonnet provides a perfect definition of a supremely important problem that has never as yet been properly studied. Genius is, in terms of biological normality, a disease. It often appears as a living contradiction of all that we generally call 'maturity', because it remains unsettled. But this is only because its supreme maturity, or wholeness, its 'riper days' (102), is a *dynamic wholeness* that cannot rest content: it must be allowed to spill over. This fulness, this restlessly expansive immaturity, is both its signature and aim, and that is precisely why Shakespeare loved the growing rather than the grown, the rose-bud rather than the flower. Behind the Sonnets lies what is called a 'perverted' love, a non-sexual, yet sexually impregnated, adoration for a boy. Such a passion many people today would regard as a psychological illness, and had Shakespeare, in modern style, been given professional treatment in good time, he might have been satisfactorily cured of such bisexual tendencies and all desire for dramatic composition. We may say the same of other examples of artistic, or religious, genius: as science grows more efficient, they will cease to trouble us.

We next come to a passionate outburst recording an agony of conflict. Shakespeare finds himself 'still losing when I saw myself to win'; presumably losing his friend's love in proportion as he has been advancing in other ways. He had been happy in success, but now—there is certainly pathos and may be irony in the thought—he cries:

> What wretched errors hath my heart committed
> Whilst it hath thought itself so blessed never!
>
> (119)

He concludes by expectation of rebuilding their love stronger than before. Next, he indulges in recriminations. Since 'you' were 'once unkind' to me, he says, I now must, 'unless my nerves were brass or hammer'd steel', admit my 'transgression' and sympathise with you. He records 'how once I suffer'd in your crime' (though 'crime' need mean no more than 'serious

fault'; see Tucker's note to 124, ll, 13–14). If you now suffer
as much, he says, under 'my unkindness', I must indeed be
sorry for you. He recalls how his friend then offered him his
'humble salve', and admits that he should have done the same.
He concludes by suggesting a mutual exchange of faults (120).

Our next is that great piece of self-assertion starting:

> 'Tis better to be vile than vile esteemed.
>
> (121)

This we have already (pp. 49–53) analysed. In it Shakespeare,
with a grim anger, asserts his own basic integrity, whatever
scandals may say of him. He must, and will, go his own way:
'I am that I am.' The sonnet develops with a far greater power
and subtlety his earlier thoughts regarding the 'sin of self-love'
so firmly 'grounded inward' in his 'soul' and 'heart' that there
was no remedy for it (62; p. 44). If our present piece refers
to some variety of licentious behaviour, it may be worth
reminding ourselves once again that what we have called the
'higher', or 'bisexual', integration does not necessarily pre-
clude such lapses. We claim that Shakespeare touched it in his
love, and in his creative work, but we have every reason, from
our recent analyses, to suppose that he had fallen below it in
action. Had he been able to possess in full and stabilised integration his own tumultuous and expansive self, he would have
been, not a poet, but something else, which we can leave it to
Nietzsche to define for us.

We find him next apologising, as best he may, for having
given away one of his friend's gifts (122; p. 96).

We pass to the 'pyramid' sonnet quoted above (p. 95),
starting 'No, Time, thou shalt not boast that I do change.'
Here Shakespeare asserts the superiority of his own soul, or
soul-love, his eternal insight or achievement—it is not precisely defined for us—against grand symbols of lastingness, old
or new. He is writing at high pressure again, attacking Time
with the words, 'Thy registers and thee I both defy.' He says
nothing directly of his love, but is concerned mainly with his
own integrity, concluding:

> This I do vow, and this shall ever be,
> I will be true, despite thy scythe and thee.
>
> (123)

What exactly he now means by 'true' is uncertain. I suspect it means 'true to the essence of my love, even though my friend cannot see it'. Grandeur, royalty, national themes, distract him.

Our last sonnet was weighted with symbols of temporal persistence and our next two concentrate on state affairs. Here is the first:

> If my dear love were but the child of state,
> It might for Fortune's bastard be unfather'd,
> As subject to Time's love or to Time's hate,
> Weeds among weeds, or flowers with flowers gather'd.
> No, it was builded far from accident;
> It suffers not in smiling pomp, nor falls
> Under the blow of thralled discontent,
> Whereto the inviting time our fashion calls:
> It fears not policy, that heretic
> Which works on leases of short-number'd hours,
> But all alone stands hugely politic,
> That it nor grows with heat, nor drowns with showers.
>   To this I witness call the fools of time,
>   Who die for goodness, who have lived for crime.
>
> (124)

'Dear love' means 'highly valued love', and not 'dear loved person'. This love is to be contrasted with 'state', and all such temporal and ephemeral valuations. The phrases are not all clear: 'suffers not in smiling pomp' might mean, as C. Knox Pooler takes it, 'is not withered by the sun of prosperity' (*Arden* Edn., 1918); or, more probably, 'does not suffer from the insecurity that attends on greatness'. Love itself is in Shakespeare a kind of royalty, and royalty in Shakespeare has its burdens. So this and the next line may mean: 'It does not endure the uncertainty attending the supposed blessings of pomp and world-glory, nor risks falling under the attack of a discontented subject.' Royalty is clearly within the lines, the troubled royalty of Richard II's meditation on tragic kingship and Henry V's on 'ceremony' (*Richard II*, III, ii, 155–77; *Henry V*, IV, i, 250–304).

The love, or spiritual state, indicated is to be contrasted with 'Fortune', 'Time', nature (in 'weeds' and 'flowers'), 'accident', 'time' (as contemporary time) and 'fashion', 'policy' (which carried a derogatory, Machiavellian, sense), 'heretic',

10

and all short temporal calculations. These are rationalistic entities, Iago-forms. They occur powerfully within *Antony and Cleopatra* as love's antagonists, where 'fortune' is important as 'chance', and favours Caesar (e.g. ii, iii, 16). But at love's sacrificial victory Caesar is nevertheless an 'ass unpolicied' (v, ii, 309). Such love is 'builded far from accident', in the eternal dimension. 'Accident' recalls Cleopatra's

> And it is great
> To do that thing which ends all other deeds,
> Which shackles accidents and bolts up change . . .
> (v, ii, 4)

In *Antony and Cleopatra* love is given an imperial setting above which it rises as a super-imperial splendour (*The Imperial Theme*, vii), rather as when Donne in *The Sun Rising* writes 'She is all States, and all Princes, I', or Marvell in *To his Coy Mistress* dreams of a love 'vaster than empires'. So in our sonnet the love-state 'all alone stands hugely politic', independent of growing or drowning, heat or showers; independent, that is, of the natural order. But we must assume that this was a soul-state having room for nature and for state-affairs, and could moreover survey them with superb clarity and ease precisely because it had risen above them; for such was, surely, the state from which Shakespeare's dramas, and *Antony and Cleopatra* pre-eminently, were composed.

The concluding couplet has baffled the commentators, who usually see in it a strong aspersion on those who 'die for goodness'. This appears to me unlikely. Butler, pointing out, I think justly, that Shakespeare 'would never call a man a fool for dying well after living ill', changes the Quarto's 'foles of time' to 'soles oftime' (i.e. 'oft-time'), arguing that 'f' and 's' were, in the old typography, readily confused. But 'fools' might contain no insult, in the manner of Lear's 'my poor fool' (i.e. Cordelia) 'is hang'd' (*King Lear*, v, iii, 307); and for 'fools of time' we could perhaps, remembering 'love's not time's fool' (116), and Hotspur's 'Thought's the slave of life, and life time's fool' (*1 Henry IV*, v, iv, 81), offer the quite general rendering, 'those who have suffered under the complexities of temporal conditions'. Anyway, no dishonour need be supposed as accorded to the witnesses called on: they are those who, having, like the poet, wavered under temporal conditions, finally, as he does, reassert their integrity, dying, like Cawdor, in a state of grace. In such instances, the assurance given by the Church asserts the littleness of the temporal order, and that is why Shakespeare uses the comparison. We shall also observe how exactly, within the value-context of her play, Cleopatra performs this part: she becomes one of our witnesses. The sonnet says '*Antony and Cleopatra*' as clearly as Sonnet 66 says '*Hamlet*'.

Our last two sonnets have been heavily weighted with what might be called the 'vast externals' of monuments and state in contrast, shall we say, to the 'vast eternal' of love. The last of the three, which interlink neatly, renders the content of the others immediate and personal. It goes:

> Were't aught to me I bore the canopy,
> With my extern the outward honouring,
> Or laid great bases for eternity
> Which proves more short than waste or ruining?
> Have I not seen dwellers on form and favour
> Lose all, and more, by paying too much rent—
> For compound sweet foregoing simple savour—
> Pitiful thrivers, in their gazing spent?
> No, let me be obsequious in thy heart,
> And take thou my oblation, poor but free,
> Which is not mix'd with seconds, knows no art
> But mutual render, only me for thee.
>> Hence, thou suborn'd informer! a true soul
>> When most impeach'd stands least in thy control.
>
>   (125)

Again, we have an important, and far from easy, sonnet.

In some of our most significant pieces, including the last, Tucker's close self-confinement to the words appears to cut out too many obvious meanings. Thinking mainly of the central love-affair, he dissolves concrete suggestion or description into metaphor in such a way that the statement dwindles into insignificance. Metaphor there may be, but the thing used for comparison is first concretely established, and must be so understood. His comments on language are, as always, a valuable check on any facile reading, as when he here translates 'were't' not as 'was it' but as 'would it be', and 'I bore' as 'if I bore': i.e. 'Would it be anything to me if I were to bear the canopy?' But bearing the canopy he takes as simply a metaphor for elaborate praise. He agrees that the 'canopy' means a canopy 'carried over a sovereign in procession', but says that it is 'here, of course, purely figurative'. 'Figurative' it may, indeed, be; but why 'of course'? Butler, however, observes that 'there is a reference to the bearing of a certain canopy, apparently on some very great occasion, over some great personage'. He thinks that Shakespeare either bore it, or wanted to, and was foiled in his ambition; and proceeds to quote Stow's *Annals* in support of his own dating (xi, 145–7). Line 2 certainly suggests an actual incident, but lines 3 and 4 are more vague and general. Without engaging too far in exact speculations, we can content ourselves with some such rendering as this: 'Engaging in matters of ceremony means nothing to me, nor do I set store by any attempts of mine to establish monuments supposed to be everlasting, but really as short-lived as are all such things.' It must, at least, mean something like that. Whether Shakespeare had had anything to do with some foundation ceremony for a great building, or whether the 'bases' are metaphorical and apply to his poetry, is not clear. There may be a reference to the dedication of poems to the Earl of Southampton, or to Shakespeare's national dramas. The poet is claiming, in the manner of many famous passages in the plays, to set little store by external honours. Both this and the preceding sonnet are suggested in Henry VI's:

> Gives not the hawthorn bush a sweeter shade
> To shepherds, looking on their silly sheep,
> Than doth a rich embroider'd canopy
> To kings, that fear their subjects' treachery?
> (*3 Henry VI*; ii, v, 42)

Such 'ceremony', to use Henry V's term (iv, i, 250–304), is, from every view, deceptive, and so we are next told that those who rely on outward shows often actually lose everything by working too hard (i.e. by flattery) in the cause of their own desires. We next have a contrast of all such elaborate cookery ('compound sweet') with things of simpler taste, and as against such 'pitiful thrivers', with their Rosencrantz and Guildenstern tricks—all this must be read as a warning to himself—he would aim at love's more inward, spiritual, humility and worship.

Tucker reads 'form and favour' as 'shape and beauty'. It may mean that: 'favour' and 'form' are applied to a 'fair occasion' in *King John* (v, iv, 50). But 'form' can apply to ceremonial, and 'favour' mean what it means today, as in Timon's

> Thou art a slave, whom Fortune's tender arm
> With favour never clasp'd . . .
> *(Timon of Athens*, iv, iii, 251)

Lines 5–8, moreover, arouse in our minds so many Shakespearian parallels, from *Timon of Athens* and elsewhere, concerning court-flattery, that it is difficult to deny such a reference here. Compare these with Hamlet's words to Rosencrantz:

ROSENCRANTZ: Take you me for a sponge, my lord?
HAMLET: Ay, sir, that soaks up the King's countenance, his rewards, his authorities. But such officers do the King best service in the end: he keeps them, like an ape, in the corner of his jaw; first mouthed, to be last swallowed. When he needs what you have gleaned, it is but squeezing you, and, sponge, you shall be dry again.

> *(Hamlet*, iv, ii, 15)

See how 'countenance' here corresponds exactly to 'favour' in its dual content of 'facial expression' and 'approval'. Again, consider Wolsey's soliloquy at his fall:

> Vain pomp and glory of this world, I hate ye!
> I feel my heart new open'd. O, how wretched
> Is that poor man that hangs on princes' favours!
> There is, betwixt that smile we would aspire to,
> That sweet aspect of princes, and their ruin,
> More pangs and fears than wars or women have;
> And when he falls, he falls like Lucifer,
> Never to hope again.
> *(Henry VIII*, iii, ii, 366)

Here 'favours' means just what 'favour' might mean in our sonnet. We have an earlier sonnet on this theme:

> Let those who are in favour with their stars
> Of public honour and proud titles boast,
> Whilst I, whom Fortune of such triumph bars,
> Unlook'd for joy in that I honour most.

Great princes' favourites their fair leaves spread
But as the marigold at the sun's eye,
And in themselves their pride lies buried,
For at a frown they in their glory die.

(25)

'Favour' again. Here, exactly as in our later sonnet, love's simplicity is contrasted with worldly honour.

What biographical conclusion shall we draw? Clearly, nothing of certainty. The contrast of 'heart' with 'gazing' suits Tucker's, the usual and logical, reading as a transition from physical to spiritual adoration; but 'dwellers', 'rent' and 'thrivers' suggest patronage. We *slide* from ceremonial and monuments, through the ambiguity of 'favour', to an inward love. Anyway, these last sonnets are so weighted with world-glory that, metaphor or no, we must acknowledge its impact.

That granted, we may perhaps suppose that Shakespeare, for whom the Fair Youth had once, whatever his exact status, acted as an introduction to the refinements of society, had now advanced far higher. He had, we know, been accepted as a poet by Southampton. The young man, if indeed the affair dates back so far, may have read with some bitterness the dedication to *The Rape of Lucrece*, which some commentators have regarded as a variant of Sonnet 26:

The love I dedicate to your lordship is without end; whereof this pamphlet, without beginning, is but a superfluous moiety. The warrant I have of your honourable disposition, not the worth of my untutored lines, makes it assured of acceptance. What I have done is yours; what I have to do is yours; being part in all I have, devoted yours. Were my worth greater, my duty would show greater; meantime, as it is, it is bound to your lordship, to whom I wish long life, still lengthened with happiness.

That is, of course, quite mild as dedications go, or went, but it is considerably warmer and more personal than the dedication to *Venus and Adonis*. It is the dedication of someone who has been accepted; not, of course, as a social equal, but as a poet of consequence. Shakespeare's national compositions must also have attracted notice. It is quite likely that he had indeed taken part, or had been hoping to take part, in a royal ceremony. The service of favoured actors might well have been found useful when exact effects of pageantry were wanted.

Such details remain hypothetical. But the Sonnet certainly appears to record Shakespeare's claim to remain true to his love's essence, without being deflected, though these sonnets suggest that he was tempted, by the glitter of externals. After *The Rape of Lucrece* we have no evidence of flattery. Despite its success—and his poems were successful—Shakespeare henceforward appears to have kept himself steadily to what would have been regarded as a lower form of composition, drama; though Southampton certainly loved the theatre, and the dramas were national achievements. But Shakespeare's dramatic work shows no *forced* contemporary reference, and no instances at all of any subjugation of dramatic truth to self-seeking. He may certainly have parted with his friend, but never for long with all for which his treasured and inspiring love of him had stood. For now love and royalty were one.

Our final couplet is difficult. Who, or what, is the 'suborn'd informer'? We may relate him to 'policy' and 'heretic' in the preceding sonnet. He is some sort of Iago-form, some antagonist to truth and love, Goethe's 'spirit of negation'. He is the principle of critical rationality that has persuaded the youth that Shakespeare is unfaithful and only out for his own ambitions; more, he has all but persuaded Shakespeare himself of it. Remember our earlier conclusion: 'I *will* be true, despite thy scythe and thee' (123). Shakespeare, engaging in 'public manners' (111), had fallen below the high 'married chastity' (*The Phoenix and the Turtle*), the ideal truth and beauty (pp. 45, 67–8), of his love; he had also, in the world's eyes, begun to rise far above it. He had 'hoisted sail' (117) to the winds of patronage, and his ambitions are still active, causing him a keen sense of guilt when he thinks of the past. Though now mixing with the great, and perhaps indulging in all the licence that such an advance would have encouraged, he nevertheless feels himself, from that first high standard, most seriously 'impeach'd'. But, deep down, he knows his course: 'I am that I am' (121). He insists that his 'soul' remains 'true'. And we, who can see what came of it, may well agree that he was right.

There is one more sonnet, the *envoi* or farewell, concluding the series. This we have already (p. 97) discussed. It breathes a sweet spirit of resignation, acceptance, and farewell. All past thoughts of the boy's beauty, growth and waning as a creature of nature bound for eternity are contained and placed. It expresses a love at once impersonal and sincere; a love, to use a well-known distinction, nearer *agapé* than *eros*. It is a perfect end.

VI

CONCLUSION

All gems are cordial and of an influence religious.
These elemental flowering lights almost persuade us of a
serene eternity.

Arabia Deserta

IT has been my aim to discuss this last sequence without com-
mitting myself to an exact, or even an approximate, dating.
But our analysis certainly tends to suggest that the experience
behind the Sonnets was fairly early. If they indeed record a
single relationship, we might suppose them to be an artistic
working up, or re-working, of its significance at some later date
—for the main sequence, as a whole, shows artistic form—for
private circulation. That the two sonnets (138 and 144) printed
in Jaggard's *The Passionate Pilgrim* in 1599 show variants from
Thorpe's text is perhaps some evidence of a revisionary process.
The subject handled might well have precluded publication of
the whole sequence by Shakespeare himself. There was quite
enough in them to cause a certain diffidence. Michelangelo's
sonnets caused embarrassment to their first editor, his great-
nephew, who accordingly played tricks with genders in the text
(Symonds, Int., II; and see his note to Sonnet 8 on the boy
Cecchino Bracci). So did Benson, the second editor of Shakespeare's Sonnets in 1640

Precise biographical deductions are necessarily hazardous.
Our own analyses have tried to remain true to the poetry, whilst
refusing any close involvement in factual narrative, and it is
hoped that they may at least hold a negative value in serving
to check certain facile approaches that fail to recognise the
subtleties involved.

Shakespeare's personality has for so long remained enigmatic that we perhaps too readily assume that it was, by nature,
dispassionate and uninvolved. We do not think of him as interested in, or even aware of, his own mental and spiritual development. But it would really be strange if he were not. The

137

sequence from Sonnets to Drama is really simple enough and
has parallels in Vergil's transition from *Eclogues* to *Aeneid*, and
within the structure of Goethe's *Faust* (p. 124). Other great
poets in modern literature, Dante, Milton, Goethe, Byron and
Ibsen, knew well enough what they were doing: we have
claimed no self-consciousness for Shakespeare greater than
theirs.

Shakespeare does moreover elsewhere describe thoughts
very like his own creative processes. Meditating at Pomfret,
Richard II wishes to compare his solitary prison to the
'populous' world of men. He finds it hard:

> Yet I'll hammer it out.
> My brain I'll prove the female to my soul;
> My soul the father: and these two beget
> A generation of still-breeding thoughts,
> And these same thoughts people this little world
> In humours like the people of this world
> For no thought is contented.
> (*Richard II*, v, v, 5)

This is followed, as I have shown in *The Imperial Theme* (xi),
by a speech forecasting the sequence of Shakespeare's greater
work up to his final period. The 'brain' is here the 'female to
the soul'. We have already argued that the feminine element in
Shakespeare which loved his friend can be detected at work
within the dramas (pp. 30–3); and we shall recall that his friend
is identified, again and again, either directly, or in effect, with
both his 'soul' and his 'muse' (pp. 42–3, 106–13). Richard's
speech makes a neat correspondence with certain processes
which we have discovered within the Sonnets.

What else have we discovered? Let us, for clarity, recapitul-
ate a point or two that might otherwise be forgotten.

The Sonnets define the spiritual principle behind all Shakespeare's work.

It all started with the bisexual image of the Fair Youth.
Recognition of its excelling beauty and significance aroused
Shakespeare's love; through that love an inward bisexuality,
already dormant, was rapidly developed within the poet's soul or
mind, or rather 'soul-mind'; unity was glassed in unity (pp.
35–7). But the purity and perfection of the experience could

not be maintained: each lover in turn seems to accuse the other of falling below it into sexual vice, or suspicion of it (see p. 25 above). To Shakespeare, the incandescent purity could even be felt as a kind of disease (p. 125): being an insight into the eternal meaning of the creative process, all he could do was to create from it. He created love-plays and king-plays.

The great dramas were composed from a bisexual understanding. They can be comprehensively read in terms of the sexes, since we have either the bringing together of the sexes in romance, or the interweaving of masculine and feminine, which are the Apollonian and the Dionysian, principles in the Histories and the Tragedies. Feminine pathos is subjected to suffering by masculine action, or the tragic hero is overthrown by some feminine, and cosmic, invader. Dramatically, this interweaving labours for the fusion of power-with-love, or strength-with-grace (p. 112). That is a, perhaps the, main result of Shakespearian drama. Nor is this surprising: we may remember that Nietzsche's visionary description of the Superman in *Thus Spake Zarathustra* (II, 13) is couched in terms blending power with grace.

Having in his idealised passion for the beloved boy so touched the bisexual heart, or goal, of human striving, Shakespeare could write with ease of great affairs. From the start he had scorned to change his 'state' with 'kings' (p. 61); his love was less subject to temporal accident than were their high-sounded 'decrees' (p. 122). With an *Antony and Cleopatra* scorn of temporal engagements, he nevertheless enjoys a consciousness itself now 'hugely politic' (p. 129), over-arching empires. He is himself a super-king, so 'crowned' (p. 120) with the miraculous youth's eternal significance that all creation now salutes him and discloses its splendours (p. 119). This experience he expressed, years later, through Miranda:

> O, wonder!
> How many goodly creatures are there here!
> How beauteous mankind is! O brave new world,
> That has such people in it.
> *(The Tempest, v, i, 181)*

That was natural enough, for Miranda, within the integration-pattern of *The Tempest*, is, as we have seen (p. 55), precisely

that within Shakespeare which makes the sweet surrender and
resplendent discovery from which the Sonnets and Dramas
were composed. The nature of it is defined for us, as I have
shown in *Christ and Nietzsche* (1, 18–27), in Pope's *Essay on
Man* and Shelley's *Defence of Poetry* (p. 121, note). It is born
from what Shelley calls 'that imperial faculty whose throne is
curtained within the invisible nature of man', laying bare 'the
naked and sleeping beauty' which is 'the spirit' of all 'forms',
and so showing us the 'wonder of our being'. This 'imperial
faculty' it is of which Shakespeare writes in the line, 'And my
great mind most kingly drinks it up' (p. 120); like the Sun
drawing the Ocean, to let it fall as rain. And all this once
recognised, we shall not forget that it applies throughout: every
least person in Shakespeare enjoys this royalty, shares in the
elixir, is known by the *atman*, or divine spark, within.

There is within Shakespeare's humanism a central gem,
hard as rock, and yet burning with internal flame. You feel it in
The Phoenix and the Turtle, a condensed miniature of our whole
story. Generally it is working below, or within, hidden from
view. Most of Shakespeare's work is characterised by a seemingly inexhaustible outpouring, but we do not see the glittering source. It is all flesh and blood, and we do not actually see
the *atman*, or spark, and no one but Henry VI talks of it:

> My crown is in my heart, not on my head;
> Not deck'd with diamonds and Indian stones,
> Nor to be seen.
>
> (*3 Henry VI*, III, i, 62)

But the divine thing is always there, and we find it unearthed
for us in the last plays. It is in Marina as 'a palace for the
crown'd Truth to dwell in' (*Pericles*, v, i, 123) and looking

> Like Patience gazing on kings' graves and smiling
> Extremity out of act.
>
> (*Pericles*, v, i, 140)

It is in the 'fairy gold' and 'great creating Nature' of *The
Winter's Tale* (III, iii, 127; IV, iii, 88; and see *The Crown of Life*,
III, 120), where so much of the nature-thought of the Sonnets
reaches fulfilment; it is in the rugged mountain fastness of the
royal boys in *Cymbeline*; it is in Caliban's speech on Ariel's

music (*The Tempest*, III, ii, 147–55); and in the description of
the Field of the Cloth of Gold in *Henry VIII* (I, i, 13–38). In
all these, you get a magic beyond all normal Shakespearian
poetry, a sense of the wondrously eternal more potent than
dramatic gods and goddesses, even than Prospero's—the magic
we are describing is perhaps nearer Cerimon's—art. These
wonders are not obviously transcendental, or what we call
'spiritual'; they are close to earth. They are like gems (pp. 66,
159), where the divine sparkles; hard, glittering, indestructible.
This is a magic not actually realised in the Sonnets, but it is
verbally approached, and realisation groped for. We accordingly move easily from the Sonnets to *Antony and Cleopatra*,
which has another excellence, all its own. So, too, has the
resurrection of Hermione. The Final Plays follow naturally
enough. As he looks on Marina, you could almost see in the
old and worn Pericles, remembering the recurring emphasis on
age in the Sonnets, the poet *discovering his own soul*, as in T. S.
Eliot's poem; the thing which had been alive in his first great
love, had been expanded in the dramas, and was found, at last,
intact, as Prospero keeps Miranda intact, in *The Tempest*. At
this moment of recognition Pericles hears 'the music of the
spheres' (*Pericles*, V, i, 231).

We have covered in our survey much of Shakespeare's
work, but not all. We have said nothing whatsoever of his
humour. There seems little to say of it here, except to observe
that our story holds many elements of humour, and that it is
probable enough that Shakespeare, in Byronic mood, may have
noticed them. Of that, however, we have no evidence, and it is
more to the point to suggest that perhaps, after all, he was
himself behind Thorpe's publication of the Sonnets, covering
his traces by an imperfect text, and intentionally devising the
dedication in such a way as to mystify posterity. If so, he has
succeeded.

Mystified though we must remain as to much of the biography, and despite our not knowing with any certainty when
the Sonnets were composed or how far they preserve, or were
even meant to preserve, truth to fact, we can at least conclude
that Keats was not wholly wrong—though he was quite wrong
about Byron, whom the words suit even better—in suggesting
that Shakespeare 'led a life of allegory', and that his dramatic

work was a 'commentary' on it; and that Wordsworth came still nearer the truth in saying that in the Sonnets Shakespeare 'unlocked his heart'.

As for the metaphysical problems which they pose, these are best answered through the symbolism of the Phoenix.

Part II

PHOENIX AND TURTLE

I

PRELIMINARY REMARKS

WE have more than once referred to *The Phoenix and the Turtle*, and shall now attempt a brief discussion of this difficult poem.

As a metaphysical work celebrating a perfected love it responds readily to a generalised interpretation. But, after working through the Sonnets, we may wish to enquire a little further, and see whether we can arrive at a more exact definition of its symbolism. What is the meaning of 'Phoenix'? Has this particular symbol anything to do with the kind of love celebrated in Shakespeare's Sonnets?

Our discussion is complicated by the context in which Shakespeare's poem first appeared. In 1601 there was published a long poetic narrative by a certain Robert Chester, called *Love's Martyr, or Rosalin's Complaint*, defined on the title-page as 'allegorically shadowing the truth of Love', together with shorter works by Shakespeare, Marston, Chapman and Jonson, all turning on the one subject of Phoenix and Turtle, and all together dedicated to Sir John Salusbury. Anything beyond a generalised, philosophical, interpretation, must take this volume into account. The collection was edited by the Rev. A. B. Grosart in 1878 for The New Shakespeare Society. It had been reissued in 1611 without Chester's name, or the preliminary dedication and address, as—misprinting 'annals'—*The Anuals of great Britainne*, followed by a lengthy sub-title, the whole title-page concentrating on what is no more than a subsidiary theme (pp. 159, 178 below). To this reissue, which was bound up from some of the original sheets (Grosart, Int., lxi; Rollins, *New Variorum*, 559) I shall later (pp. 169–70) have occasion to refer. For the rest, my quotations will follow Grosart's text, except for a modernisation of spelling and punctuation, and the occasional correction of some obvious blunder. Since the pages bear two sets of numbers, my references give both.

Grosart argues that this poem, and indeed the whole collection, refers to the tragedy of Queen Elizabeth's love for Essex. This is however hard to accept. There are far too many lines which contradict the thesis. Once when the Phoenix, being shown London, starts to praise it and its governors as a place with 'all things to beautify a Royal Throne', Nature cuts in with: 'Leave off thy praises, till we have more leisure' (78/86). This would scarcely have pleased the Queen. Nor would the emphasis on 'a more perfect creature' (132/140) said to rise from the ashes of Phoenix and Turtle. Nor would she have been thrilled by the suggestion that the Turtle (= Essex) was to teach her 'knowledge', should she surrender the 'secrets' of her youth, her beauty being 'fresh as May' (137/145). Since Essex was under condemnation, if he had not already been executed, by the ageing queen, such stanzas would be in questionable taste.

But there was some reason for Grosart's theory. The Phoenix, though feminine, is 'princely' (134/142); she is associated with such phrases as 'empiring honour' (146/154) and 'thy imperial crown' (155/163). We hear that, 'Thee hath the world admired for clemency' (148/156); and that, 'To thee all human knees proffer their duty' (157/165). If a single, human, woman is being so addressed in a collection of poems by various authors—for the others write in roughly similar strain—one might well suppose that no one less than the Queen could be intended. Grosart (xxiv–xxxiv) supports his argument by many quotations from Thomas Churchyard's *Challenge* (1593), where the equation Phoenix = Elizabeth I is explicit.

In 1914 appeared Carleton Brown's valuable collection *Poems by Sir John Salusbury and Robert Chester*, printed for the Early English Text Society, and containing a number of previously unpublished pieces by the two men. Of Sir John himself quite a lot is known; but Robert Chester remains an enigmatic personality, about whom we shall say a word or two later (p. 175).

In his introduction Carleton Brown shows clearly that *Love's Martyr* cannot be intended to represent Elizabeth and Essex, since Salusbury was bitterly opposed to Essex' party (Int., xi). He suggests instead that Turtle and Phoenix represent Sir John and his wife, Ursula Stanley, who claimed royal

blood, being a natural daughter of Henry Stanley, Fourth Earl
of Derby, by Jane Halsall (Int., xv). He quotes lines to her by
'Danielle', included in his volume, running:

> From princely blood and royal stock she came,
>   Of eagle's brood hatch'd in a lofty nest.
> The earl of Derby and the King of Man
>   Her father was . . .
>   (Int., lxiv; and see 31)

Sir John was married in 1586; his first child, Jane, was born
in 1587, and a son, Harry, in 1589. Carleton Brown supposes
that *Love's Martyr* was composed ten or more years before
its publication in 1601, and argues that Marston's reference to
the new Phoenix as 'grown to maturity' in 1601 would suit Sir
John's daughter, then aged fourteen (Int., lxiv, lxix, lxxi-lxxii).
Whether his description of it as 'god, man nor woman, but
elix'd of all' (p. 183 below) would be equally suitable may,
however, be questioned.

We can also question whether the title *Love's Martyr*
makes the best possible device for a poem honouring a patron's
marriage, the more so since we know from a number of Sir
John's own acrostic lyrics, included in the collection, that he
was, at one period at least, passionately devoted to Dorothy
Halsall, his wife's sister (Int., xxxviii). One poem of considerable force entitled *J. S. his Amazement* is an agonised soliloquy
about some *secret* love (Christ Church MS. xxiv; *Poems of
Salusbury and Chester*, 33–5; see p. 179 below). The lines by
Danielle might conceivably be intended for his sister-in-law
rather than his wife: in Brown's text 'm(istress) Salusbury' may
even represent some innuendo (Christ Church MS. xxii, 31).
But it is very doubtful whether Salusbury or his ladies have anything to do with the book's contents. After all, dedication does
not necessarily involve identification.

Brown is, necessarily, baffled by Shakespeare's contribution: 'Shakespeare', he writes, 'chose to develop his theme along
a widely diverging line. In his poem the note from first to last
is funereal' (Int., lxxii).

Shakespeare's poem has received a very fair critical attention. In a valuable essay called 'The Nature of Poetry' in his
Discoveries (1924), J. Middleton Murry regards it as pivotal in

Shakespeare's emotional and imaginative development pointing on to the great tragedies. In *The Voyage to Illyria* (1937)
Kenneth Muir and Sean O'Loughlin interpreted it as a record
of Shakespeare's final break with Southampton, taken to be the
Fair Youth of the Sonnets:

> Though love has been betrayed brutally, even sordidly, the fact that
> it once existed is sufficient assurance to the poet that 'love hath reason',
> that is to say, is an absolute.
>
> (v, 132)

The deaths of Phoenix and Turtle signify the tragedy of this
love, but perfect love somehow continues to exist 'in eternity'
(v, 132).

Without confining ourselves to any exact biographical pattern, we can agree that some such experience may lie behind
the poem. But the Sonnets certainly suggest that there was
'betrayal', if so strong a word be in place, on both sides. Nor
can we be sure that Shakespeare's emotional experiences were
limited to a single affair: he may have had many.

Southampton is again the centre of interest in Walter
Thomson's *The Sonnets of William Shakespeare and Henry
Wriothesley* (1938).[1] Thomson (IX, 63–74) brushes aside
Chester's *Love's Martyr*, but regards the following *Poetical
Essays* as a surreptitious method used by his stage friends to
send a message of sympathy to Southampton when in prison
on a charge of treason. For reasons of prudence, the meanings
are veiled; the female sex of the Phoenix is a mask, the more
easily used since 'the sex of the mythical Phoenix was an uncertain and variable quantity'. The author lays especial stress on
Jonson's short poem *The Phoenix Analysed* (p. 188 below) as
giving a key to this particular masking.

There is yet another candidate. In his edition *Poems of Ben
Jonson* (1936), Bernard H. Newdigate notes that one of Ben
Jonson's contributions, the *Ode Enthousiastiké* (p. 190 below),
is found in manuscript addressed to Lucy, Countess of Bedford;[2] and from this he deduces that the whole volume may

---

[1] Walter Thomson argues that some of Shakespeare's Sonnets were written by
Southampton.

[2] An account of this MS. was given by Newdigate in an article on '*The Phoenix and
the Turtle*' in *The Times Literary Supplement*, 24 Oct., 1936; 862.

have been composed in her honour, calling Chester's *Love's Martyr* 'an allegory of married love' (365–6). He has since developed his argument further in his *The Phoenix and Turtle* (1937). But it is hard to see any of these poems as a celebration of *married* love. The lady had been married in 1594, but since there was no child to correspond to it, the reference to the new Phoenix, said to have 'grown into maturity' in Marston's contribution (p. 184 below), forces Newdigate into a metaphysical interpretation (*The Phoenix and Turtle*, Int., xxiii) ill-suited to a biographical allegory. Jonson's poem may, indeed, have been at one time offered to this lady, but in our present context it surely holds its own significance. To this problem we shall return (pp. 190–1).[1]

In his monograph *Phönix und Taube* (1953) Heinrich Straumann does well to remind us that *Love's Martyr* was, in fact, dedicated to Sir John Salusbury. The dedication, though this need not involve identification within the fictions, is phrased in no uncertain terms, which suggest a devotion and admiration corroborated by the adulatory verses of Chester and others, including Jonson, published in Carleton Brown's *Poems by Salusbury and Chester*. Whatever be the validity of our various ascriptions, we can surely agree with Prof. Straumann that different levels of meaning may co-exist in Shakespeare's poem; and if in Shakespeare's, then perhaps in the others too. What we really want to decide is this: What meanings can the poems hold for *us*? There is something universal about our Phoenix-and-Turtle collection, and it is on this universal that we must concentrate. The main myth will be found to have little in common with married love; and whatever oblique truths the various personal attributions and identifications which have been put forward may once have held, they have been burned by the poetic fires generated, and cannot, for us, be the main thing. Even so, we cannot quite work independently of them.

Our enquiry may be directed by a valuable passage from Emerson's *Parnassus*, quoted by Grosart (Int., xliv):

I should like to have the Academy of Letters propose a prize for an essay on Shakespeare's poem, *Let the bird of loudest lay*, and the *Threnos*

---

[1] Objections to Newdigate's theory were put forward by R. W. Short in *The Times Literary Supplement*, 13 Feb., 1937; 111; and answered by Newdigate on 20 Feb., 1937; 131.

with which it closes, the aim of the essay being to explain, by a historical research into the poetic myths and tendencies of the age in which it was written, the frame and allusions of the poem. I have not seen Chester's *Love's Martyr* and the 'Additional Poems' (1601), in which it appeared. Perhaps that book will suggest all the explanation this poem requires. To unassisted readers, it would appear to be a lament on the death of a poet, and of his poetic mistress. But the poem is so quaint, and charming in diction tone, and allusions, and in its perfect metre and harmony, that I would gladly have the fullest illustration yet attainable. I consider this piece a good example of the rule, that there is a poetry for bards proper, as well as a poetry for the world of readers. This poem, if published for the first time, and without a known author's name, would find no general reception. Only the poets would save it.

Note the phrase 'poetic mistress', and the emphasis throughout on poets. The various contributors certainly appear to be speaking a rather abstruse language understood by themselves and Sir John Salusbury, but likely to be obscure to the general reader. Note, too, the words 'poetic myths and tendencies of the age'. Their very imprecision hints a direction and a discipline. We shall try, without aiming at an exhaustive treatment, to follow Emerson's advice.

We shall assume that the Phoenix holds a significance in its own right. Of this primary significance any comparisons with Queen Elizabeth, as in Churchyard's *Challenge* and at *Henry VIII*, v, v, 41, or any particular lord, lady, friend or lover, will be a derivative.

In his introduction to his edition (1931) of the 1593 Elizabethan anthology called *The Phoenix' Nest*, Hyder Edward Rollins refers to the bird's popularity in Petrarch, Ronsard and Desportes, and traces its English ancestry back to the expansion of Lactantius' *Carmen de Phoenice* as an allegory of Christ by an anonymous Old English poet of the eighth or ninth century. 'Perhaps, too', he writes, thinking of the elegy and epitaphs to Sidney in the anthology, 'Sir Philip Sidney was connected with the Phoenix' (Int., x). Certainly the first poem is addressed to his memory. The Phoenix is a semi-transcendental creature; but in Elizabethan poetry divine and human converge. Christ, sovereign, aristocrat and lover exist on a single imaginative circuit; but the main poetic emphasis of the period falls on near-distance humanity; intuitions of the divine are transmitted through human stuff, or experience. On certain choice occasions of this kind the Phoenix may appear.

The Phoenix (i) rouses an extreme poetical, almost mystical, devotion; (ii) is naturally associated with excelling love, including chastity; and (iii) has immortal powers. Clearly, **we are** close to Shakespeare's sonnets. Its original title-page explicitly defined *Love's Martyr* as '*allegorically shadowing the truth of Love*'. This does not necessarily rule out devotion to sovereign or aristocrat, since to the Elizabethan mind both were romantically charged; but the Phoenix is certainly a symbol of personal, indeed intimate, experience.

It is transcendent without ceasing to be physical. When in *The Author's Request to the Phoenix* Chester as Turtle-Dove, for so he calls himself, dedicates his 'praises' to one 'that feed'st all earthly senses with thy savour', 'all' indicates a universality, whilst 'senses' preserves physical impact. Chester may have been referring here to Lady, or perhaps to Sir John, Salusbury, or to Dorothy Halsall. One of them is *at this moment* functioning as Phoenix with respect to Chester as Turtle. Phoenix and Turtle indicate really not so much persons, as a kind of *relationship*. In study of these poems we are continually forced to the equation Dove = Poet. In this '*Request to the Phoenix*' it is explicit, the poet asking for the Phoenix' 'kind acceptance of thy Turtle-Dove'. It has even been argued that the now generally recognised as fictional name Torquato Caeliano given on the title-page of *Love's Martyr* as the original source-author, in old Italian, of the main narrative is intended to be 'a Latinised form for "silver-coloured" or "heavenly dove"' (Irma R. White, *T.L.S.*, 1932, 532; quoted Rollins, *New Variorum*, 582).

The birds' sexes throughout our collection appear baffling. 'Contrary to ordinary usage', writes Grosart, 'the Turtle-Dove is distinctly sung of as a male' (Int., xxxiv). The Dove is Venus' bird, and we expect it to be poetically female. It is regularly a symbol of peace, as in Shakespeare's 'the dove' and 'blessed spirit of peace', at *2 Henry IV*, iv, i, 46: or as when 'meek-eye'd Peace', as a lady, is compared with it in Milton's *Nativity Ode* (iii). But in our Phoenix-and-Turtle poems it functions throughout as the male.

The Phoenix, though the female partner, is a creature of royal power, as well as beauty. It is mentioned by Hesiod

(Fragment 171), and also in the Book of Job (xxix, 18; R.V., margin). Herodotus (ii, 73) says that it resembles an eagle in shape and size and has feathers of red and gold. Pliny describes it in similar terms, and so does Petrarch (Sonnet 185; also 321, 323). The Old English poem on the Phoenix, following and expanding Lactantius, gives it connotations of pride and leadership, and describes it pre-eminently as a bird always desirous of the Sun, whose rising it anxiously awaits. When the time comes, the Sun fires its nest, and the new Phoenix is as an eaglet, growing to an eagle. As for its sex, we are told that only God knows what its sex is. But it certainly hits the imagination with a suggestion of male virility; it is male in Hesiod and Herodotus; and in ancient Greece 'Phoenix' was a male name.[1]

In the elegy for Sir Philip Sidney in *The Phoenix' Nest* we find the Eagle instead of the Phoenix as partner to the Dove:

> The sky-bred Eagle, royal bird,
> Perch'd there upon an oak above,
> The Turtle by him never stirr'd,
> Example of immortal love.
>   The Swan that sings about to die,
>   Leaving Meander, stood thereby.

> And that which was of wonder most,
> The Phoenix left sweet Araby,
> And on a cedar in this coast,
> Built up her tomb of spicery,
>   As I conjecture by the same,
>   Prepared to take her dying flame.

The Phoenix is here separated from the others. When, as in the various poems which we are to analyse, we find it rather than the Eagle as mate to the Turtle, we naturally expect it to be the male partner. But it is not.[2] Again, the Dove is sometimes called

---

[1] For the origins, see *Le Mythe de Phénix* . . ., Jean Hubaux and Maxine Leroy, Paris, 1939; reviewed W. F. J. Knight, *Classical Weekly*, xxxiv, 5; Nov., 1940; also Sir Osbert Sitwell and others, *The Times Literary Supplement*, 1941; 199, 203, 251, 287, 347, 352, 364 and 397; and T. W. Baldwin's *Literary Genetics*, xvi, 377, note, referring to Miss M. C. Fitzpatrick's edition of Lactantius' poem.

[2] I do not know whether there are other examples of Eagle and Turtle-Dove. The love-association of Parrot and Turtle-Dove is found in Ovid and Pliny; see Baldwin's *Literary Genetics*, xvi, 365.

'silver' and perhaps bears to the female Phoenix the relation of Moon to Sun (pp. 151, 157, 180, 196, 207). These sexual transferences must be supposed significant.

Whenever the Phoenix is mentioned we must suppose that a universal meaning of some kind is being conveyed. The bird's flaming spirituality appears to cover the whole range of Spenser's four *Hymns* in honour of Beauty and Love, Earthly and Divine. Being the essence of love-beauty, as the Dove is the essence of love-truth, both are regularly contrasted with lust, and chastity is a reiterated emphasis. The experience is rich, yet, even if praise to a patron be involved, somehow intimate and inward: to Danielle Salusbury is 'beautiful' as Paris and called 'sweet Salusbury' (Christ Church MS. xxi; *Poems by Salusbury and Chester*, 30). In his poetic address 'to the kind reader' of *Love's Martyr*, Chester asserts that he is aiming not at any great epic themes, but at fantasies more delicate: 'Of none of these, of sweet conceit I sing'. The experience must, I think, be in general distinguished from any ordinary marriage, or celebration of a marriage: the Phoenix would scarcely be at home within Spenser's *Epithalamion*.[1] It is at once tragic and brilliant, and may be related, variously, to Platonic love and its reflection in Castiglione's *Courtier*; to the courtly love, in so far as sexual consummation was not attained, of medievalism; and to Christian mysticism, in so far as it approaches the flaming mysticism of a Crashaw. Among the poems which we are considering it enjoys a certain immediacy of physical impact peculiar to a period when the divine was felt as incarnate, in queen, aristocrat, or lover. That is why the poetry rises on occasion to so extreme an excitement.

But the love is generally thwarted of any easy, non-poetic, expression. The lover's soul may be an anguished work-shop of sublimation and idealisation. The process is evident in Drayton's *Idea's Mirror*, *Amour* 32 (1594):

Those tears which quench my hope still kindle my desire,
Those sighs which cool my heart are coals unto my love,
Disdain, ice to my life, is to my soul a fire;
With tears, sighs and disdain, this contrary I prove.

---

[1] It does, however, occur, for a reason, in an *Epithalamion* of Donne's. See pp. 206–8.

Quenchless desire makes hope burn, dries my tears;
Love heats my heart, my heart-heat my sighs warmeth;
With my soul's fire, my life disdain out-wears,
Desire, my love, my soul, my hope, heart and life charmeth.

My hope becomes a friend to my desire,
My heart embraceth Love, Love doth embrace my heart;
My life a Phoenix is in my soul's fire,
From thence, they vow, they never will depart.

Desire, my love, my soul, my hope, my heart, my life,
With tears, sighs, and disdain, shall have immortal strife.

And here is a more settled expression at *Amour* 6:

In one whole world is but one Phoenix found,
A Phoenix thou, this Phoenix then alone,
By thy rare plume thy kind is easily known,
With heavenly colours dye'd, with nature's wonder crown'd.

Heap thine own virtues, seasoned by their sun,
On heavenly top of thy divine desire:
Then with thy beauty set the same on fire,
So by thy death, thy life shall be begun.

Thyself thus burned in this sacred flame,
With thine own sweetness all the heavens perfuming,
And still increasing as thou art consuming[1],
Shalt spring again from the ashes of thy fame;

And, mounting up, shalt to the heavens ascend.
So may'st thou live, past world, past fame, past end.

This piece recurs in a revised form emphasising fiery chastity in *Idea*, 16 (1619). The emphasis on 'sweetness' is important. Something infinitely sweet, beyond all normal biological creation, is being created. It is not all fruitless yearning: something is *made* by it. Part, but not all, of what is made is, of course, the poetry.

Such ideal and bravely tragic loves may exist between persons either of different sexes or of the same sex: in Dante we

---

[1] With l. 11 we might compare the sense of loss and gain within the temporal process discussed above (pp. 72, 91–2).

have it with Beatrice, in Shakespeare with the Fair Youth, in Michelangelo with both man and woman. And where there is no external evidence of sex we can never be sure that the poet is not using female terms as a mask. A suggestion of the kind was hinted by George Wyndham in *The Poems of Shakespeare*. In a discussion of Shakespeare's sonnets in his introduction (cv-cvi) he makes the point with reference to Drayton's *Idea* 10 (1619):

> Drayton, like Shakespeare, upbraids someone, whom he compares to the son—and the sex is significant—'of some rich penny-father', for wasting his 'Love' and 'Beauty', which Time must conquer, 'on the unworthy', who cannot make him 'survive' in 'immortal song'. And the next number sounds familiar, with its curious metaphysical conceit of identity between the beloved one and the poet who sings him. If anyone had thought it worth his while to investigate the biographical problems of Drayton's obviously doctored *Idea*, he would have found nuts to crack as hard as any in Shakespeare's sonnets. It is best, perhaps, to take Sidney's advice, and to believe with him that 'there are many mysteries contained in Poetry, which of purpose were written darkly'.

There are no easy solutions to the multi-facial potentialities of the Phoenix-symbol in this period, but the suggestions of that passage should be held in mind throughout our study.

The main point to remember is that the Phoenix suggests a difficult, tragic, and yet victorious experience. In fact, if Chester's main poem is intended to represent Sir John as Turtle, the Phoenix, if correctly used, would be more likely to be his sister-in-law (p. 147 above), to whom Sir John composed many ardent lyrics in the tradition we are discussing, than his wife. Such examples of poetic passion are always more likely to refer to some elevated and ideal, or otherwise difficult, and perhaps dangerous, relationship—Sir John's own acrostic lyrics show many evidences of secrecy—than to a settled marriage; the relationship may be homosexual or heterosexual, but it must be hampered, you must have a maximum of ardour with a minimum of possible accomplishment, so that desire is forced into eye and mind to create—whatever it *does* create: the new Phoenix.

II

LOVE'S MARTYR

CHESTER'S main narrative tells us how Nature, also called Rosalin, solicits the help of Jove to perpetuate a wonderful female creature called the Phoenix whom she has created. She is authorised to take this Phoenix to Venus' island, Paphos, where it meets a male Turtle-Dove mourning for its dead lover, which is considered variously as another Phoenix and as a Dove. The two living birds at once, and on the briefest acquaintance, decide to immolate themselves on a pyre, and a new Phoenix arises. Cantos follow containing praise 'to fair Phoenix made by the Paphian Dove'.

Though a male is mentioned (5/13),[1] Chester's main Phoenix is feminine. Its physical excellences are carefully described. But some of these certainly suggest male beauty. It has golden locks stolen from Apollo, a forehead like that of 'princely Jove' fit to 'censure matters of import', 'princely eyes like carbuncles', 'two rich imperial lights' brighter than 'moon and glorious sun'; and its lips speak 'true learned eloquence and poetry' (2/10; 3/11). The Phoenix is regularly to be associated with poetry; 'gold' and 'golden' are recurring impressions in poems on this theme, and Apollo generally the presiding deity.

But much of Chester's description of the Phoenix' expressly *delicate* physical charms is feminine enough. Its chin is 'a little little pretty thing' (3/11), and the breasts 'two crystal orbs of whitest white' (4/12). When, after a point-by-point analysis, he comes to the sexual centres, he says 'Be still my thoughts, be silent all ye Muses', invokes Homer's aid, and continues:

> There is a place in lovely paradise,
> From whence the golden Gehon overflows,
> A fountain of such honourable prize,

---

[1] For my double-page references to *Love's Martyr* see p. 145 above.

That none the sacred, sacred, virtues knows,
Walled about, betok'ning sure defence,
With trees of life, to keep bad errors thence.
(5/13)

That is, I suppose, sexually non-committal. The weak repetition of 'sacred', as of 'little' above, appears to be a characteristic of Chester's work (and see my quotation on p. 175 below).

The more feminine descriptions indicate a fragile loveliness; but then we have the brow made to 'censure matters of
import' (2/10) and the general effect is called 'majestical'
(7/15). It all reads rather as a blend of statesman and chorus-
girl, and the implications are bisexual. The Phoenix is an
'angel' alone on earth (6/14). Its loneliness is important,
Nature grieving, not unlike the Shakespeare of the Sonnets,
at its inability to find a mate, and the probability of its death
without perpetuation (7/15; 9/17).

It is arranged that it shall meet 'Honour's lovely squire',
the Turtle-Dove, who is said to be keeping for it 'Prometheus'
fire', a male creature of 'liberal honour' and 'faithful service'
(11/19). This dove may be said to correspond roughly to the
poet in Shakespeare's Sonnets. Chester has already equated
himself as poet with the Turtle (p. 151).

Once Phoenix and Turtle are bafflingly confused. We have
during the narrative: 'A Prayer made for the prosperity of a
silver coloured Dove, applied to the beauteous Phoenix'
(13/21). The dove is, as in Shakespeare (p. 196 below), *silver*,
as against the *gold* of the Phoenix. There is an address 'To
those of light belief', aimed at persuading the reader to 'read
gently' (i.e. sensitively and sympathetically) 'what you read,
this next conceit', since it is 'framed of pure love' (15/23); and
there follows a dialogue (17/25) by Nature and the Phoenix,
concerned with the inherent *dangers* of the Phoenix' beauty.
The Phoenix tells Nature, who has been praising it, that
'raising me thou dost corrupt thy song', that 'honey' is mixed
with 'poison' in its beauty, and that its admirer fails to see
'how I do bait my hook'. It knows its beauty to be 'a fading
flower', and that, though its 'sun-bred looks' win it devoted
admirers, yet, where it would love, 'foul blear-eyed Envy doth
my thoughts reprove'. This appears to be a recurring thought
in Phoenix poems: the creature, though superlative, is in

danger of being slandered. C. Knox Pooler notes 'that James I
published in 1585 a poem on the Phoenix in which he represented her as assailed by malice and envy' (*Shakespeare's
Poems*, Arden edn., 1911; Int., xci). The love of Chester's
Phoenix, though backed and praised by Nature, or instinct, is
yet, it seems, thwarted by society, and all its 'wit' accordingly
but an 'inhuman glory', though it would indeed wish 'to my
kind dear friends to proffer peace' (17/25). But already it fears
that it has gone too far, and warns itself:

> Malice perchance doth hearken to thy words
> That cuts thy thread of love with twenty swords.
>
> (18/26)

Nature—remember that it is *Nature* that speaks—cannot
understand all this:

> Tell me, O Mirror of our earthly time,
> Tell me, sweet Phoenix, glory of mine age,
> Who blots thy beauty with foul envy's crime,
> And locks thee up in fond suspicion's cage?
> Can any human heart bear thee such rage?
>   Daunt their proud stomachs with thy piercing eye,
>   Unchain love's sweetness at thy liberty.
>
> (18/26)

The Phoenix is a creature of virile power and 'piercing eye'.
The poetry is often powerful; some of it is reminiscent, and
parts not unworthy, of Shakespeare; and whatever be the exact
meaning, the Sonnets are continually recalled.

Nature goes on to assure the Phoenix that she will over-
rule Envy, Malice, Hate and Suspicion:

> Thou art but young, fresh, green and must not pass,
> But catch the hot sun with thy steeled glass.
>
> (18/26)

The poetry is on occasion fiercely fine:

> Stand by, fair Phoenix, spread thy wings of gold,
> And daunt the face of Heaven with thine eye . . .
>
> (19/27)

'Eye' again. So Nature will take the Phoenix in 'Phoebus'
coach', Apollo being our deity, to where it may 'taste a secret

fire' that shall add 'spreading life' to its 'desire' (19/27); just as Shakespeare's 'secret fire' expanded to his life-work. More stanzas are given to Envy, who comes in a 'foggy cloud' to 'tyrranise' over the bright Phoenix, is shown in a state of repellent self-torment ('how the villain sweats', 20/28), and is finally driven off by Nature.

So they journey to Paphos. On the historical disquisitions and descriptions which follow we need not linger, except to observe that at one point nine famous *women of action* are listed, continuing the bisexual emphasis (29/37–32/40). There is also a tribute paid to Edward III and 'Knights of the Garter and St. George's Cross' (34/42), and a long section on the life and death of King Arthur. Any chivalric emphasis, in its blend of gentleness with strength, Christianity with power, can, if we like, be integrated into our theme, but the length of these sections is disproportionate and tedious.

Nature sings a ditty on trivial kinds of love, with Cupid as symbol, saying that all this is thoroughly 'unwholesome' and profanes 'the sacred name of Love', which is her only real theme and 'golden Truth'; and the Phoenix follows on with a song about such greater love, Platonically and religiously conceived (79/87–80/88).

On arrival at Paphos, we are given a long description of its vegetation and bird-life, with much rather irksome lore. The Phoenix is interested in stories of Narcissus and of Apollo and Hyacinthus, and speaks some interesting stanzas on them (86/94–87/95; 89/97). With reference to the myrtle, we have a legend about a girl called Mersin favoured by Pallas Athene or Minerva. She is another woman of action, who so 'excelled' in masculine games, that she aroused jealousy, and was killed (96/104–97/105). The bisexual emphasis is again noteworthy. So are some remarkable stanzas on the diamond as the origin of all learning and art, since it is worshipped rather as is the Phoenix, itself such a symbol (103/111).[1]

Eventually, at Paphos, we meet the male Turtle-Dove, called 'Cupid's child' (125/133. The text is confusing, but the words are spoken by the Phoenix; Grosart, notes, 233). Nature leaves the two birds together.

[1] Compare my remarks on such stones (e.g. in Sir Herbert Read's *The Green Child*) in *Christ and Nietzsche*, V, 193–4; and see pp. 66, 137, 141 above.

The Turtle, found grieving for a lost mate or companion, is at once struck by the Phoenix' beauty, calling it an 'eye-dazzling sun', a perfect child of Nature and thing of wit and virtue (124/132). The Turtle's lost mate is considered first female ('her') and next male ('him') within a single stanza (125/133).

Carleton Brown says that the discrepancy 'defies explanation'; notes that Furnivall altered 'him' to 'her'; but, in pursuance of his own theory, equates the dead Turtle with Sir John Salusbury's dead brother, and changes 'her' to 'him' (*Poems by Salusbury and Chester*; Int., lviii, note; lxiii–lxiv). It is true that we have no evidence that the Turtle's lost dear one was his spouse, though it is natural to suppose so, and later in the book we come across, as a purely general thought, 'Thou art a turtle wanting of thy mate' (139/147; and compare my quotation from *The Winter's Tale* on p. 195 below). Early in the poem our Turtle-Dove was called by Jove 'a second Phoenix' love' (9/17; 'Argument', 10, 14), which suggests that its mate had been a Phoenix. However that may be, the birds' sexes throughout these poems are a positive torment. We shall find more instances.

Now that they have met, the Phoenix and the Turtle arrange to die together as speedily as possible, though the Phoenix first warns the Turtle against 'impure thoughts or unclean chastity', since the burning, which is equated with 'true love's desire', will not succeed otherwise. The Turtle denies any such thoughts (127/135–128/136). The Phoenix (129/137) dedicates their joint sacrifice to the Sun as Apollo —Apollo, the god of male beauty and art, is throughout our presiding deity—and fire is invoked:

> Accept into your ever hallowed flame,
> Two bodies, from the which may spring one name.
>
> (130/138)

There is little about all this to suggest a poem in honour of any normal marriage. It is tragic, yet bright, and the sacrifice charmingly handled, with one of Chester's more successful repetitions:

> See, beauteous Phoenix, it begins to burn!
> O blessed Phoebus, happy, happy light ...
>
> (130/138)

The Turtle is glad to be 'a partner in this happy tragedy'
(130/138). The Phoenix' last words include:

> I hope of these another Creature springs,
> That shall possess both our authority.
>
> (131/139)

That, with the 'one name' before, suggests the key and core
of all our Phoenix-symbolism, and its emphatic place here
underlines its importance.

The tragic sacrifice is commented on, not inappropriately, by
a Pelican, a bird accustomed to give its life for its children, and,
indeed, only allowed to watch the sacrifice by reason of its own
sacrificial propensities (129/137). It says, rather obscurely:

> O if the rarest creatures of the earth,
> Because but one at once did ere take breath
> Within the world, should with a second he,
> A perfect form of love and amity,
> Burn both together, what should there arise,
> And be presented to our mortal eyes,
> Out of the fire, but a more perfect creature?
>
> (132/140)

The meaning is: The Phoenix and Turtle are 'rarest', because
hitherto there has only been one Phoenix at a time, but now,
in the Turtle, we have 'a second he'. Both Turtle and Phoenix,
unless we understand the phrase as meaning 'a second who
happens to be a "he",' are here accordingly male. The general
suggestion is that, instead of a single perfected unity, we have
now watched, to use my earlier phrase (p. 112), 'unity glassed
in unity'.

The more perfect creature is to have the 'beauty', 'wit's
rarity' and 'virtue' of the Phoenix, together with the love,
chastity, constancy, and wit's *guiding power*, or reason, of the
Turtle (132/140). The attributes can be said to divide
sexually, but would also fit the Fair Youth and Shakespeare,
from the poet's viewpoint. The new creature must presumably
be imagined as androgynous, or bisexual, since it *is* love:
'without these two no love at all can be' (132/140). This 'love'
may be equated with Donne's 'great Prince' (p. 61). The
burning is called a matter of 'true desire', with a final emphasis
on 'chastity' (133/141).

12

A 'conclusion', signed by Chester, addresses, once again, 'gentle conceivers of true-meaning wit'; which means that he hopes for a sensitive and refined response to a meaningful and worth-while poem (133/141). He tells us that 'another princely Phoenix upright stood', even more brilliant than 'her late-burned mother', with, in her heart, 'a perpetual love', said to be 'sprung from the bosom of the Turtle-Dove'. This could be read as a description of Shakespeare's development from the experience behind the Sonnets to his greater work; what was evanescent, becomes 'perpetual'. But I am not arguing that Chester's poetry intended anything of the sort. Rather we must suppose it to be describing some great universal of which Shakespeare's development exists merely as one particular manifestation; though, when he prays that 'long may the new uprising bird increase', it does, rather remarkably, fit Shakespeare's career in 1601. He concludes by hoping again for 'gentle minds' to accept his work.

There follow the 'cantos' made by 'the Paphian Dove' to 'fair Phoenix'. This is, presumably, our first Phoenix, but poetically that is of no consequence. These cantos may be called straight devotional poems by the poet as Turtle to the Phoenix-conception-in-general.

The first sequence of cantos is arranged alphabetically, the lines of each stanza starting with the same letter. Much of the poetry fits the love-theme of Shakespeare's sonnets:

> Ah, be my Phoenix, I will be thy Dove,
> And thou and I in secrecy will love.
>
> (134/142)

The love must not be publicised: 'Blaze not my love, thou herald of the day'. The poetry enjoys a freedom of suggestion that contrasts with the chastity elsewhere so emphatic in treatment of the Phoenix: C. Knox Pooler calls the Dove of these cantos 'a maker of dissolute proposals' (*Shakespeare's Poems*, Arden edn., 1911; Int., xcii). Whether dissolute or not they are insistent:

> Devout obedience on my knees I proffer,
> Delight match with delight, if thou do crave it,
> Deny not, gentle Phoenix, my sweet offer,
> Despair not in my love, for thou shalt have it,

> Damn not the soul to woe if thou canst save it:
> Doves pray devoutly, O let me request,
> Delicious love to build within thy nest.
>   (135/143)

'Envy' is banished; there is now no need for Phoenix to fear that 'evil motions tempt thee sooner than the good'; there may be some suggestion that a higher state has now been attained in which more freedom is allowable; so it is asked to 'esteem the thing that cannot be withstood', to

> Esteem of me, and I will lend thee fire,
> Even of mine own to fit thy sweet desire.
>   (135/143)

The 'faint-hearted soul' is implored not to blush and be 'fearful of that which will revive thy sense' (i.e. perhaps, 'stimulate physical excitement'); 'faith and obedience' is asking it; it is a matter of 'friends' plighted war'. So

> Fear not at all, 'tis but sweet Love's offence,
> Fit to be done, so doing 'tis not seen.
>   (136/144)

The 'gold beautifying Phoenix' is, as in Shakespeare's Sonnets, the poet's 'muse', able to give him 'old Homer's spirit'. Therefore, with perhaps an innuendo and double meaning, 'grant me to play my sonnet on thy harp', and 'hide not thy secret glory, lest he' (i.e. the Turtle) 'die' (136/144). 'Secret glory', in such a context, appears rather male than female. A difficult stanza delicately defines a balance of ardour and inhibition:

> I love, O Love, how thou abusest me,
> I feel the fire, and warm me with the flame,
> I note the errors of thy deity:
> In Vesta's honour, Venus' lusts to tame,
> I in my humours yield thee not a name,
>   I count thee foolish, fie, adulterous boy,
>   I touch the sweet, but cannot taste the joy.
>   (136/144)

It is suggested that Phoenix might at least kiss the Turtle, and not continue to withhold from him 'the secrets of thy youth'. The Turtle will teach it everything, and no one need know: 'Kend shalt thou be of no man' (137/145). Kisses are craved again later, with the offer to bring *fuel for the Phoenix' fire* (i.e.,

perhaps, to help preserve its integrity) in return (140/148)·
There are various phrases of physical innuendo. Shakespeare's
sonnets are recalled, though suggestion is stronger, as in the
'sapless flower' of these lines:

> Love is my great Advotrix, at thy shrine
> Love pleads for me, and from my tongue doth say,
> Lie where thou wilt, my heart shall sleep with thine,
> Lamenting of thy beauty fresh as May.
> Look, Phoenix, to thy self do not decay:
>> Let me but water thy dead sapless flower,
>> Love gives me hope 'twill flourish in an hour.
>>> (137/145)

Do not, says the Dove, be 'mis-led by folly and a kind of fear'
(137/145). Phoenix' 'chastity' is 'too precise' (138/146).
    Its beauty is for some reason said to be 'abused', and
'rack'd on the tenter-hooks of foul disgrace'. It must revive
itself: 'refresh thy feathers, beautify thy face' (138/146–
139/147). Its reluctance is positively woman-like:

> Shame is ashamed to see thee obstinate,
> Smiling at thy womanish conceit . . .
>> (139/147)

There the suggestion is male, but the thought recurs with more
feminine impact when the same quality is called simply
'woman's peevishness' (150/158). Phoenix, we gather, is
lonely, and cannot 'find another' for its 'sweet self', being, perhaps, untuned to sexual relationships, but in the Turtle it will
find one to relieve its 'smart'. There follows a stanza holding
obscene connotations:[1]

> Upon a day I sought to scale a fort,
> United with a tower of sure defence;
> Uncomfortable trees did mar my sport,
> Unlucky Fortune with my woes expense,
> Venus with Mars would not sweet war commence,
>> Upon an altar would I offer love,
>> And sacrifice my soul, poor Turtle-Dove.
>>> (139/147)

[1] For the physical impressions often mapped out through natural imagery in
Elizabethan literature, see Eric Partridge's *Shakespeare's Bawdy* (New York, 1948). A
good example occurs at *Venus and Adonis*, 229–40. See also Chester's description of the
Phoenix already quoted (pp. 156–7).

Compare Tarquin's 'am I come to scale thy never-conquer'd fort' (*The Rape of Lucrece*, 481). Something appears to have gone wrong in the fourth line. The exact text of the last line is: 'And sacrifice my soule poore Turtle Dove'. The Turtle is the poet's *soul*, corresponding to Psyche as Phoenix to Eros.

There is what sounds like a feminine reference in the 'Y' stanza:

> Yf thou have pity, pity my complaining,
> Yt is a badge of virtue in thy sex . . .
> (140/148)

And yet it might conceivably, though less naturally, suit a male. The last stanza is addressed to Zenobia, the only 'Z' the poet can find, presumably as a synonym for Phoenix, calling her 'queen and empress of my heart'; and concludes with a prayer to her to 'accept my meaning as it fits my turn' (140/148).

The alphabetical cantos are followed by others 'verbally written', where the first words of each line compose a sentence relevant to the stanza concerned (an example is given below, p. 166).

'You women' (141/149) preserves female reference, and so does 'maiden eye' (161/169). One stanza beginning 'Be the poor bee, suck honey from the flower' (149/157) suggests, without finality, the female sex. But, whether the object be male or female, and it is certainly supposed to be female, the tonings are virile. Here are some: 'Vouchsafe with splendour of thy gracious look' (142/150); 'Thee on the stage of honour have I mounted' (142/150); 'Thee hath the world admir'd for clemency' (148/156); 'Great mistress, matchless in thy sovereignty' (158/166). Phrases such as 'empiring honour' (146/154), 'thy imperial crown' (155/163), and 'eye-dazzling mistress' (147/155) start up naturally. But all these are part of an intimate personal impressionism like that of Shakespeare's Sonnets that also gives us 'thine ever-growing beauty, like the rose' (146/154). Eyes, as in the Sonnets, are emphatic: 'My Phoenix hath two star-resembling eyes' (154/162). Elsewhere they are 'sun-resembling' (161/169). Eyes are, as in Shakespeare, active and power-impregnated:

> Disgrace be banish'd from thy heavenly brow,
> Not entertained of thy piercing eye . . .
> (145/153)

Again,

> The eye-balls in your head are Cupid's fire
> Darting such hot sparkles at my breast . . .
>
> (146/154)

How closely these eye-pieces recall *2 Henry VI*: 'Beaufort's red sparkling eyes blab his heart's malice' (III, i, 154); 'mine eyes should sparkle like the beaten flint' (III, ii, 317); and

> Upon thy eyeballs murderous tyranny
> Sits in grim majesty to fright the world.
>
> (III, ii, 49)

Eyes are vigorous in our Cantos: 'Your eye-balls do enwrap my destiny' (147/155).

Sun-reference is strong. The poet is a harvest-man, glad of sunshine, and

> You are my Sun, my day's delightsome queen,
> I am your harvest labourer almost mad . . .
>
> (150/158)

Compare Shakespeare's Sonnets: 'In the distraction of this madding fever' (119), and 'frantic-mad with everymore unrest' (147). The Phoenix is a 'glorious comet'. It is told to 'be not Narcissus', and to be glad 'to obtain the thing thou ne'er [1] could'st find' (150/158); that is, to enjoy love despite all psychological hindrances, since the loved one is apparently, as we have already (p. 164) suggested, supposed by the Turtle to be in a state of inhibited desire. The impressions sometimes become positively metallic:

> Within the circuit of a crystal sphere
> Thy eyes are plac'd, and underneath those eyes,
> Breast of hard flint, ears that do scorn to hear
> My day's sad groanings and night-waking cries,
> Heart-sore sick passions, and love's agonies.
>   Doth it become thy beauty? No, a stain
>   Rests on thy bright brow, wrinkled with disdain.
>
> (148/156)

That is close to Shakespeare. For the use of 'sphere' with 'eyes' compare Sonnet 119, 'How have mine eyes out of their spheres been fitted'; for 'disdain' compare the similar impressions of 'scorn' in Sonnet 88, and 'disdain' and 'scorn' at *Venus and*

---

[1] The text reads: neare.

Adonis, 241, 252. The object may possibly be a woman, but there is little specifically feminine impact:

> Then let our holy true aspiring love,
> Frame us the sweetest music of desire:
> Thy words shall make true concord, and remove
> Self-will itself, for Venus doth require
> To be acquainted with thy beauty's fire . . .
>
> (154/162)

There is a strangely compacted force in that last line, deriving from the will to subjective sensuous experience of some essentially visual, objective, and therefore unapproachable, beauty. 'Fire' is the language not of sexual union but of idealism, and the word 'acquainted' indicates the diffidence and daring of the proposal. This juxtaposition of incompatibles, extremes of the Apollonian and the Dionysian, the simultaneous forcing together of objective, intellectual beauty and intimate, sensuous, desire, strikes a peculiarly vivid flash.[1] 'Music' is used here as in 'grant me to play my sonnet on thy harp' earlier (p. 163). Though the style is sharper, the general pleading is in the manner of Venus in *Venus* and *Adonis*.

We have one piece of direct evidence that the Phoenix' feminine attributes are part of a mask:

> I being forc'd to carry Venus' shield
> Had rather bear a Phoenix for my crest . . .
>
> (143/151)

For, we are told, 'her beauty is the best':

> Though some desire fair Vesta's turtle-dove,
> In my bird's bosom resteth perfect love.
>
> (143/151)

The thought and metaphor are extended:

> Vain is that blind unskilful heraldry
> That will not cause my bird that is so rare
> Face all the world for her rariety,
> Then who with her for honour may compare?
>   Have we one like her for her pride of beauty,
>   Of all the feather'd quire in the air?
>
> (143/151)

---

[1] A rather similar effect is found in the work of C. P. Cavafy (e.g. *To Remain* and *Days of 1908*, Nos. 86 and 153 in the translation by John Mavrocordato, London, 1951).

Which might mean, 'This kind of love, coming from intellect and vision, is at once choice and honourable, and should not have to remain secret'. Elsewhere we find suggestion of secrecy, as in 'me may you count your unknown Turtle-Dove' (152/160), and

> Other sweet motions now I will conceal;
> Grace these rude lines that my heart's thoughts reveal.
>
> (144/152)

'Pride' in 'pride of beauty' suggested male power. For 'rare' and 'rariety', we might compare Marvell's *Definition of Love*:

> My love is of a birth as rare
>   As 'tis for object strange and high:
> It was begotten by despair
>   Upon impossibility.

Marvell's poem reveals a new poignancy if read in the context of our present discussion. Observe that, like Chester's sub-title, he claims to be defining love; but the definition outspaces love as we normally think of it.

The phraseology often leaves us guessing. When the poet writes:

> Change when thou wilt, it is but cruelty,
> Though unto women it is given by fate,
> Some gentle minds these ranging thoughts do hate . . .
>
> (153/161)

the loved one may be being contrasted with women ('gentle' meaning not 'mild', but 'well-bred' or 'sensitive'), or you could read it the other way. 'Friend' and 'friendship' are used at 17/25, 136/144, 152/160, 156/164; but the word was then more all-embracing than it is today, and could cover sexual love, as in Juliet's

> Art thou gone so? my lord, my love, my friend!
>   (*Romeo and Juliet*, III, v, 43)

The loved one is rich 'in all learned arts' (157/165); but so was Elizabeth I, and other ladies of the period. Possible confusions are continual.

Once the poet faces us with a series of paralysing posers.

Here, except for the modernised 's', I follow the 1611 text exactly.[1]

First, we have four lines representing the acrostic lines to follow. They are:

> *Ah quoth she, but where is true Loue?*
> *Where quoth he? where you and I loue.*
> *I quoth she, were thine like my loue.*
> *Why quoth he, as you loue I loue.*

The four main stanzas follow, with the usual sentences in the margin, corresponding to the first words of the stanzas:

Ah	Ah thou imperious high commaunding Lord,
quoth	(Quoth he) to *Cupid* gentle god of Loue,
he,	He that I honor most will not accord,
but	But strives against thy Iustice from aboue,
where	Where I haue promist faith, my plighted word
is	Is quite refused with a base reproue:
true	True louing honour this I onely will thee,
loue?	Loue thy true loue, or else false loue will kill me.

Where	Where shall I find a heart that's free from guile?
quoth	Quoth Faithfulnesse, within my louers brest.
he	He at these pleasing words began to smile,
where	Where Anguish wrapt his thoughts in much vnrest:
you	You did with pretie tales the time beguile,
and	And made him in conceited pleasure blest,
I	I grac'd the words spoke with so sweet a tong,
Ioue,	Loue being the holy burden of your song.

I	I grac'd your song of Loue, but by the way,
quoth	(Quoth true Experience,) sit and you shall see,
she	She will enchaunt you with her heauenly lay:
were	Were you fram'd all of heauenly Pollicie,
thine	Thine eares should drinke the poison of Delay,
like	Like as I said, so did it proue to be,
my	My Mistris beautie grac'd my Mistris song,
loue.	Loue pleas'd more with her Eyes than with her Tong.

[1] This text belongs to the same printing as the 1601 text: see p. 145 above. There is a copy in the British Museum. No copy of the 1601 Volume is known to exist in England. There are two in America.

Why	Why then in deepenesse of sweete Loues delight,
quoth	Quoth she, the perfect Mistris of Desire,
he	He that I honor most bard from my sight,
as	As a bright Lampe kindles Affections fire:
you	You Magicke operations worke your spight,
loue	Loue to the mountaine top of will aspires:
I	I chalenge all in all, and this I sing,
loue.	Loue is a holy Saint, a Lord, a King.

(157–8; Grosart, 161/169–162/170)

The general drift appears to be an argument between Phoenix and Turtle as to the purity of the Turtle's intentions. But it is not always clear who is speaking, and problems abound.

In the marginal acrostic of the first main stanza Grosart quite unjustifiably prints '(s)he', using an old 's'. His note runs: ' "He", as in the margin, and as required by the sense, should be "she".' I had to look up the 1611 text to discover whether it originally had 'he', 'she', or '(s)he'.

If 'she' is correct, then there is a duplicated misprint, but, since the text has also departed from the first line of the acrostic stanza, it is difficult to suppose it no more than a printer's slip. If, as the sense suggests, the Turtle speaks in the main stanza, and if the 'he' of line 3 is not a blunder, both lovers are male.

Alternatively, we could, following the acrostic stanza, hand the whole stanza to the Phoenix, who then speaks, contrasting the Turtle's licentious proposals, as 'base reprove' and 'false love', with the Platonic ideal of 'true love'. But the Phoenix is again male in line 2, and the acrostic *cannot* say 'quoth *she*' because 'he' in line 3 is the Turtle.

In stanza 2, if 'Faithfulnesse' is the Turtle, the Phoenix is male in line 3. Or it may be the other way round. Or 'Faithfulnesse' may be a third person.

In stanza 3 'Experience', who may, or may not, be the Phoenix, speaks at least up to line 5, 'poison of delay' suggesting a salutary torment in line with 'heavenly policy'. The last couplet may be the Turtle's. It draws a distinction between sensuous ('eyes') and intellectual delights.

Stanza 4 is the most baffling of all. If for 'she' in line 2 we read 'he', all is clear, and the acrostic harmonizes, with the 'he' of line 3, meaning the Phoenix, again male: observe that

'He that I honour most' repeats the phrase from stanza 1 opposite Grosart's marginal change. We now read: 'the perfect mistress of desire, he that I honour most, barr'd . . .' We cannot change 'he' to 'she', because of the acrostic. The fire-suggestion suits the Phoenix as the person addressed.

Alternatively, we can ignore the acrostic and give the stanza to the Phoenix. Then 'he' and 'she' are normal, and we read: 'He that I honour most when he is debarred from my sight', suggesting a denial of sense-enjoyment as a positive value: the Phoenix charitably enjoys seeing the Turtle burn with thwarted desires for its own good.

Whoever speaks ends by invoking the 'magic operations' to do their worst ('spite') in driving the love *upwards* to a Platonic culmination and achievement.

The sexual and other confusions are throughout so closely inwoven that they appear to be part of the plan. There is a limit beyond which analysis becomes unprofitable. Certainly the acrostics do not simply reflect the text.

For our present purpose, it is enough to note the sexual ambiguities. We might compare the contention of Kenneth Muir and Sean O'Loughlin in *The Voyage to Illyria* (vi, 145) that the erroneous use of 'his' for 'her' in Orlando's verses to Rosalind (*As You Like It*, 111, ii, 154) represents an unconscious self-revelation on the part of the dramatist, for whom Rosalind in boy's dress inevitably recalled the Fair Youth of the Sonnets. But this is rather an analogy to our earlier confusions (pp. 160–1). In our present example, there seems to be little unconsciousness about it: the stanzas have been deliberately constructed in this way.

We have already observed certain Shakespearian reminiscences (e.g. especially the metaphor of scaling a fort; p. 165 above). There are many more. With 'death's arrest' (133/141) compare 'as this fell sergeant death is strict in his arrest' at *Hamlet*, v, ii, 350, and 'that fell arrest without all bail' at Sonnet 74; with 'map of sorrow' (125/133) and 'great map of beauty' (136/144), both applied to a person's outward appearance, compare 'Thus is his cheek the map of days outworn' in Sonnet 68, and 'thou map of honour' at *Richard II*, v, i, 12; with 'Fall thou a tear' (125/133) compare Antony's 'Fall not a tear' at *Antony and Cleopatra*, 111, ix, 69. Phoenix' breasts as 'two crystal orbs of whitest white' (4/12) recall the 'ivory globes' of *The Rape of Lucrece*, 407. 'Thoughts are his heralds, flying to my breast' (151/159) recalls Juliet's 'Love's heralds should be thoughts', and 'Shame is ashamed to see thee obstinate' (139/147) recalls her line, 'Upon his brow shame is ashamed to sit', at *Romeo and Juliet*, II, v, 4 and III, ii, 92. 'Quite captivate and prisoner at thy call' (138/146) parallels 'Leading him prisoner in a red-rose chain' at *Venus and Adonis*, 110, and the 'liquid prisoner pent in walls of glass' of Sonnet 5. Early Shakespeare appears to predominate. With 'my love-lays in my love's praise always written' (143/151) compare Sonnet 76, especially 'you and love are still my argument'; also Sonnet 108 (p. 115). With 'singing thy pride of beauty in her height' (139/147), compare 'now stand you on the top of happy hours' in Sonnet 16, and also 'this thy golden time' and 'crowning the present' in Sonnets 3 and 115. 'To thy sweet self' (139/147) reminds us of 'sweet self' in Sonnet 114 and 'as thy sweet self grow'st' in Sonnet 126. With 'thou art that all-in-all that I love best' (151/159) compare:

> For nothing this wide universe I call
> Save thou, my rose; in it thou art my all.
> (Sonnet 109)

Lines start up in Shakespearian rhythm, such as 'Die perjur'd envy, for thy late offence' (147/155), and 'Have, from the deepest closet of your heart' (152/160), which recalls 'Within the gentle closure of my breast' in Sonnet 48. 'Breast' and 'heart' are used as Shakespeare uses such physical seats as repositories of inward experience. Again:

> For in my bosom's chamber, I enroll
> Your deep love-darting eye, and still will be
> Own of your own, despite extremity.
> (152/160)

We think of Juliet's 'death-darting eye of cockatrice' at *Romeo and Juliet*, III, ii, 47. 'Own of your own' suggests 'thou mine, I thine' of Sonnet 108 and much of the Sonnets' thought elsewhere; and 'extremity' is used as in 'smiling extremity out of act' at *Pericles*, v, i, 140. Thought is Shakespearian:

> Being enamour'd of rich Beauty's pride,
> Absent, I freeze in winter's pining cold.
> (147/155)

Compare the comparison of 'absence' to December's 'freezings' in Sonnet 97 (pp. 70–1 above). 'Pride' is a recurring word in the Sonnets. 'Pining' recalls Richard's

> I towards the north,
> Where shivering cold and sickness pines the clime. . . .
> *(Richard II, v, i, 76)*

If all the world offers 'disgrace' to 'my Turtle-Dove' (i.e., perhaps, 'my soul') nothing matters 'so that thou smile on me and be my love' (158/166): the thought is that of 'When in disgrace with fortune and men's eyes' (Sonnet 29). This is pure Shakespeare:

> Hell round enwraps my body by disdain,
> And then a Heaven, if thou love again.
> (159/167)

So are certain impressions of the rose, as in 'the fresh-bloom'd rose within her pride' (137/145), and 'thine ever-growing beauty, like the rose' (146/154).

Even the circumstances of the Sonnets appear to be recalled. Shakespeare's Fair Youth was repeatedly charged with growing 'common' and losing his good name, so that people are 'making lascivious comments' on his 'sport', and so on (69, 94, 95). Here we have

> Remember how thy beauty is abused,
> Rack'd on the tenter-hooks of foul disgrace.
> (138/146)

About this Shakespeare felt bitterly. So is it with the Turtle, anxious for his precious Phoenix:

> My care to have my blooming rose not wither,
> Self-loving envy shall it not deny,
> And that base weed thy growth doth seek to hinder,
> Mine hands shall pull him up immediately.
> Are they not envious monsters in thine eye,
>   Always with vain occasions to enclose
>   Thine ever-growing beauty, like the rose?
> (145/153)

Exactly so Shakespeare wrote of his Fair Youth being tramelled by various dangers in Sonnets 69 and 70 (pp. 13, 43); with 'base weed' compare 'lilies that fester smell far worse than weeds' in Sonnet 94.

The thoughts and impressions continually suggest the theme of Shakespeare's Sonnets. Phrases such as 'the fresh bloom'd rose within her pride' (137/145) and 'singing thy pride of beauty in her height' (139/147), recalling the 'youth's proud livery so gaz'd on now' of Sonnet 2, are more obviously applicable to a youth whose charm is evanescent than to a lady whose beauty might be supposed to grow from strength to strength. It is a brief chance, not to be missed: 'Look, Phoenix, to thyself do not decay' (137/145); Phoenix is a rose which, if not gathered at the time of 'chiefest beauty', will be thereafter neglected (137/145–138/146). All this recalls Shakespeare.

Shakespeare may, indeed, have written, or doctored, some of it. Even parts of the main narrative are not unworthy of him. Of the Cantos Grosart wrote: 'I think I can detect in some of his lines a reflex or remembrance of the rhythm of Shakespeare's lines' (Int., lxvii). His notes show a number of Shakespearian correspondences to Chester's verbal usage. C. Knox Pooler, in the *Arden* edition (1911) of Shakespeare's poems, asks, semi-humorously, if Shakespeare was concerned in the composition of one of the early semi-Shakespearian, and yet faulty, stanzas, and wonders whether 'such assistance, if asked for', was 'honestly given' (Int., xcii).

There is, clearly, some sort of a mystery. Carleton Brown, observing that the 'Cantos Alphabet-wise' are declared to be 'made by the Paphian Dove', suggests that they may have been written by Salusbury himself, though he notes that at the conclusion of those 'verbally written' Chester's name is subscribed. Chester's poems in Carleton Brown's collection are far weaker than Sir John Salusbury's, and do little to associate him with any of the best pieces of *Love's Martyr*. Here is a sample of Chester's work:

> I charm the coldness to forsake my hand,
> I conjure up my spirits at this time.
> Good-meaning tells me he my friend will stand,
> To under-prop my tottering rotten rhyme;
>   And I being arm'd with a presumptuous love,
>   From my goodwill disdainfulness will shove:

Therefore to thee, sole patron of my good,
I proffer up the proffer of my heart,
My undeserved favours understood
To thee and none but thee I will impart.
    O grace them with thy gratious gracing look
    That in pure kindness much have undertook.
(Christ Church MS. x; *Poems by Salusbury and Chester*, 15)

How does the writer's paucity of vocabulary[1] compare with the technical virtuosity of our Cantos, whether 'alphabetically' or 'verbally' devised? A note to 'kindness' tells us that it is crossed out in the manuscript; and so might more have been. Peter Quince could have done as well.

Chester's identity has not been with any certainty established. Grosart's tentative relation of him to the Chesters of Royston, or Roysdon, in Hertfordshire, appears to have been followed by Sir Gurney Benham in *The Times Literary Supplement* on 26 July 1941 (364),[2] and also by F. E. Halliday in his *A Shakespeare Companion* (1952). But surely Carleton Brown's insistence in *Poems of Salusbury and Chester* (1914) that he was probably a humble dependent of Sir John Salusbury at his home seat in Wales, Lleweni, appears, his adulatory poems in Brown's collection duly considered (especially his *Welcome Home*; Christ Church MS. xvii; 23), to be incontrovertible. In *The Author's Request to the Phoenix* (p. 151) Chester himself refers to his 'home-writ praises'. Brown thinks that Salusbury 'in order to gratify the literary ambition of Chester . . . took the MS. of the poem with him, on one of his journeys from Lleweni to London', and asked 'a few of the most prominent poets' to 'lend their names and verses to the success of the volume' (Int., liii–liv). This theory was accepted by Sir Israel Gollancz (*T.L.S.*, 26 Jan., 1922, 56; quoted Rollins, *New Variorum*, 577).

One way of resolving our various sexual and stylistic problems would be to suppose that Chester's work had been crudely

---

[1] The verbal repetitions may be compared with those already observed on pp. 156–7, 160. But such repetitions are only occasional in *Love's Martyr*, and never quite so bad as this.

[2] Sir Gurney Benham calls him *Sir* Robert (which he became later; see Grosart, Int., ix–x), and regards him as a man of consequence and a patron of Shakespeare. This I cannot follow. Surely it is Sir John Salusbury who is, in this context, acting as patron? There appears to be some confusion here.

devised to pay compliments to Sir John Salusbury and his wife
or sister-in-law (p. 155), and that Shakespeare, or some other
able poet well acquainted with Shakespeare's work, having
undertaken to polish the lines, succeeded only too well, using
the Phoenix-symbol witn a greater respect for its bisexual
nature, and working into the finished version much of his
own experience. In his dedication to Sir John Salusbury
Chester speaks of his 'long-expected labour' as having been
completed 'according to the directions of some of my best-
minded friends'. Shakespeare may have been one of them; or,
if not, the necessity of revision may have been so obvious to
the various poets lending their names to the publication that
Shakespeare was asked to do some final polishing, and, once
started, he might not have known where to stop. In the 1611
reissue Chester's name does not even appear on the title-page.
It is certainly almost impossible to credit him with lines like
these:

> Yet, my soul's life to my dear life's concluding,
> Ne'er let Absurdity, that villain, thief,
> The monster of our time, men's praise deriding,
> Less in perseverance, of small knowledge chief,
> Keep the base gate to things that are excelling.
> Thou by fair virtue's praise may'st yield relief;
> My lines are thine, then tell Absurdity
> Heart of my dear shall blot his villainy.
>
> (163/171)

The punctuation is mine. 'My soul's life' is the Phoenix; 'to'
means 'up to'. There is a quality here in the use of abstrac-
tion and personification that I would call deeply Shakespearian.
The firm statement, so vividly recalling Sonnet 121 (p. 49),
finds exact place in the poetic argument.[1]

Certainly you could have no finer re-expression of the
deepest convictions of the Sonnets than you get here. Death is
similarly reviled:

> Till that lean, fleshless, cripple, pale-fac'd Death,
> Thy lovely Dove shall pierce with his fell dart . . .
>
> (164/172)

[1] The association of 'Absurdity' and 'thief' occurs in Chester's dedication to Sir John
Salusbury: '. . . knowing that if Absurdity like a thief have crept into any part of these
poems, your well-graced name . . .'

Compare Romeo's 'Death's pale flag', and Death as 'the lean abhorred monster' at *Romeo and Juliet*, v, iii, 96 and 104. 'Lovely', presumably referring here to the poet as 'loving'—in the Sonnets it tends to mean 'lovable' (see Tucker's word-index)—may be a blemish, placed as it is by 'Dove'. But we shall find no complaint with this:

> Death is amazed, viewing of thy beauty,
> Thinking thyself perfect eternity.
> (159/167)

Nowhere in the Sonnets is their whole theme so exquisitely and compactly expressed.

Towards the close, love becomes definitely religious. 'Adoration' is a 'holy art' (149/157). Again:

> Most reverend mistress, honour of mine eye,
> Divine, most holy in religious love,
> And lord itself of my heart's empery,
> Sacred in thoughts admitted from above . . .
> (165/173)

Compare 'religious love' in *A Lover's Complaint* (250), 'dear religious love' in Sonnet 31, and also 'religious in mine error' at *All's Well that Ends Well*, i, iii, 213. The loved one is both 'mistress' and 'lord', like the Fair Youth, who is called the 'master-mistress of my passion' in Sonnet 20. He is 'my Saint, my bosom's lord' (166/174; compare 'my bosom's lord', meaning 'heart', at *Romeo and Juliet*, v, i, 3). The final stanza sums it all up:

> Where two hearts are united all in one,
> Love like a King, a Lord, a Sovereign,
> Enjoys the throne of bliss to sit upon,
> Each sad heart craving aid, by Cupid slain.
>   Lovers, be merry: Love being dignified,
>   Wish what you will, it shall not be denied.
> (167/175)

This great 'Love' is, again, Donne's 'great Prince' (p. 61), the super-personal reality created by love. 'Dignified' means 'rendered respectable'.

Whatever be the truth, we have a love with similar sun and

13

gold imagery to Shakespeare's and a similar insistance on constancy and truth, concepts so obvious and frequent as applied to the Turtle-Dove that quotation is unnecessary. It must be admitted that these Cantos witness a more intimately physical eroticism than the other Phoenix poems of our collection; but satisfaction appears to be withheld. The distinction is beautifully clear when the Dove offers to bring fuel for the Phoenix' fire, that is, to help preserve the loved-one's Phoenix-integrity, in exchange for a kiss (140/148).[1] About the love, or loves, recorded, there is certainly a mystery of sorts, or all these poetic contortions would be waste of time. The sexes are bafflingly used. We expect the Turtle-Dove to be feminine, but it is masculine. The Phoenix, though called feminine, often radiates lines of force rather male than female, and much of the attendant imagery drives home the impact. As for the acrostics, they leave the mind dizzy.

We must nevertheless remember that in Elizabethan poetry Love itself is, as in Spenser's *Hymns*, a great sovereign, and may be felt as a male power even when its object is female. We must beware of any too precise definitions in sexual, homosexual, or bisexual terms; but in interpretation our thoughts must be allowed freely to explore all possibilities. It may be significant that in the 1611 re-issue (p. 145) Chester's name and the dedicatory matter to Sir John Salusbury were suppressed, and a new title-page used, concerned only with the quite secondary narrative of the 'annals' of Britain, as though to mask the real content of the collection, which is an attempt, as the original 1601 title-page told us, to shadow 'allegorically' the 'truth of Love'. But that may perhaps involve rather more than is usually supposed.

[1] For the moral valuation of kisses in our Phoenix poems, see pp. 89, 199.

III

THE *POETICAL ESSAYS*

WE now come to the additional poems by Shakespeare, Marston, Chapman and Jonson. The superscription, modernised, goes:

Hereafter follow Divers Poetical Essays on the former subject, viz: the Turtle and Phoenix. Done by the best and chiefest of our modern writers, with their names subscribed to their particular works; never before extant; and now first consecrated by them all generally to the love and merit of the true-noble Knight, Sir John Salusbury.

These Poetical Essays are prefaced by an '*Invocatio*' to Apollo and the Muses ('Pierides'), and a dedicatory poem to Sir John Salusbury, both signed 'Vatum Chorus'. There follow two stanzas on the Phoenix by 'Ignoto'; Shakespeare's poem, over his name; four poems on the Phoenix and the Turtle, and the resultant 'Perfection', by John Marston; one called *Peristeros, or the Male Turtle*, by George Chapman; and four pieces by Ben Jonson. These various poems appear to be symbolical definitions of experiences not too dissimilar, whatever the sex of the loved one, from that celebrated in Shakespeare's Sonnets, and therefore also of what I have called (pp. 36, 44) 'the higher, or bisexual, integration'. This 'integration' has much to do with the psychology of poetic creation, and we may suppose that Sir John Salusbury and the various poets had reason to be interested in the subject. We know from Sir John's rough but powerful *Amazement* (p. 147) that he was himself at one time tormented by a hidden and 'ancient' love, which he would not have 'in the popular open-mouth'd world be blown' till 'time' and 'place' should serve, and whose secret celebration demanded the poetic aid of 'great Apollo', with Venus left 'mute' and 'blushing' at the loved-one's 'glory' (Christ Church MS. xxiv; *Poems of Salusbury and Chester*, 33–5). All this, whatever the sex involved, is Phoenix-stuff. In our poems the Phoenix is regularly referred to as though everyone concerned knew precisely what it was.

The *Invocatio* by 'Vatum Chorus' is addressed to the god of male beauty, Apollo, and the Muses. The first of its two stanzas is difficult:

> Good Fate, fair Thespian deities,
> And thou, bright God, whose golden eyes
>   Serve as a mirror to the silver Morn,
>   When, in the height of grace, she doth adorn
> Her crystal presence, and invites
> The ever-youthful Bromius to delights,
> Sprinkling his suit of vert with pearl,
> And, like a loose enamour'd girl,
>   Ingles his cheek; which, waxing red with shame,
>   Instincts the senseless grapes to do the same,
> Till, by his sweet reflection fed,
>   They gather spirit, and grow discoloured.

The Morn, as lady, for whom Apollo's eyes are, strangely enough, the 'mirror', sprinkles the green ('vert') earth (here indicated by Bromius, or Dionysus-Bacchus, deity of fecundity) with dewy pearl. It is a flirtation, rousing shame, rather paradoxically, in the deity of sexual abandon; and the laboured imagery of the grapes turning red and gathering 'spirit' from Bromius' 'reflection'(? = throwing colour, *O.E.D.*) is difficult.

Suppose, however, we allow an interthreading of another meaning, we have a better sense. Here I tread dangerous ground, and would ask that my suggestions be regarded as no more than tentative. I read the lines as describing the lover's solitary experience at early morning.

Apollo with his 'golden eyes' then signifies the loved one, or Phoenix, and the 'silver' Morn the Dove, using again the correct gold and silver terms (for 'silver' applied to the Dove, see p. 153). The Morn represents the lonely lover, or lover's soul, with 'mirror' carrying on the usual imagery of eyes mirrored in eyes (pp. 37–42). The time is early morning, and to interpret the experience I would quote the words of the lonely lover-prophet in Nietzsche's *Thus Spake Zarathustra*:

> For I am particularly wicked in the morning; at that early hour when the pail clattereth at the well and the horses whinny warm breath in the grey alleys.
>
> (III, 6; trans. Tille and Bozman; *Everyman* edn.)

The 'ever-youthful Bromius', stimulated by the lover's dawn-soul to vitality, assumes an obvious meaning. 'Ingles his cheek' is the more significant in that, though 'ingle' as a verb became a general term for 'fondle', it derives from a noun which means 'catamite' (*O.E.D.*, giving appropriate dates). Grosart, not, of course, making my reading, translates: 'Treats his cheek as one does one's ingle or delight, or loved youth; playfully pinches or strokes it' (the semi-colon after 'youth' is my, surely necessary, insertion). Possible, but perhaps not wholly satisfactory, meanings can be looked for in 'pearl', 'red', and *'senseless grapes'*. For 'reflection' we have: 'The action of bending, turning, or folding back; recurvation 1553' (*O.E.D.*). 'Sweet reflection' might accordingly denote the subsequent quiescence. The solitary engagement has somehow fed back into the organism *a gathering of spiritual power* ('gather spirit'). If such a reading be accepted, we can next observe that, however emphatic are our emphases in these poems on chastity, it is not to be supposed, any more than in the lives of ascetics, that there is no physical functioning and accomplishment.

Our second stanza is easier. It contains the thought of propagation, praying to Apollo and the Muses to 'propagate' with their 'illustrate faculties' the various poets' 'mental powers', so that they may 'gratulate an honourable friend' (i.e. Sir John Salusbury) by creating poetry 'varied from the multitude'; that is, perhaps, 'of a secret and esoteric kind'.

The following address to Sir John Salusbury, also by Vatum Chorus, is easy. The poetry is to be 'pure juice' (purity is a recurring thought) from 'Pierian springs', not imitative, but direct from the 'flame-hair'd Apollo', 'infus'd' into the poets' brains and 'distill'd thence' in writing (for 'distill'd' compare Sonnet 54; and pp. 47, 88 above). It is sharply distinguished from any sort of 'mercenary hope'. The 'invention', or poetic creations, to follow is to be 'freer than the times'; that is, bolder than convention normally allows.

Ignoto's contribution runs:

The First

> The silver vault of heaven hath but one eye,
> And that's the Sun: the foul-mask'd Lady, Night
> (Which blots the clouds, the white book of the sky),
> But one sick Phoebe, fever-shaking light:

The heart, one string: so, thus in single turns,
The world one Phoenix, till another burns.

The Burning

Suppose here burns this wonder of a breath,
In righteous flames, and holy-heated fires
(Like Music which doth rapt itself to death,
Sweet'ning the inward room of man's desires);
  So she wastes both her wings in piteous strife;
  The flame that eats her, feeds the other's life:
    Her rare-dead ashes fill a rare-live urn:
    One Phoenix born, another Phoenix burn.

As in the *Invocatio*, our deity is the male Sun (discussed on pp. 62–5 above). Night, with her 'sick' moon, corresponds to the 'fever-shaking' experiences noted in Shakespeare's engagement with the Dark Lady. Beyond sexes, sun and moon, lies the more spiritual ('heart') unity (pp. 35–9); under it the whole 'world' becomes 'one Phoenix'. We have various analogies in Shakespeare's Sonnets (31, 53, 84 98 109, 112, 113, 114; pp. 118–21); in a sonnet of Drayton's already (p. 154) quoted; and in the world-absorbing experience of Donne's *The Sun Rising*. The experience is one of 'righteous flames and holy-heated fires', corresponding to the 'sunny pleasure-dome with caves of ice' in *Kubla Khan* (*The Starlit Dome*, II, 91–7). The result is a death through *plenitude*, through over-much 'inward' *sweetness* of desire (as in Sonnet 118; also 23, 56; pp. 125–6; and compare Marvell's 'lilies without, roses within' in *The Nymph Complaining for the Death of her Fawn*). There is suffering, but the suffering is creative, as it was with Shakespeare. The Phoenix becomes here a symbol of creative suffering.

Shakespeare's poem, which follows, we shall discuss later. Our next contribution is Marston's. It is headed: *A narration and description of a most exact wondrous creature, arising out of the Phoenix' and Turtle-Dove's ashes*. Notice the word 'exact' (= 'perfected', 'highly wrought', *O.E.D.*) Superlatives alone fit this new creature. The reality celebrated is a reality growing from both partners in death; a new 'creature' is thereby made; and we can compare the 'creation' maturing from integration in Wordsworth's *Recluse* fragment (*The Starlit Dome*, I, 1–2; *Christ and Nietzsche*, IV, 133–4). Here it is a 'rare creation' beyond the attacks of 'fire', 'time', or 'blackest fate'; 'corruption' will not touch this 'excellence', this 'glorious issue' brighter than 'fire', and whiter in its purity than 'Dian's tire'; indeed a 'measureless pure rarity'. We continue:

> Lo now, th' extracture of divinest essence,
> The soul of Heaven's labour'd quintessence
> (Paeans to Phoebus) from dear lovers' death,
> Takes sweet creation and all blessing breath.
>   What strangeness is't that from the Turtle's ashes
> Assumes such form, whose splendour clearer flashes,
> Than mounted Delius? Tell me, genuine Muse.
>   Now yield your aids, you spirits that infuse
> A sacred rapture, light my weaker eye:
> Raise my invention on swift phantasy,
> That whilst of this same metaphysical
> God, Man, nor Woman, but elix'd of all,
> My labouring thoughts, with strained ardour sing,
> My Muse may mount with an uncommon wing.

Compare with those last lines, Shelley's in *Epipsychidion*:

> The winged words on which my soul would pierce
> Into the height of Love's rare universe
> Are chains of lead around its flight of fire . . .
>
> (588)

The intuitions, or experiences, are similar. In Marston the new creation is not god, nor man, nor woman, but somehow 'elix'd of all'. So, too, in the *Fragments* connected with *Epipsychidion*, Shelley, as we shall see, plays with thoughts of a Hermaphrodite, and the creation, through love, of a 'naked seraph' (pp. 213–4 below). Such is the fine-wrought ('labour'd') 'quintessence' which Heaven extracts from 'lovers' death' to make the 'sweet creation'; and we may recall the phrase 'my verse distills your truth' in Shakespeare's sonnets (54). 'Paeans to Phoebus' suggests a connection with poetry. Poetic, or some other artistic, creation may clearly be, at the least, an aspect, or derivative, of the new birth.

   However we define it, and clearly nothing less than poetry can finally do that, the result is a strange 'perfection', and Marston's second poem is called *The description of this Perfection*. The word which, according to Sir Gurney Benham (*T.L.S.*,

19 July, 1941; 352), had for centuries been applied to the Phoenix (cp. pp. 71–2), is similarly used by Drayton, *Amour* 17:

> Were not invention stall'd, treading invention's maze,
> Or my swift-winged Muse tired by too high flying,
> Did not perfection still on her perfection gaze,
> Whilst Love (my Phoenix bird) in her own flame is dying,
>   Invention and my Muse, perfection and her love,
>   Should teach the world to know the wonder that I prove.

Marston's Perfection, defined as 'that boundless *Ens* that amplest thought transcendeth', is a marvel that cannot be held by mental concepts, a 'divinest beauty' compared with which 'Earth's purest' is 'unclean'. But it is dimly known *through* creation, since 'by it all beings' are 'deck'd and stain'd'; that is, all created forms incarnated and coloured. Now it is not enough for us to say, simply and academically, that all this is Platonism, since that is to replace Plato's living experience by mere book-reading. That is why the poet next insists that, 'Ideas that are idly feigned only here subsist invested'; which means, 'The Platonic Ideas about which we talk so glibly can only be found in living actuality in this creature of which I am speaking.' The creature concerned is the new Phoenix, Shelley's 'naked seraph', that which is born of the Platonic love. For it, no praise, says the poet, can be called 'hyperbolicall'.

There follows a sonnet *To Perfection*, which grumbles at the amount of ugliness on earth, especially 'hard-favour'd Feminines' (our second aspersion on the feminine sex); at the general lack of 'virtues' now current in the world, the scarcity of 'wit' and 'defects of mind'. The poet suggests that these must be designed as 'foils', or happy contrasts, to the 'rareness' he is celebrating.

He concludes with *Perfectioni Hymnus*, in adoration of this 'creature' now 'grown into maturity'. It is a creature 'as firm and constant as Eternity'. 'Perfection', 'Heaven's mirror', 'Beauty's resistless thunder' are all called inadequate definitions. But 'deep Contemplation's wonder' is accepted. It is limited by 'all best', and contains nothing else. He concludes: 'All is *Mind*, as far from spot as possible defining'. It is a *mental* experience.

Chapman contributes a single, rather rugged, piece, called *Peristeros: or the Male Turtle*. So far the *Poetical Essays* have not forced us to consider the sexes of the birds. The Greek word for dove is *peristera*, and it is only found in the feminine. As Sir Gurney Benham observes (*T.L.S.*, 19 July, 1941; 352), Chapman has, deliberately, coined a masculine form of it. His title accordingly serves to remind us, as though with a conscious paradox, that the Turtle signifies the female aspect of the male poet's soul. The use of 'male turtle' makes a significant emphasis.

The poem starts by attacking love-affairs of the normal kind, with all their superficial ups and downs. There is reference to mistresses, conceits and fashions, with a slighting of all who depend 'upon their lover's pomp'. All this is a matter of 'outward worth' only, and liable to be 'tomb'd in wrinkles'. In contrast, we have our Phoenix and Turtle, introduced by a quatrain syntactically adrift and unrelated, but otherwise clear:

> But like the consecrated Bird of Love,
>   Whose whole life's hap to his sole-mate alluded,
> Whom no proud flocks of other fowls could move,
>   But in herself all company concluded.

Here the Turtle is devoted to his 'sole' (or 'soul'?) mate, the Phoenix, all other 'company' neglected, or rather contained. She is to him 'th' analys'd world of pleasure', and we are told that 'her firmness cloth'd him in variety'. The mental, philsophic, impact of the first phrase recalls Marston's 'deep Contemplation's wonder'; the second reminds us of how Shakespeare's single love expanded to the multiple world of his plays (pp. 104–36). Chapman concludes his poem by comparing himself to the Turtle and expressing the devotion of all his 'powers' to her who 'bounds the Empire of desert'. Neither time nor change can affect 'truth eterniz'd in a constant heart'. The Phoenix is his 'form' (i.e. informing principle), and 'gives my being spirit'. We may compare the use of 'spirit' in the *Invocatio*.

Our last contributor is Ben Jonson, who expands more voluminously. His *Praeludium* rejects one deity after another as 'countenance' for our 'active Muse'; that is, perhaps, our poetry at work to create the thing it writes of. The rejection includes Hercules, Phoebus, so honoured elsewhere, Bacchus, Pallas Athene, Mars, 'light Venus', Cupid ('his absence in our verse is all we ask'), Hermes, and 'all the ladies of the Thespian lake'. These will not do:

> No, we bring
> Our own true fire. Now our thought takes wing,
> And now an epode to deep ears we sing.

Our obvious analogy here is Keats' *Ode to Psyche*, where mythical deities are similarly replaced by inward and poetic experience leading to the growth of 'branched thoughts' in 'some untrodden region of my mind'; that is, poetry. Phoenix and Turtle have clear analogies in the myth of Eros and Psyche. Psyche denotes 'soul', and is called a dove in Keats' poem. Eros within the myth must be firmly distinguished from normal sexual experience.[1]

The *Epos* devotes considerable space to some rather obvious moralising against the 'affections' and 'passions', with 'conscience' and 'reason' as their antagonists. The poet insists that love is to be firmly distinguished from 'blind desire', which only plunges you in torment:

> Now true Love
> No such effects doth prove:
> That is an essence most gentle, and fine;
> Pure, perfect; nay divine.
> It is a golden chain let down from Heaven,
> Whose links are bright, and even,
> That falls like sleep on lovers; and combines
> The soft and sweetest minds
> In equal knots. This bears no brands nor darts
> To murder different hearts,
> But, in a calm and God-like unity,
> Preserves community.
> O who is he that, in this peace, enjoys
> The elixir of all joys?
> A Form more fresh than are the Eden bowers,
> And lasting, as her flowers;
> Richer than Time, and, as Time's virtue, rare;
> Sober, as saddest care;
> A fixed thought, an eye untaught to glance.
> Who, blest with such high chance,

[1] For a study of the implications of Keats' *Ode*, and its place within the 'Eros and Psyche' myth, see *The Starlit Dome*, IV, 301–4 and *Christ and Nietzsche*, IV, 136.

Would at suggestion of a steep desire,
    Cast himself from the spire
Of all his happiness?

The poem proceeds to assert the reality of 'chaste Love', insisting that, whatever may be true of sparrows, 'Turtles can
chastely die', and proceeding to a disquisition on the merits of
different kinds of chastity. The poem's climax is powerful and
difficult:

But we propose a person like our Dove,
    Grac'd with a Phoenix' love;
A beauty of that clear and sparkling light,
    Would make a day of night,
And turn the blackest sorrows to bright joys;
    Whose od'rous breath destroys
All taste of bitterness, and makes the air
    As sweet, as she is fair;
A body so harmoniously compos'd,
    As if Nature disclos'd
All her best symmetry in that one feature.
    O, so divine a creature,
Who could be false to? chiefly when he knows
    How only she bestows
The wealthy treasure of her love in him,
    Making his fortunes swim
In the full flood of her admir'd perfection?
    What savage, brute affection
Would not be fearful to offend a dame
    Of this excelling frame?
Much more a noble and right generous mind,
    To virtuous moods inclin'd,
That knows the weight of guilt. He will refrain
    From thoughts of such a strain,
And to his sense object this sentence ever,
    Man may securely sin, but safely never.

The 'sparkling' beauty is the Phoenix, illuminating the Turtle's
world. The Phoenix is still considered feminine. I can give no
clear reason why the 'harmoniously composed' body compacting all Nature's 'best symmetry' (cp. Byron's 'o'er limbs whose
symmetry set off the silk', referring to his hero, *Don Juan*, IX,
43) should suggest the male form; but it may do so, the word
'symmetry' being more applicable to flatness than to rondure.

If it does, we can see why it is said that no brutal 'affection', or lust (*O.E.D.*, 1596; and see Leontes' use, *The Winter's Tale*, I, ii, 139), could be so bold as to offend 'a dame of this excelling frame', the meaning being, perhaps, that this is a body that should not be approached by sexual passion. A noble 'mind' will recognise 'guilt' in such a contact, and not let it enter his thoughts.

This may, perhaps, be the meaning. I cannot see that the lines would be much of a compliment to a lady, though to the Elizabethans, who could write of a lady's chastity in terms that to us appear crude, they might pass. The use of 'dame' may be a mask. It seems that the *Epos* was not specifically written for this occasion. According to Sir Israel Gollancz there is evidence that it had circulated among Jonson's friends before its publication with *Love's Martyr* in 1601, and he notes that its last gnomic line, which certainly suits our reading, had been quoted in *England's Parnassus* in 1600 (*T.L.S.*, 8 Oct., 1925; 655). This can have little bearing on our interpretation, except to remind us that the kind of work we are discussing was, like Shakespeare's 'sugred Sonnets', *coterie* poetry, with its own free-masonry of allusion and intent. Jonson's *Praeludium* specifically told us that his *Epode*, or *Epos*, was designed for 'deep ears'; that is, contained statements in which, as Milton has it in *Il Penseroso*, 'more is meant than meets the eye'. These suggestions are put forward for what they may be worth: there can be no certainty.

Jonson's next piece may, or may not, provide a key. It is called *The Phoenix Analysed*, and goes:

> Now, after all, let no man
>   Receive it for a fable,
>   If a bird so amiable
> Do turn into a woman.
>
> Or (by our Turtle's augur)
>   That Nature's fairest creature
>   Prove of his mistress' feature,
> But a bare type and figure.

These are brain-taxing verses. The obvious meaning is: 'Do not be surprised if by this symbolical bird one's lady-love is really intended; it is all a figure of speech.' But can any reader be sup-

posed to have plodded through all these arduous poems under
the impression that they are giving ornithological information?
Besides, if these abstruse and tiring symbolisms are merely
indirect ways of writing conventional love-poetry, they are
surely wasting our time.

The lines may, like the *Invocatio*, hold a secondary meaning
for those prepared to receive it. Jonson, writes Sir Gurney
Benham (*T.L.S.*, 19 July, 1941; 352), 'seems a little exercised
about the sex of Chester's Phoenix'. Walter Thomson in his
study of the Sonnets had been more explicit. He argues that
our collection of poems is being addressed to Southampton as
Phoenix, whilst he was in prison. He explicitly disassociates
his reading from any sort of passionate romance: the veiling,
for him, is a matter of political expediency, Southampton's
friends wishing to communicate surreptitiously with a man
convicted of treason. Nevertheless, his argument (IX, 71–2)
that these lines are a veiled assertion that the Phoenix' female
sex is a mask falls into line with, and indeed prompted, my
own understanding of them, though their secondary meaning
appears less simple than his brief paraphrase suggests.

The first stanza might mean: 'Do not think it absurd that
one so essentially lovable should be presented as a woman.' A
deeper meaning might be something like: 'Do not think it
utterly impossible that somehow, if not in this life, then perhaps
in another, the love in question shall be satisfied'; as the boy
Cesario turns out, to Orsino's advantage, to be a girl in
Twelfth Night. So much is easy, but the second stanza remains
baffling. We might read:

> Or, to look at the matter from another angle—the angle of those who
> really thought that it was a woman—let no one be surprised that the
> 'Nature's fairest creature' so continually being referred to in these poems
> should, with the help of our various poets' hints, prove concerning *his*
> appearance of a mistress that this appearance is a mere figure of speech.

The length of my paraphrase argues its insecurity. 'Turtle's' I
take to refer to one or more of the poets: that is obvious.
Grosart refers it in particular to Chester. Whether 'of' can mean
'concerning' here, I am not sure: the comma after 'feature',
which I have preserved for my purpose, might support the
reading, could we put any faith in Elizabethan punctuation.

But we cannot: Grosart (Notes, 243) observes that 'the compositor of *Love's Martyr* was especially fond of a comma at the end of a verse-line'.

There is a third possibility. These stanzas come directly before the concluding ode, which we have reason to suppose was at one time offered to the Countess of Bedford (p. 148). They might therefore mean: 'Do not be surprised if our next Phoenix poem is one *really* about a woman.' 'By our Turtle's augur', could then be rendered: 'on the example of Sir John Salusbury'; that is, 'we have a precedent for it in Sir John's secret love of Dorothy Halsall, which is the Turtle-Phoenix relationship in whose honour this collection is being made.' For Dorothy Halsall, a mere hazard, see pp. 147, 155 above.

This concluding poem, called *Ode Enthousiastiké*, celebrates once again the 'more than mortal', female, 'splendour'. It is distinguished from 'sin'; is a matter of 'wit as quick and spriteful as fire', and more pleasant than lovers' nocturnal engagements. We think of Shakespeare's mentally alert heroines, of Berowne and Mercutio, of Elizabethan drama in general, and the Mermaid Tavern. The matured result is wisdom:

> Judgment, adorned with learning,
> Doth shine in her discerning,
> Clear as a naked vestal
> Clos'd in an orb of crystal.

Her 'breath' is sweet beyond anything reported of the Phoenix' mythological home (compare the 'nest of spicery' at *Richard III*, iv, iv, 425, and the 'tomb of spicery' in *The Phoenix' Nest*, 2, l.15; see p. 152); and, when 'mixt with sound' (i.e. presumably, speech), 'transcending' all attempts at praise. Her 'graces' are more profound, more spiritual, than their surface suggests, though she is never anxious to advertise, nor even takes 'pride to know', them.

That this poem was discovered in manuscript addressed to Lucy, Countess of Bedford, serves to show how rash any exact attribution of the various poets' 'intentions' may be. The Phoenix is only obliquely referred to, but the poem, with its emphasis on beauty, virtue, wit, learning and eloquence, makes a neat enough conclusion to our sequence. For whatever be the sexes involved in our various love-impressions, the Phoenix itself is close to the poetic essence; is to be related very exactly to what we call 'genius'; and is really all but a symbol *of* poetry.

Whether I am right that, in some of our pieces, the female sex is being used as a mask is, of course, arguable. It might perhaps appear strange that in a period so rich in romantic friendships any poet should be concerned to disguise the sex of the person addressed. But I think that we may be over-emphasising the freedom allowed by convention; severe penalties were in force for extreme forms of vice; even among the Greeks, male effeminacy in such relationships met the criticism of Aristophanes,[1] and it is perhaps wisest to assume that in such matters all ages are very much alike. Shakespeare's Sonnets are outspoken, but they were only circulated among an inner circle of friends, and their publication in 1609, long after *Love's Martyr*, may have been an embarrassment to the poet.

A note or two on Michelangelo's sonnets (which I quote in J. A. Symonds' translation) may help us. He certainly was afraid of misunderstanding and misrepresentation, and his first editor and great-nephew was, as we have seen (p. 137), embarrassed. He himself uses the Phoenix. Reason argues:

> What else but death will that sun deal to thee—
> Nor like the Phoenix in her flaming nest?
>
> (39)

From his love's eyes, he says,

> I might have drawn new strength my race to run,
> Burning as burns the Phoenix ere it dies.
>
> (50)

In Sonnet 60, probably addressing a man, he asks why, if 'all human loves were impious', God has created the world, and goes on to insist that he loves with 'chaste fires' (60). Such love may be misinterpreted by its object, as in Sonnet 36, where the loved one is definitely male:

> How then, ah wo is me! shall that chaste fire,
> Which burns the heart within me, be made known,
> If sense finds only sense in what it sees?

[1] I am thinking of the reference to Antimachus in the educational contest of *The Clouds*.

All my fair hours are turned to miseries
With my loved lord, who minds but lies alone;
For, truth to tell, who trusts not is a liar.

(36)

'Sense', he writes, 'is not love,' but rather 'lawlessness accurst',
killing the 'soul', while love is said to lift 'our friends on earth'
'higher in heaven through death'; that is, Phoenix-wise (52).
The 'fair face' of his beloved 'lord' lifts him to 'God':

And though the vulgar, vain, malignant horde
Attribute what their grosser wills obey,
Yet shall this fervent homage that I pay,
This love, this faith, pure joys for us afford.

(54)

And so death will be 'sweet'. Death is, continually, the consummation, the way:

Because in thee I love, O my loved lord,
What thou best lovest, be not therefore stern:
Souls burn for souls, spirits to spirits cry!

I seek the splendour in thy fair face stored;
Yet living man that beauty scarce can learn,
And he who fain would find it, first must die.

(55)

The soul 'flies free', like 'gold refined in flame' (58). This is a
favourite image. Only through 'fire' can the artist work 'gold to
its utmost purity of hue':

Nay, nor the unmatched Phoenix lives anew,
Unless she burn: if then I am distraught
By fire, I may to better life be brought
Like those whom death restores nor years undo.

(59)

The experience behind these sonnets, many of which derive
from a man-to-man relationship, is of similar sort to that celebrated in our various Phoenix-and-Turtle poems.

IV

SHAKESPEARE'S POEM

THIS, then, is the context in which we must study Shake-speare's contribution. *The Phoenix and the Turtle* has received a sensitive handling. John Masefield accorded it high praise in his *William Shakespeare* (1911). In *Discoveries* (1924) J. Middleton Murry wrote that 'it gives us the highest experi-ence which it is possible for poetry to give, and it gives it without intermission'. It was the subject of an interesting monograph by 'Ranjee' (Ranjee G. Shahani) in *Towards the Stars* (which I reviewed in *The Criterion*, April, 1931). I have myself written of it in *The Shakespearian Tempest* (1932; App. A, 320–5) and *The Christian Renaissance* (1933; XII, 327–9). It was an impor-tant step in the general argument of Kenneth Muir and Sean O'Loughlin in *The Voyage to Illyria* (1937). Cleanth Brooks has touched it in *The Well-Wrought Urn* (1947); Bonamy Dobrée has broadcast an appreciation of its music (1948); and we now have Heinrich Straumann's monograph (p. 149). But these are only a few examples of the interpretations that have from time to time been offered, many of which are crisply sum-marised in the *New Variorum* (1938) edition of Shakespeare's *Poems* by Hyder Edward Rollins. Among these was an interesting essay by Alfred von Mauntz in 1893 (*Shakespeare Jahrbuch*, XXVIII, 308–10), seeing the poem, rather as did *The Voyage to Illyria* later, as a symbolic representation of Shake-speare's estrangement from Southampton, regarded as the friend of the Sonnets; and a significant contribution by Charles Downing (*The Shrine*; May, 1902; 34–7), reading the various poems of our collection in terms of ideal and idealist, suggesting the equation of Shakespeare's Phoenix with the Fair Youth of the Sonnets, and regarding his dramatic work as a develop-ment from this central inspiration. To these we may add the discussion of Shakespeare's source, or background, material in T. W. Baldwin's *On the Literary Genetics of Shakespeare's Poems and Sonnets* (1950).

14

We need commit ourselves to no biographical details. Shakespeare may have had more than one ardent love, and *The Phoenix and the Turtle* need be referred to no particular person or event. Even so, we shall, I think, be right in allowing it to include, to gather up and transmute, the experience of the Sonnets, in its own particular fashion. It is quite different in tone. 'Its very concinnity and restraint', wrote Grosart, 'compared with the fecundity of *Venus and Adonis* and *Lucrece*, differentiate it from all other of Shakespeare's writings. I discern a sense of personal heart-ache and loss in these sifted and attuned stanzas, unutterably precious' (Int., xlv). Ranjee compared it to 'the mystic fire in the heart of the opal' (60); and in reviewing his essay I found it natural to define the quality of Shakespeare's poem by quoting Donne's line from *A Valediction* 'like gold to airy thinness beat'. Its quality is well characterised by one of Michelangelo's finest sonnets:

> So friendly is the fire to flinty stone,
> That, struck therefrom and kindled to a blaze,
> It burns the stone, and from the ash doth raise
> What lives thenceforward binding stones in one.
>
> Kiln-hardened this resists both frost and sun,
> Acquiring higher worth for endless days—
> As the purged soul from hell returns with praise,
> Amid the heavenly host to take her throne.
>
> E'en so the fire struck from my soul, that lay
> Close-hidden in my heart, may temper me,
> Till burned and slaked to better life I rise.
>
> If, made mere smoke and dust, I live today,
> Fire-hardened I shall live eternally;
> Such gold, not iron, my spirit strikes and tries.
>
> (34)

Such is the hard, resistant, tempered quality of the poetry in *The Phoenix and the Turtle*.

It is not obviously optimistic. If Marston's contribution is the most ecstatic and Jonson's the most moral, Shakespeare's may be called, as Carleton Brown observed, the most tragic. Such love as the love of the Sonnets is, as we have seen (p. 69), naturally tragic, and we may profitably compare *The Phoenix and the Turtle* with Marvell's *A Definition of Love*. Of the poem's paradoxes I have elsewhere (see p. 200 below) written. Much of it, in substance, if not in form, recalls the Sonnets. We have 'truth' and 'beauty' together as in the Sonnets (p. 45), and a similar, and greater, stress on chastity.

Carleton Brown finds the birds' failure to leave 'any posterity' a stumbling-block. 'This last stanza', he writes, 'is especially remarkable, for it flatly contradicts Marston and Chester, both of whom, as we have seen, give account of a fair creature which issued from the ashes of the Phoenix' (*Poems by Salusbury and Chester*, Int., lxxiii). His comment well illustrates the inadequacy of the biographical approach. The new Phoenix is as surely present within Shakespeare's poem as in the lyric ecstasy of Marston which *follows*; the sequence is vital. Besides, as we shall see, the 'bird of loudest lay' is itself a likely candidate.

We have already (pp. 48, 185) equated the Turtle, or Turtle-Dove, with the female element in the Shakespearian bisexuality which loved the Fair Youth and composed the plays. The Turtle-Dove is a normal Shakespearian symbol of love-constancy, as at *1 Henry VI*, ii, ii, 30–1. The dove is Venus' bird: her car is drawn by 'two strengthless doves' at *Venus and Adonis*, 153; the association recurs elsewhere (e.g. *The Rape of Lucrece*, 58; *Romeo and Juliet*, ii, v, 7); and in *The Tempest* (iv, i, 94) Venus' dove is associated directly with her island, Paphos, as in *Love's Martyr*. We should normally in Shakespeare expect a single Turtle-Dove to be female, as in Paulina's lines:

> I, an old turtle,
> Will wing me to some wither'd bough, and there
> My mate, that's never to be found again,
> Lament till I am lost.
> (*The Winter's Tale*, v, iii, 132)

The bird itself is female even when compared with a male, as when Troilus insists that he is as true 'as turtle to *her* mate' (*Troilus and Cressida*, iii, ii, 185). But here, on the pattern of our other poems, the Turtle is the male partner. That this is not quite natural within Shakespeare's world may be seen from the equation of the dove with gentleness underlying Juliet's agonised, 'Dove-feather'd raven! wolvish-ravening lamb!' (*Romeo and Juliet*, iii, ii, 76); and, still more, by the series of paradoxes developed by Helena in *A Midsummer Night's Dream* when, with a significant grouping of effects, she compares herself ironically to Daphne chasing Apollo, the dove pursuing a griffin, or a 'mild hind' the tiger (ii, i, 231–3). We do not *expect* our Turtle to be, in any obvious sense, a typical male: that is certain.

As for the Phoenix, it is always, and necessarily, baffling. It occurs in the Sonnets:

> Devouring time, blunt thou the lion's paws,
> And make the earth devour her own sweet brood;
> Pluck the keen teeth from the fierce tiger's jaws,
> ⁴And burn the long-liv'd Phoenix in her blood . . .
>
> (19)

Lion and tiger are natural associations, and we must never forget that it is itself a kind of eagle. It is pre-eminently royal and golden, whereas the Dove is 'silver' (*Venus and Adonis*; 366, 1190; and see p. 153, references). In *A Lover's Complaint*, the 'beauteous' and 'maiden-tongued' (99–100) youth, who so resembles the young man of the Sonnets, is given a phoenix-comparison:

> Small show of man was yet upon his chin;
> His phoenix down began but to appear
> Like unshorn velvet on that termless skin,
> Whose bare out-bragg'd the web it seem'd to wear;
> Yet show'd his visage by that cost more dear,
> And nice affections wavering stood in doubt
> If best were as it was, or best without.
>
> (92)

The Phoenix is used here the more naturally for the border-line, and so in a sense bisexual, age of the youth, set between boyhood and manhood, and we may observe how precisely this border-line state of 'down' is, as in the Sonnets, shown as the secret of the attraction, and how exactly it is related to the Phoenix. But the Phoenix may also be a creature of militant virility, as in *3 Henry VI*:

YORK: My ashes, as the Phoenix, may bring forth
            A bird that will revenge upon you all,
            And in that hope I throw mine eyes to heaven
            Scorning whate'er you can afflict me with.
            Why come you not? what! multitudes, and fear?
CLIFFORD: So cowards fight when they can fly no further;
            So doves do peck the falcon's piercing talons;
            So desperate thieves, all hopeless of their lives,
            Breathe out invectives 'gainst the officers.

                                             (I, iv, 35)

Compare Enobarbus', 'In that mood, the dove will peck the estridge' (*Antony and Cleopatra*, III, xi, 195). The Phoenix is associated with strong action, backed by 'heaven'; the Dove with female weakness, in contrast to the falcon's 'talons'. Traditionally the Phoenix is represented as an eagle-like bird, with just such talons of its own.

In *Richard III* the Phoenix' 'nest of spicery' is once compared by Richard to natural procreation, with the womb as both the grave of old bitterness and the nurture-ground of comfort (IV, iv, 424). The context is dramatically ironical.

Shakespeare's two most resplendent male lovers, Timon and Antony, are compared with it. Timon, who 'flashes now a Phoenix' (II, i, 32), enjoys the comparison the more appropriately in that his love and personality are abnormal: he has, in fact, precisely those magical qualities, that blend of sweetness with virility, that lonely completion, which the bird symbolises. The comparison of Antony to 'thou Arabian Bird' (*Antony and Cleopatra*, III, ii, 12), humorously reported as coming from Lepidus, is relevant, though less important.

Female and royal persons of chastity and virtue may also receive the comparison. Imogen, with her 'mind so rare', is 'alone the Arabian bird' (*Cymbeline*, I, vi, 17); and in Cranmer's prophecy at the conclusion to *Henry VIII*, Queen Elizabeth is compared to 'the bird of wonder' or 'maiden Phoenix', from 'the sacred ashes' of whose 'honour'—it is a *spiritual* propagation—a new sovereign is to rise in 'star-like' majesty (*Henry VIII*, v, v, 40–8).

The bird can be crisply defined as a creature of highest virtue, in both the old and the modern senses of the word. It holds magical properties; power must be contained; and it is

M.F.—14

significant that our two female candidates are royal. Its presence
in *The Tempest* is natural:

> Now I will believe
> That there are unicorns; that in Arabia
> There is one tree, the Phoenix' throne, one Phoenix
> At this hour reigning there.
>
> (III, iii, 21)

Observe the 'throne': it is a royal bird, a kind of super-eagle.
   The Phoenix and the Turtle itself gives us some help. The
Phoenix, though female, comes first, as the leading partner; but
the Dove's 'loyal breast' (57) also suggests the female sex. The
Phoenix is the Turtle's 'queen' (31), royalty being preserved.
The poem, too, opens with a list of mourners, and these are
important. One, the crow, is called 'treble-dated', which means
unusually long-lived. It is sexually abnormal:

> That thy sable gender mak'st
> With the breath thou giv'st and tak'st . . .
>
> (18)

This has been interpreted in three ways: that the bird, crow or
raven, (i) changes its sex at will, which Grosart (242) recorded
as still a popular belief concerning the crow; (ii) conceives not
'by conjunction of male and female', but by 'a kind of billing
at the mouth' (Swan's *Speculum Mundi*, 1635; 397); (iii) conceives and lays its eggs at the bill (*Hortus Sanitatis*, III, 34). The
first reading involves a dubiously correct translation of 'gender',
and Grosart apparently, according to Hyder Edward Rollins,
changed his mind; the other two may be grouped together. The
various references are given in Rollins' *New Variorum* notes, to
which I must refer the reader.[1]
   We therefore have an interesting sequence. The mourners
of the opening stanzas hold exact significances. Our first
stanza emphasises chastity ('chaste wings'); the second banishes
evil and death (the owl); the third, after rejecting tyranny
('tyrant wing'), preserves royalty in the eagle; the fourth sounds
the music of immortality in the 'death-divining' swan; and the
crow signifies long life and sexual abnormality (bisexuality,

---

[1] See too *Shakespeare's Poems* in The Yale Shakespeare, ed. Albert Feuillerat, 1927;
165–6; T. W. Baldwin and D'Arcy W. Thompson in *The Times Literary Supplement*,
1941, 287 and 397; and Baldwin's *Literary Genetics*, XVI, 372.

propagation by *kisses* only,[1] or propagation without any sexual partner). Our positive values are: chastity, royalty, immortality, and some form of non-sexual or bisexual unity and propagation, *related, as in poetry, to both music and breath*. These, being the primary constituents of the Phoenix itself, are correctly represented in our ceremonial.

All our many sexual confusions and abnormalities are component to the poem's central purpose in celebration of a mystical love-union beyond sex, as we understand it, and all normal biological categories. I cannot then agree with Ranjee that 'the very title suggests the sex duality', nor that it is 'a sex poem, albeit in a very special sense' (36), unless we mean that it is sexually paradoxical, and that that paradox is the heart of it. Here are our central stanzas:

> Here the anthem doth commence:
> Love and constancy is dead;
> Phoenix and the Turtle fled
> In a mutual flame from hence.
>
> So they lov'd, as love in twain
> Had the essence but in one;
> Two distincts, division none:
> Number there in love was slain.
>
> Hearts remote, yet not asunder;
> Distance, and no space was seen
> 'Twixt the Turtle and his queen:
> But in them it were a wonder.
>
> So between them love did shine,
> That the Turtle saw his right
> Flaming in the Phoenix' sight;
> Either was the other's mine.
>
> Property was thus appall'd
> That the self was not the same;
> Single nature's double name
> Neither two nor one was call'd.
>   (21)

---

[1] For kisses as a legitimate form of soul-contact in what might be called the Phoenix' field of moral valuation see Baldwin's *Literary Genetics*, XVI, 372 and 375. Compare, too, our references to kisses in the Cantos, pp. 163–4, 178 above; also p. 89, note.

These lines should by now need little comment. Ranjee (42–5) well discusses the words 'essence', 'distincts', 'division' and 'property' in terms of scholastic thought. The general conclusion of the whole poem is, as I put it in *The Shakespearian Tempest* (App. A, 324), that 'the very death of truth and beauty creates a third unknown immortality'. But, though to this extent optimistic, the experience is firmly *objectified*, and the frame-work correspondingly tragic. The lovers are *seen* to disappear, having fled this dimension in a 'mutual flame'. The transcending of numerical distinction is our central thought. Ranjee (40) says, 'it is not two who have gone—it is *one*'; and yet there is really more in it than the simple resolution of duality in unity. In *The Christian Renaissance*, during a comparison of the poem with Christian symbolism (the Trinity, the Incarnation, Dante's Gryphon, etc.)—Ranjee (42) also made a cross-reference to Trinitarian doctrine—I wrote: 'Here we see not merely a transcending of duality: rather the duality-unity dualism is itself transcended' ('The Eternal Triangle', xii, 329). This is what our stanzas are trying to define. For 'distance, and no space was seen', we might compare T. S. Eliot's 'more distant than stars and nearer than the eye' in *Marina*.[1]

We have already (pp. 42, 61) compared the love shining 'between' them to Sonnet 24 and Donne's 'great Prince' of *The Ecstasy*. It is a 'flaming' reality born from the union of eyes, the Turtle's 'right' (i.e. perhaps, what is properly its own) being seen by the Turtle burning within the Phoenix' 'sight', or act of seeing, as in Sonnet 24 (p. 40).[2] Such lovers see themselves not merely reflected in the other's eyes, but in the other's sight. With 'either was the other's mine' we can compare 'thou mine, I thine' of Sonnet 108. On 'Property . . . appall'd' Ranjee comments: 'Existence in its metaphysical aspect was scandalised at this impossible condition' (44).

So the paradoxes go on. For 'if what parts can so remain' (48) we may compare Shelley's definition of love in *Epipsychidion*

---

[1] Walter Whiter concluded his *A Specimen of a Commentary on Shakespeare* (1794) with a note on *The Phoenix and the Turtle* as a reflection of Christian dogma. For the poem's scholastic affinities, see also J. V. Cunningham in *E.L.H.*, xix; 4; Dec., 1952; 265–76.

[2] T. W. Baldwin notes here that 'the Phoenix, as bird of the Sun, had flaming eyes' (*Literary Genetics*, xvi, 374). According to Ranjee, the Turtle saw his 'justification for existence in the appreciation with which the Phoenix regarded him' (43).

as a reality where 'to divide is not to take away' (161). Within
all this there is really only the one paradox, and for its elucidation we may again turn to Michelangelo:

> If love be chaste, if virtue conquer ill,
> If fortune bind both lovers in one bond,
> If either at the other's grief despond,
> If both be governed by one life, one will;
>
> If in two bodies one soul triumph still,
> Raising the twain from earth to heaven beyond,
> If Love with one blow and one golden wand
> Have power both smitten breasts to pierce and thrill;
>
> If each the other love, himself forgoing,
> With such delight, such savour, and so well,
> That both to one sole end their wills combine;
>
> If thousands of these thoughts, all thought outgoing,
> Fail the least part of their firm love to tell,
> Say, can mere angry spite this knot untwine?
>
> (32)

Here, instead of paradox, we have, in the fifth line, the transcendental word 'soul'. Once agree that each person has, or is
related to, some higher soul-self holding its being in another
dimension, and all becomes clear. Donne regularly thinks in
these terms; as in *A Valediction* and throughout *The Ecstasy*.
Lovelace, in *To Lucasta, Going beyond the Seas*, says that Faith
and Troth, 'like separated souls', can yet meet, beyond space,
'above the highest sphere', greeting each other as angels, even
though 'unknown' (i.e. to the earthly consciousness). We may
suppose that true lovers are attuned, through love, to this
dimension; in each other's eyes, to use Shakespeare's imagery,
they see the dimension in which exist both souls in unison and
unity. The two personalities remain distinct, until in death they
attain each their greater selves, which are one: hence our
various unity-affirmations, as in 'The world one Phoenix, till
another burns' (p. 182, with accompanying references). Something of this massive unity can be glimpsed before death, and
that is the meaning of Michelangelo's 'one life', 'one will', 'one
soul'; but the 'smitten breasts' remain two.

In such terms you can also see why the lover's love of the loved one is *simultaneously self-union and integration* (pp. 35–7) *within his own total self*.

The concluding *Threnos*, spoken by Reason, maintains a strict objectivity and pathos, peculiarly evident in 'cinders' (55) and 'buried' (64). 'Eternity' (58) comes in naturally, with whatever assurance it can give. 'Chastity' (61) recurs, the lack of 'posterity' (59) fitting well enough the story of the Sonnets. 'Truth' and 'Beauty' (64) refer respectively to Dove and Phoenix, and, though a reference to Keats' *Grecian Urn* is natural, we must here read 'truth' in terms of loyalty as well as metaphysical insight. Truth 'cannot be', because in temporal terms loyalty, as the Sonnets suggest, will inevitably weaken; though this is not to say that the more metaphysical meaning is not also contained. The 'prayer' (67) points on to Prospero's epilogue in *The Tempest*. With a fine reserve the poet leaves us, as does Pope in *Eloisa to Abelard*, with a tragic conclusion, but we get the essence of neither poem by remaining content with that, and here, should we wish to know more, we may concentrate on the lines

> Phoenix and the Turtle fled
> In a mutual flame from hence.
>
> (23)

These suggest, as indeed many earlier phrases in *Love's Martyr* have suggested (e.g. 163–4, 178), that the flame of the Phoenix' burning is also the flame of mutual, but sexually separated, love, corresponding to the 'joy's bonfire' in Donne's image of 'one fire of four inflaming eyes, and of two loving hearts' (*Epithalamion*, xi); always fleeing 'from hence', and piercing dimensions beyond earthly computation.

A question arises concerning the 'bird of loudest lay' who introduces the poem and summons the various mourners. Grosart suggests the nightingale, and he was followed by Ranjee. Sir Osbert Sitwell offers the Peacock (see *T.L.S.*, 1941, 199, 203, 352, 359, 364). In my 'additional note' to Appendix A of the 1953 re-issue of *The Shakespearian Tempest*, I returned to the older view, supported by the use of 'sole Arabian tree' (2), so exactly corresponding as it does to the bird's description in *The Tempest* (p. 198), that this bird is *the*

Phoenix itself. T. W. Baldwin notes that the Phoenix is a song-bird in Lactantius' *Carmen de Phoenice* (*T.L.S.*, 1941, 287; and see his relation of Shakespeare's 'trumpet' to Ovid in his *Literary Genetics*, xvi, 363–4 and 368). In the old English poem based on Lactantius it is certainly credited with wondrous vocal powers:

> As soon as the Sun o'er the salty streams,
> On high doth soar, the haughty bird
> Joyfully leaves his lofty perch,
> Darting upward on dauntless wing,
> And singing exultant, seeks the light.
> Glorious the greeting he giveth the Sun,
> His spirit athrill with rapture of bliss;
> Warbling melodies wondrous sweet,
> With various art and voice more clear
> Than ever men heard the heavens beneath,
> Since the King of Glory, the great Creator,
> Established the world. More winsome far
> Than any music that men may make;
> And sweeter than any earthly strain,
> This trancing song. No sound of trump
> Or horn or harp, or harmonies clear
> Of organ-pipes, or purest tones
> Of mortal voice, or music of the swan,
> Or aught that God hath given to cheer
> Earth's heavy toil, may touch this song.
> He carols and sings in unceasing delight
> Till the Sun descends in the southern sky;
> Then sinketh his song and silent falls,
> The beautiful bird then bows his head
> And listening alert lifteth his wings
> Beating them thrice, then bideth at rest.
>   (120; trans, J. Duncan Spaeth [1])

The references to the trumpet and swan's music are interesting, since we find them in Shakespeare's poem.

If this reading be accepted, we find the Phoenix celebrating the obsequies of itself and the Turtle. For a bird accustomed to rise from its own ashes, this need not be considered a task beyond its power. Besides, the process neatly balances the process found later (first, I think, observed by Middleton Murry

---

[1] Princeton University Press, 1921.

in *Discoveries*; 1924), when Reason 'in itself confounded' (41) sings in the concluding 'theme' (49) the triumph-song of its own death-knell. It is primarily to these two mechanisms that we owe our sense, resembling that given by Blake's *Mental Traveller*, of self-regeneration and revolving movement.

But surely, within the poem, the establishing of a living Phoenix rather weakens the point and pathos of the close? In so far, however, as we are prepared to agree with those (pp. 105–7, 147–8, 193) who see Shakespeare's dramas as flowering from whatever love experience, or experiences, lie behind the Sonnets and *The Phoenix and the Turtle*, there is a possible answer. The 'bird of loudest lay' becomes Shakespeare's greater poetry, rising from the ashes of the love from which it draws its inspiration. Many years ago I suggested, in *The Shakespearian Tempest* (App. A, 323–4), that stanzas 2 to 6, being made of leading Shakespearian themes and symbols, might be said to constitute a brief summing up of Shakespeare's total work. Since this work must be supposed to represent a fall from the perfection which prompts and inspires it—for it is Beatrice, not Vergil, who guides Dante through Paradise—we can indeed call it one vast threnody on the wondrous thing—love, vision, divine insight, names do not matter—which, once, twice, or perhaps more often still, came, stayed for a while, and was gone.

But that is not the whole truth. In *Timon of Athens* and *Antony and Cleopatra* we feel as, later, in Byron's *Sardanapalus*, 'the mutual flame' itself; we are within its warmth, its sphere of radiation; and in the Final Plays, concluding with *Cymbeline*, *The Tempest* and *Henry VIII*, we are aware of some new Phoenix, some new, earthly and yet unearthly, perfection, rising from the flame. Each of these five plays just mentioned contains one of our few Phoenix references.

V

OTHER POETS

THE Phoenix is more than a symbol of love as usually understood: it, and its Turtle, symbolise rather, as Chester's
title-page puts it, 'the truth of love'. This truth is most clearly
seen and experienced in the less obviously biological forms;
but it may be supposed to cover all love, wherever love is true.
Our male tonings need not always be interpreted according to
the letter: to the Elizabethan, as Spenser's *Hymns* suggest,
Love itself was a great Lord, Captain or King, whatever the
sex of its immediate object, or symbol. To Shakespeare it is
'lord Love' (*The Merchant of Venice*, ii, ix, 101), and the lover
naturally abashed, as before a sovereign (*The Merchant of Venice*,
iii, ii, 176–84; *Troilus and Cressida*, iii, ii, 35–9; see pp. 60–1).
And yet this poetic tendency also reminds us that the imagination of the period could also idealise, romanticise, and think
erotically of, a man-to-man relationship. Matthew Roydon's
poem in *The Phoenix' Nest* on the death of Sir Philip Sidney in
the collection of that title (p. 150) is called 'an elegy, or friend's
passion, for his Astrophill'. We have already (p. 69) observed
that such idealisations are easier to write of after the subject's
death. But even when there was little romance, the most
extreme terms could be used for a great man, as they were for
Leicester, in *The Dead Man's Right* of the same collection. As
for the Queen, there was no limit. Extravagance of praise
proves little, or rather, perhaps, too much. Romantic feelings
were close-twisted with aristocratic and royal valuations. Duty
to a lord, friendship, and sexual love, are often poetically indis-
tinguishable; 'friend' was an even stronger term than 'lover'.
But all this works both ways. The age was an age of human
idealism from which many most potent, wonderful, and even
transcendental personal experiences could mature, and such are
the experiences behind the 'Phoenix'. It was a peculiarly poetic
period; and, as Ranjee (25) puts it, 'poets hover round the

Phoenix as the bees hover round the flower that gives them honey'.

We shall advance little by attempting to relate each Phoenix poem in turn to a biographical exactitude. What rouses our interest in these poems is their power and conviction, and our best way to attain understanding is to compare them with their like: with Plato, Petrarch, Dante, Michelangelo; with Donne and Marvell, Shelley and Browning. These speak, in different ways, of a single mystery; and if with some the experience appears to be heterosexual, and with some homosexual, such details are subsidiary. But it is all-important that we should realise that they *are* subsidiary; that we should not regard some as natural, some as unnatural; that we should not, once again, attempt, as Duke Vincentio has it,

> To draw with idle spiders' strings
> Most ponderous and substantial things.
> (*Measure for Measure*, III, ii, 297)

It is just because there is this conventional ruling, and over-ruling, that I suspect that many of our supposedly heterosexual poems in any age may have a different origin; and, if so, it is as well that we should know it.

There is nevertheless an important distinction to be drawn between the Phoenix-experience and a properly consummated heterosexual union. The one is supremely conscious, a matter mainly of eyes and soul; but, though thwarted of consummation on one plane, it has its own peculiar, and high, reward. The other enters, and enjoys, the dark world of instinct and physical consummation. Donne's poetry is remarkable for its handling, as in *The Sun Rising*, of this immersion into the twilit bliss of sexual union; and we may accordingly look to him for a precise statement on the relation of ordinary sexual experience to the Phoenix.

He has two valuable contributions for us. The first is from his *Epithalamion, or Marriage Song on the Lady Elizabeth and Count Palatine being married on St. Valentine's day*[1]. St. Valentine is addressed:

> Till now, thou warmd'st with multiplying loves
> Two larks, two sparrows, or two Doves.

---

[1] St. Valentine's Day is traditionally associated with both the choosing of sweethearts and the mating of birds.

All that is nothing unto this,
For thou this day couplest two Phoenixes;
   Thou mak'st a taper see
What the Sun never saw; and what the Ark
(Which was of fowls and beasts, the cage and park)
Did not contain, one bed contains through thee,
   Two Phoenixes whose joined breasts
Are unto one another mutual nests,
Where motion kindles such fires as shall give
Young Phoenixes, and yet the old shall live,
Whose love and courage never shall decline,
But make the whole year through, thy day, O Valentine.

                        (II)

The 'Phoenix bride' is told to rival and 'frustrate' the Sun (III). This contradicts all that we know of the Phoenix as love-symbol, as well as constituting a challenge to the Phoenix' natural companion, the Sun, elsewhere so discourteously treated by this poet; and it is clearly stated that it all *is* a result unprecedented, since the old Phoenix should die before the new appears, and these do not. Nor should there be *two* Phoenixes; one is correct according to the myth, and at the most we should expect a Turtle-Dove. Two Phoenixes are an offence against tradition and poetry alike. As for the proposed brood of young Phoenixes, the very thought of it is an outrage.

The poet probably knew what he was doing. In fact, though he appears to have slight *feeling* for them, he *understands* the symbols well enough to assist our general understanding. Though he is at pains to insist that his two lovers have more worth than 'all thy turtles and sparrows' (VII), yet his line, 'Here lies a she Sun and a he Moon here' (VII), provides the neatest possible commentary on the sexual criss-cross of our various Phoenix-and-Turtle poems, wherein a golden Phoenix is balanced against a silver (p. 153, references) Dove. And unity is finally re-established. The lovers are to meet 'as one glorious flame, meeting another, grows the same' (IV),

   And by this act of these two Phoenixes
     Nature again restored is:
    For since these two are two no more
   There's but one Phoenix still, as was before.

                        (VIII)

Though he started by treating the Phoenix-symbol with scant respect, he at least ends in conformity with its laws; but there are still the little Phoenixes to be reckoned with, and the treatment, as a whole, remains crude.

Donne is, of course, a poet of sexual, and heterosexual, achievement. Unlike most love-poets, he sings of love accomplished rather than of love-aspiring, and so stands outside the range of the Phoenix' radiation. It is perhaps significant that he can write satirically of 'frolic patricians' and 'painted courtiers' as 'strange hermaphrodites' (*Epithalamion made at Lincoln's Inn*), in the manner of Pope on Sporus. We might suggest that, just as Donne has little feeling for the rights of the Phoenix, so Shakespeare shows no sign of the mysticism of sexual intercourse: it may be the 'act of darkness' of *King Lear* (III, iv, 87) following the thought of Sonnet 129 and the self-loathing of *The Rape of Lucrece* (673–742); or, as so often in the Sonnets and elsewhere, 'sport'; but it is accorded no positive *mystique*. In *Antony and Cleopatra*, 'eternity' is present in 'lips', 'eyes' and 'brows' (I, iii, 35–6), as in the Sonnets, but the lust is sharply criticised, and the only complete union is in death. Shakespeare's most explicit statement of the inadequacy of sexual passion occurs throughout *Troilus and Cressida*, and to this I have given an extended study in *The Wheel of Fire*. D. A. Traversi notes, as a characteristic of Shakespeare's Sonnets, 'this insistent thwarting of the desire for unity and fertility'; 'this frustration', he says, 'is felt to be a *necessary* flaw at the heart of passion' (*Approach to Shakespeare*, 1938; III, 46). But this is not quite the whole story, since the experience of the Sonnets enjoys its own peculiar unity; and, indeed, fertility. There is here a necessary distinction.

Once, however, Donne does, very precisely, and without offence, define the relationship of his own heterosexual accomplishment to the Phoenix; and the definition is of considerable interest. Here it is, from *The Canonization*:

> Call us what you will, we are made such by love;
>   Call her one, me another fly;
>   We are tapers too, and at our own cost die,
> And we in us find the Eagle and the Dove.
>   The Phoenix' riddle hath more wit
>   By us; we two, being one, are it.

So, to one neutral thing, both sexes fit,
We die and rise the same, and prove
Mysterious by this love.

Here 'dove' is balanced by 'eagle', to reserve for the Phoenix
(the 'great Prince' of *The Ecstasy*, a poem packed with relevant
material) a yet greater place; and the use of 'eagle' in its stead
(as in *The Phoenix' Nest*; see p. 152 above) underlines the male
connotations elsewhere of Phoenix as against Dove. 'Hath more
wit' means 'can be more clearly understood'. We watch here a
biological expression, or shadow, of the great Phoenix mystery,
or 'riddle': in biological terms, the lover's sleep is their death,
Lawrence's dark world, and the new Phoenix, presumably, a
child. But the Phoenix is properly 'neutral', ranging beyond
this. It is a thing of wholeness, completion and consciousness.
The contrast is that of Shelley's title '*Epipsychidion*' with
Spenser's '*Epithalamion*'; the one indicating the burning
consciousness of the great spiritual experience which gives
birth to the 'naked seraph' (p. 214); the other indicating
the marriage-*bed*.

Donne's stanza makes a neat statement. The Phoenix is
properly complete and self-sufficient, made of male and female
together; but, *if the Phoenix itself finds a lover*, then indeed
we have a new dimension of most strange potentialities. That
is what happens in our Phoenix-and-Turtle, which are really
Eros-and-Psyche, poems. These exist as a half-way between
Donne's extravagant and illegitimate exploitation of *two*
Phoenixes and the original myth in which the Phoenix needs
no lover at all. In these poems a poet who has himself bisexual
affinities is faced by a human expression, or symbol, of that
bisexuality in another, whether it be lady of intellect or youth
of charm; and a conscious poetic fire is then struck beyond
all ordinary love-poetry. So is it, too, in Marvell's *Definition
of Love*, where it is said that the 'union' of 'two perfect Loves'
would be the ruin of the established order. Though possessing
the essence of all love, being its very axle and pivot, they cannot
embrace; being like, they run 'parallel'; but, though 'infinite'
in their completion, they may not meet. Such is 'the conjunction of the mind' and opposition of destiny. And yet it is
through such abnormal loves that we can best penetrate, to use

15

Chester's words, 'the truth of love'; the truth, that is, of any love, including sexual love. The Phoenix is love's wholeness, or, as we saw in discussing Shakespeare's Sonnets, love-conscious-of-love; and if you are still inclined to ask why it is so regularly associated with an abnormal love to the exclusion of the other, we can always say that normal lovers have something better to do than to be conscious.

The Phoenix-experience is very clearly expanded in Shelley's *Epipsychidion*. This I have already compared with *The Phoenix and the Turtle* in *The Starlit Dome*. Here I can only add a brief comment.

The poem tells of a dream-ideal; of various attempts throughout the poet's life to realise that ideal; and of the meeting of someone who at last appears to incarnate it, or at least acts as a release-mechanism to the poetry. The thing, or person, desired is, however, as much an aspect of the lover's own soul as an objective reality: it is all somehow *closer* than an ordinary sexual engagement. So we hear that 'the phantom is beside thee whom thou seekest' (233); it is called 'this soul out of my soul' (238); an intuition supported elsewhere by such references as 'twins' (45), 'part of thee' (52), 'my heart's sister' (415), 'twin hearts' (575). The love in question enjoys a kind of chastity, or purity:

> To whatsoe'er of dull mortality
> Is mine, remain a vestal sister still;
> To the intense, the deep, the imperishable,
> Not mine, but me, henceforth be thou united . . .
>
> (389)

The poem's climax describes a supreme union of the depths of 'being' in terms of 'passion's golden purity' (569–71). This union is as a fiery immolation. Earlier the dream-ideal made life's dead weight 'a doom as glorious as a fiery martyrdom' (214); as though a moth should crave 'a radiant death, a fiery sepulchre' in the planet Venus (223). The final union shows the lovers as 'burning, yet ever inconsumable' (579). The poetry itself is said to be taking a 'flight of fire' (590). All these are Phoenix impressions.

The experience, like that of Shakespeare's poem (pp. 199–201), is at once separate and unified:

One hope within two wills, one will beneath,
Two overshadowing minds, one life, one death . . .

(584)

The lover becomes Love itself, the 'great Prince' of Donne's
Ecstasy. Such is the meaning of 'this world of love, this *me*'
(346), and

> Let us become the overhanging day,
> The living soul of this Elysian isle,
> Conscious, inseparable, one.

(538)

Observe that they are *conscious*; it is precisely this consciousness,
on which I have already commented in writing of Shakespeare's Sonnets (pp. 65, 126), that distinguishes our love-
union from a normal sexual partnership. My comment in *The
Starlit Dome* was:

> This is the brooding 'day' of Wordsworth's *Immortality Ode*. The
> realized soul *is* the cosmic. The poet's desire is extreme: not to enjoy,
> or be lost in, the higher dimension, but to *be* that dimension; that is to
> be, not a lover, but *that love itself composed of two lovers*; and yet to
> remain fully conscious. He asks the normally impossible.

(III, 236)

Poetry is a technique for attempting this. As we have seen
(p. 183 above), Shelley's use of 'winged words' to pierce 'into
the height of Love's rare universe' (589) closely repeats the
thought of Marston in his ecstatic description of the new
Phoenix which he calls 'perfection'. And we may, once again,
remember Chester's designation of his poem as 'shadowing the
truth of love' (p. 145).

But what exactly is the ideal being which prompts these
ambitious cosmic asseverations? Here we are plunged into
*exactly the same sort of sexual confusions that we found in our
Elizabethan poets*. Within the main poem, the last love of the
sequence is, quite clearly, Emilia Viviani, and feminine impressions are preserved, though it is once suggested that the
woman's form veils a 'seraph of Heaven' (21). But this
feminine, heterosexual, yet of course thwarted, love, though
clearly our immediate release-mechanism, nevertheless does not
appear to cover everything. The poem was first published

without the author's name, and a fictitious author is put forward in the 'Advertisement', or preface, where a certain mystery is hinted:

> The present poem, like the *Vita Nuova* of Dante, is sufficiently intelligible to a certain class of readers without a matter-of-fact history of the circumstances to which it relates; and to a certain other class it must ever remain incomprehensible, from a defect of a common organ of perception for the ideas of which it treats.

That, presumably, might refer merely to its more mystic qualities. But, as soon as we turn to the remarkable '*Fragments*' connected with the poem, which were excluded from the original publication, we find a new series of problems altogether.[1]

An earlier manuscript draft of the 'advertisement' describes the pretended author as accompanied by a lady who might have been 'supposed to be his wife' and—the text is irregular—'an effeminate looking youth, to whom he showed an (attachment) so (singular) excessive an attachment as to give rise to the suspicion, that she was a woman'; and at his death, 'this suspicion was confirmed'. The *Fragments* develop these hints, with many innuendoes and much mystification:

> Here, my dear friend, is a new book for you;
> I have already dedicated two
> To other friends, one female and one male—
> What you are, is a thing that I must veil;
> What can this be to those who praise or rail?
>
> (1)

The poet repudiates the teaching that one's devotion should be limited to a single 'mistress' or 'friend' (8). 'This kind of love', though he does not precisely say what kind, is supported by 'Nature', and we are reminded that both Socrates and Christ told us to love (29–37). The person loved is younger than the writer:

> I love you!—Listen, O embodied Ray
> Of the great Brightness; I must pass away

---

[1] These *Fragments* are printed in the Oxford edition of Shelley's works. They appear to have caused a general embarrassment to Swinburne and other commentators, but have recently received a more sympathetic handling in James A. Notopoulos' monumental work, *The Platonism of Shelley* (Duke University Press, 1949).

While you remain, and these light words must be
Tokens by which you may remember me.
Start not—the thing you are is unbetrayed,
If you are human, and if but the shade
Of some sublimer spirit . . .

                                                              (38)

If a male youth be meant, the conclusion is in place, since such
loved forms may often be best interpreted symbolically, as
earthly approximations to some seraphic archetype. We
continue:

> And as to friend or mistress, 'tis a form;
> Perhaps I wish you were one . . .
>
>   (45)

These lines refer, apparently, to the 'youth' of the advertisement. There is certainly a secret: 'If you were a lady', he says,
'it were fair the world should know'; but, as things are, he is
afraid that 'the Quarterly would bait you if betrayed' (51–3).
Confusions follow:

> And if, as it will be sport to see them stumble
> Over all sorts of scandals, hear them mumble
> Their litany of curses—some guess right,
> And others swear you're a Hermaphrodite;
> Like that sweet marble monster of both sexes,
> Which looks so sweet and gentle that it vexes
> The very soul that the soul is gone
> Which lifted from her limbs the veil of stone.
>
>   (54)

This 'hermaphrodite' is important, and must be related to the
Hermaphrodite, closely symbolising poetry, in *The Witch of
Atlas*.
      'Friendship' is next 'a sweet thing' (62); 'none can ever be
more dear than you' (83); this 'lovely soul' is 'a well of sealed
and secret happiness' (88–9); the writer and the friend are
bound for 'oblivion', but a prayer is offered, recalling *The
Phoenix and the Turtle*, 'May we meet in one Elysium or one
winding-sheet' (93–6).

M.F.—15

Our next lines are more explicit:

> If any should be curious to discover
> Whether to you I am a friend or lover,
> Let them read Shakespeare's sonnets, taking thence
> A whetstone for their dull intelligence
> That tears and will not cut . . .

(97)

Or let them, he says, consider how Socrates' definition of love in *The Symposium* penetrated deeper than its praise as delivered earlier through the 'sweet lips' of the beautiful youth Agathon (101–8). The poet believes that, could 'the presumptuous pedagogues of earth' solve 'the riddle offered here', they would become very different from what they are. But, after all, 'paradise fruits are sweetest when forbidden' (116), even though people 'taunt me with your love' (123). Such phrases are valuable pointers. Perhaps the most important of all are certain lines defining the creative result in some mysterious dimension beyond the biological of the love-interchange recorded:

> And what is that most brief and bright delight
> Which rushes through the touch and through the sight,
> And stands before the spirit's inmost throne,
> A naked Seraph? None hath ever known.
> Its birth is darkness, and its growth desire;
> Untameable and fleet and fierce as fire,
> Not to be touched but to be felt alone,
> It fills the world with glory—and is gone.

(142)

This 'seraph' is Marston's 'Perfection', the new Phoenix. It is also Shakespeare's 'mutual flame'.

Some lines addressed to Emily refer to 'those exiles' (i.e., such as the lovers) from the 'dull' and 'insane' people who 'vex' the world with 'pride' and 'pain' (171–3). When these 'exiles' are called

> that band of sister-spirits known
> To one another by a voiceless tone

(173)

we have a neat use of the feminine to indicate the lovers' souls; as when our Elizabethan poets equate themselves, as lovers, with the Turtle-Dove. Among our *Fragments'* concluding thoughts is the desire to 'mix in death' (177).

I would emphasise particularly the Hermaphrodite and the 'naked Seraph'. In my discussion of *Epipsychidion* in *The Starlit Dome* I wrote:

> In two of Shelley's works, *The Revolt of Islam* and *Prometheus Unbound*, a seraphic child plays a central, guiding part, as in Isaiah; and in one, *The Witch of Atlas*, it becomes, specifically, a hermaphrodite, that is, a bisexual creation, which is there directly regarded as personifying precisely this ambitious sort of sunlight poetic assertion we are here analysing.
>
> (III, 242)

All our Phoenix poems are supremely *conscious* works, representing love fully conscious of love's transcendental implications. The child of this love-consciousness is, not a human baby, but the new Phoenix. Shelley's title *Epipsychidion* means 'on the little soul-creature'; and the 'psychidion', or 'naked seraph', is the new Phoenix.

So understood, love is naturally at home with death. When in Browning's *The Ring and the Book* the hero-lover Caponsacchi determines to sacrifice himself for his love, death means 'to spurn the ground' and soar heavenwards:

> The very immolation made the bliss;
> Death was the heart of life, and all the harm
> My folly had crouched to avoid, now proved a veil
> Hiding all gain my wisdom strove to grasp.
>
> (VI, 953)

The 'fly' is drawn to the 'intense centre' of a flame which proves to be its proper 'heaven'.

Sometimes we think of two lovers, as in *Epipsychidion* and *The Phoenix and the Turtle*, but we may instead have to regard a love-intercourse wholly within the individual, as with the 'brain' and 'soul' of Richard's soliloquy (*Richard II*, v, v, 6; p. 138), Wordsworth's *Recluse* fragment, and Keats' *Ode to Psyche* (p. 186).[1] All our thinking is summed in Nietzsche's *Thus Spake Zarathustra*, where our protagonist lover-saint is

---

[1] For a more detailed commentary on these, see *The Starlit Dome*, I, 1-2 and IV, 301-4; also *Christ and Nietzsche*, IV, 133 and 136.

at once both Phoenix and Turtle. He thinks in terms of strangely wonderful birds:

> ... this bird hath builded its nest within me: therefore I love and cherish it—now it sitteth within me upon its golden eggs.
>
> (1, 5; numbering the 'Introductory Discourse', 1, 6.)

That we can call his Phoenix. Here is his Turtle:

> ... sometimes I find a stray bird in my dovecot, that is strange to me, and that trembleth when I lay my hand upon it.
>
> (11, 17)

He is himself the apostle of sacrifice, his whole integration quest being conceived as a 'thirst' to give, to lose, himself, for some greater end, or some greater self. His drama is a drama of self-communion, a love-intercourse with his own 'soul', itself called 'the song of a lover' (11, 9); he burns for the lady 'eternity', his new Phoenix (111, 16); the 'thirst of the ring' is within him, 'for every ring striveth and turneth about that it may reach itself again' (11, 5). If we want to understand the Phoenix, we must read, and re-read, *Thus Spake Zarathustra*.[1]

Nietzsche comes at the end of our story; and at the beginning of it was, of course, Plato's *Phaedrus* and, still more important, *The Symposium*. In *The Symposium*, after others have variously contributed their praises and definitions of Love, Socrates himself offers what is probably the subtlest definition ever advanced. I shall quote from Shelley's translation.

Love is not simply 'the love of the beautiful', but rather it aims, even when it is not obviously biological, at 'generation and production in the beautiful', because 'generation is something eternal and immortal in mortality'. Love can accordingly be regarded as 'the desire of immortality'. Socrates' statement is the more valuable since it is not a statement of the supreme beauty alone, but exists rather, as do all our Phoenix symbolisms, *at the meeting-place of time and eternity*. It speaks of categories less than eternal and more than temporal. The supreme beauty is, it is true, independent of change and relativity. But just as the physical body is always 'becoming new by the loss and change of that which it possessed before', so within the soul exists a universal principle by which, 'in the place of

---

[1] For a detailed interpretation I must again point to *Christ and Nietzsche*.

what has grown old and is departed, it leaves another new, like that which it was itself'. There, clearly, we have reminders both of Shakespeare's Sonnets, and of the Phoenix. The Phoenix, though transcendent, exists in time.

Of this general truth, or process, Fame is, as in Milton's *Samson Agonistes* and Pope's *Temple of Fame*, an important element. Samson's 'fiery virtue', though thought to be 'extinguish'd', yet rises, 'with inward eyes illuminated' from its 'ashes', and is compared first to an Eagle and next to the 'self-begotten bird', the Phoenix, who 'revives' and 'reflourishes', most 'vigorous' when 'most unactive deem'd', to live on in 'fame', even 'though her body die' (*Samson Agonistes*, 1687–1707).

The thought is Socratic. In the *Symposium* fame is said to prompt men to noble deeds, and such activities are contrasted with the more elemental desires of self-perpetuation through children:

Those·whose bodies alone are pregnant with this principle of immortality are attracted by women, seeking through the production of children what they imagine to be happiness and immortality and an enduring remembrance; but they whose souls are far more pregnant than their bodies, conceive and produce that which is more suitable to the soul. What is suitable to the soul? Intelligence, and every other power and excellence of the mind; of which all poets, and all other artists who are creative and inventive, are the authors.

Poetry and the arts are our most obvious results, and thought of them is found closely entwined with the Platonic love, as when Tennyson remembers Hallam as one at home with the muses, of 'seraphic intellect and force' and 'impassion'd logic' (*In Memoriam*, cix). But education is also involved. Indeed, the Greek *paederastia*, the friendship, at once romantic and educational, of a man for a youth, shadows the essence of all education:

For, by the intercourse with, and, as it were, the very touch of that which is beautiful, he brings forth and produces what he had formerly conceived; and nourishes and educates that which is thus produced together with the object of his love, whose image, whether absent or present, is never divided from his mind. So that those who are thus united are linked by a nobler community and a firmer love, as being the common parents of a lovelier and more enduring progeny than the parents of other children.

Poets and legislators are mentioned: Homer, Hesiod, Lycurgus and Solon. The implications are of the widest, nor are they exhausted by such readily definable appearances.

In elucidation of Plato's, or Socrates', meaning I would offer a few sentences from the dialogue in my *The Dynasty of Stowe*:

> Those works of Plato have shone down the ages as a well of inexhaustible light; and indeed this very emphasis witnesses the authority of the Greeks as world-educators. To them education was inseparable from that great mystery of which the love of man for woman is merely one, biological, variation; which finds room for the pastorals of Theocritus and Vergil, for Shakespeare's Sonnets, for Leonardo da Vinci and Michelangelo. To such as those men must listen with suspended judgment, for they are the masters, and mankind their pupils.
>
> (III, 40)

Again,

> Some excellence once seen behind, or within, creation prompts the Socratic soul to further creation. Now the highly integrated man has his share of feminine perception, is, himself, both man and wife, and may the sooner recognise excellence where the germ of masculine strength exists within the as yet undifferentiated, and therefore bisexual, purity and grace; sensing therein a simulacrum of that greater humanity towards which all art and education, and all political action, travail. Such virgin excellence it is in which true wholeness, and therefore dignity, best consist. The marriage of man and wife is as the making of one whole out of two halves; but the devotion of Socrates in the *Symposium* is the reflection of unity in unity. Therefore he refuses physical contact. On this plane there should be no emotional unrest, no desire: you will just salute, and pass by.
>
> (III, 41)

Socrates' refusal of contact must certainly be faced; but it must also be remembered that everyone is not a Socrates, and that the Platonic idealism flowered from a soil where contact was allowed.

Here is my last quotation:

> What the Platonic lover begets is, admittedly, hard to define. It is, none the less, that to which all learning and all teaching, indeed, all human existence, aspires. No love can preserve its health except in con-

scious or unconscious surrender to what lies beyond, or to some shadow of it, the two partners looking together not inwards, but out, facing, as you yourself have observed, in the one direction. That temple we have just passed celebrates, for a surety, such a dedicated friendship. It is this, and this only, this joint dedication, that distinguishes the good from the bad.

And as for teaching—why, one should not fashion a growing life with too much deliberation. Such conscious didacticism is always secondary, at best a meeting place where the real things work out their unseen effects. The Greek *paederastia* was, at its best, a tutorship, but it was more than teaching. The greatest teaching recognises always the fatuities alike of mental knowledge and of moral precept; and, in basing itself on the imponderable relationships alone, may reach and impart, though still with an outward-looking eye, some drops at least of wisdom. Such wisdom, or rather wise-being, works, however humbly, towards the creation, not of some new child, but of some greater personality; a chord sounding even now in some higher dimension, or perhaps hereafter, echoing through distant generations of men in their earthly pilgrimage, or contributing to the far music of some celestial city. All art, all unseen influence, all true teaching is of this kind, and the rest nothing. That is why all true teachers must be lovers, aiming to beget something for which no definition exists in the languages of man.

(III, 42)

That is as far as I, for one, understand it. But, if we could understand it easily, there would be no need for poetic symbolisms.

The Phoenix is clearly a symbol of widest import. We are almost tempted to say that any fine human experience may be contained, with the exception of a normal, heterosexual, physically consummated, love. Such a consummation must, and should, be, as D. H. Lawrence so often emphasised, a matter of unconsciousness, of the dark world[1]; but the Phoenix is seen and known by a flooded consciousness, and he is fire-bright. He is a pre-eminently Apollonian conception, and his natural symbol is the Sun. When in discussion of *Epipsychidion* in *Shelley, His Life and Work* (1927), William Edwin Peck writes, 'Having described Mary as the Moon, it now occurs to the poet that Emilia might be the Sun' (II, 193), he appears

---

[1] It seems that Lawrence, like Donne, tried to harmonise, and may sometimes have confused, the two categories. The Phoenix was his favourite personal emblem; he wrote a poem on it; and it appears on his grave. His posthumous papers were published under the title *Phoenix*, and a valuable study of him by Miss Dallas Kenmare uses the title *Fire-Bird* (1951).

to be unaware of what is an inevitable, imaginatively forced, contrast. The Phoenix properly only exists in all its splendour when the sleeping Hermaphrodite of Shelley's *Witch of Atlas*, who is clearly a symbol of poetry, is *awakened* for supreme adventure, unfolds its heaven-coloured pinions—it is a kind of Phoenix—and ascends:

> And then it winnowed the Elysian air
>   Which ever hung about that lady bright,
> With its aethereal vans—and speeding there,
>   Like a star up the torrent of the night,
> Or a swift eagle in the morning glare
>   Breasting the whirlwind with impetuous flight,
> The pinnace, oared by those enchanted wings,
> Clove the fierce streams towards their upper springs.
>
>   (XLV)

The implications I have elsewhere discussed (*The Starlit Dome*, III, 229, 233–4): they are clearly rather visionary than sexual. We may once again compare the highly conscious love of Shakespeare's Sonnets (pp. 45, 64–5, 126, 210–11, 215).

The Phoenix is a symbol of perfection. So Donne uses the term in his *Anatomy of the World*:

> Prince, Subject, Father, Son, are things forgot,
> For every man alone thinks he hath got
> To be a Phoenix, and that then can be
> None of that kind, of which he is, but he.

Middleton wrote a complete play, *The Phoenix*, about a prince of Ferrara called Phoenix, a young man of superlative virtue and insight, who, rather like the Duke in *Measure for Measure*, moves about his father's dukedom in disguise to discover its vices and virtues. He is spoken of like this:

> Thou wonder of all princes, president and glory,
> True Phoenix, made of an unusual strain!
> Who labours to reform is fit to reign.
>   (ed. A. H. Bullen; I, i, 135)

During the action he speaks a number of moralising speeches, including a fine soliloquy on the sanctity of marriage. He is apparently beautiful both in body and in soul: by a rough and

vicious Captain he is once called 'a pretty whoreson' (ii, ii, 217).
When he finally discovers himself, and much else, involving
examples of treachery, to his father, the Duke says:

> To thee let reverence all her powers engage,
> That art in youth a miracle to age!
> State is but blindness; thou had'st piercing art:
> We only saw the knee, but thou the heart.
> To thee, then, power and dukedom we resign.
> He's fit to reign whose knowledge can refine.
>   (v, i, 177)

The play is slight, though Phoenix himself is an interesting,
and for our purpose relevant, little study.

But the Phoenix properly surpasses all normal and easily
conceived perfection. It is, indeed, a creature beyond nature
as normally understood. We may say that it is a creature that
can only be seen, understood, and loved by genius, symbolised
in the Turtle-Dove; for without the humility, faith, and constancy of the Turtle-Dove genius cannot function, and for those
lacking these qualities the Phoenix will not exist.

The Phoenix is both 'self-begotten' (*Samson Agonistes*,
1699) and bisexual. As the old English poet tells us:

> Only God, the almighty King, knows what its sex is, female or male;
> none of mankind knows, save God alone, how wondrous are the rulings,
> the fair decree of old, concerning that bird's birth.
>   (trans. R. K. Gordon)

We on earth are split into sexes, but completeness, despite
Donne's slighting of hermaphrodites (p. 208), must be conceived, as Aristophanes explains in *The Symposium*, as, in some
way, androgynous or bisexual. It is that completeness, or 'perfection', which the Phoenix possesses. That is why Ovid calls
it 'unica semper avis', or 'a bird ever alone of its kind' (Baldwin,
quoting Showerman, *Heroides and Amores*, pp. 400–3; *Literary
Genetics*, xvi, 365). It is of the same race as the Sphinx and
the Unicorn, and occurs with the Unicorn—as well as being
significantly associated with Ganymede—in George Darley's
Nepenthe; or the Gryphon, so important in Dante's *Purgatorio*
(xxxi) as a symbol of the Incarnation. Ranjee tells us that
the Phoenix was at one time associated with the Virgin
Mother, and that, in an emblem for John Hawkin's *The Virgin*,

it is depicted with two hearts, 'which are as one', symbolising the Virgin Mother and her Son (14, and note). In terms of Phoenix-and-Turtle we can say that Christ would be Phoenix, and his Church, the Turtle: the Phoenix is a symbol of Christ in the old English poem, and the Church is 'thy' (i.e. Christ's) 'mild Dove' in one of Donne's Holy Sonnets (XVIII). In Dekker's *Four Birds of Noah's Ark* (ed. F. P. Wilson, 1924), we have a collection of devotional pieces under the headings of Dove, Eagle, Pelican and Phoenix. The Dove covers prayers conceived in softness and pity for children, women, the sick, and all whose lot is cast in danger or suffering. The Eagle covers prayers for royalty, aristocracy, clergy, judges, universities, and the nation. Under the Pelican, called a figure of Christ on the Cross, we have prayers against various vices. Last, we are told simply, and without reservation, that the Phoenix is a figure of Christ; and it covers thanksgivings for the benefits of Christ's *sacrifice*, with pieces on the resurrection and ascension, and Christ's coming in 'glory' hereafter. This little collection of devotional passages serves admirably to define the meanings of the various birds.

The Phoenix-symbol can obviously bear the weightiest meanings. The alchemists identified it with the Philosopher's Stone; and with reference to the great 'third Empire' of Ibsen's *Emperor and Galilean*, we have, at a climax: 'But from the ashes shall arise—like that marvellous bird—the God of Earth and the Emperor of the Spirit in one, in one, in one!' (*The Emperor Julian*, IV, iii).

We may, in conclusion, and for the sake of simplicity, give the Phoenix a certain negative definition in terms of Shakespeare's Sonnets. As a symbol both of spiritual propagation and of the eternal self-regeneration of nature hinted in Sonnet 126 (p. 97), it is a creature in whom the problems of the Sonnets are answered. It is the supreme positive to which these problems negatively point. Through it the wonder is perpetuated, not by marriage and a child, but by the new Phoenix; the loved thing is preserved, not merely by the 'black ink' of poetry (pp. 86, 90), but within that other dimension to which Phoenix and Turtle are for ever fleeing in their 'mutual flame', and of which the greatest poetry is but a miserable reflection. In it eternity and immortality are manifested, not as ghostly

concepts, but as a marvellous fire-nested bird of eagle eye and
wondrous plumage.

Whenever poetry has vigour, the Phoenix may come. It
lives today. W. B. Yeats' exquisite poem *His Phoenix*, contrasting its 'lonely' excellence with all more normal '*engines* of
delight', recalls lines of 'Ignoto', Marston and Chapman in the
Poetical Essays (pp. 181–5); and Edith Sitwell's poetry is often
on a Phoenix wave-length. It is certainly no distant splendour.
Rather call it the blazing heart of creation, flesh, blood, and
fire, both fierce and sweet, as in Francis Berry's *Phoenix*[1]:

> Flourish the bird of plumage fine,
> Golden and red,
> Brave Phoenix of the crimson vine,
> Living yet dead;
> Dweller in Arabian sun,
> Vivid in air,
> Rich with all richness, rich in song,
> Richer than birds you sing among;
> Phoenix of the savage grace
> And rudely fair,
> Solitary living—then you die
> Murdered by your flaming artistry.
>
> Phoenix in luxuriant wilderness,
> Of the flushed and barbarous grace,
> Once in five hundred years
> Praising youth—until the Wars.
> Then ceases heart, you burning die
> Spent by your own hot blazonry.
> Cold your ashes on the earth
> Grey and cold the vine of birth.
>
> Bird of blazon, come again,
> Ardent in Sun, Arabian pain,
> Pillage your heart for golden songs,
> Marshall your blood, and start like gongs
> Dared canzons gay, like torrent wine
> Purpling a river on the plain,
> Full joyous agony to gain.

[1] *The Galloping Centaur*; the collected poems of Francis Berry; Methuen & Co. Ltd.,
1952. Francis Berry's work, lying as it does in the central tradition of poetic symbolism,
is likely to survive after much of our modern poetry is forgotten.

Now smoulder ashes on the earth—
Then leap stab-flames to fusion birth
Of Phoenix, my gay—oh, trenchant—Cavalier,
This handsome minute of the suffering year.

There, today, in the words of a master-poet, is our Phoenix.

Having seen this marvel, our Elizabethan poets have left us words tinctured by its splendour; and, being themselves honest turtle-doves, whenever they recognised its self-sufficing royalty shining from queen or lord, brilliant lady or splendid youth, they wrote it down as 'Phoenix'.

PRINCIPAL WORKS CITED

The Sonnets of Shakespeare; ed. T. G. Tucker; Cambridge, 1924.

The Poems of Shakespeare (includes the Sonnets, but not *The Phoenix and the Turtle*); ed. George Wyndham; London, 1898.

Shakespeare's Sonnets Reconsidered; Samuel Butler; London, 1927 (orig. 1899).

A New Variorum Edition of Shakespeare: the Sonnets; ed. Hyder Edward Rollins; Philadelphia; 2 vols., 1944.

The Arden Shakespeare: the Sonnets; ed. C. Knox Pooler, 1918.

The Sonnets of William Shakespeare and Henry Wriothesley, Third Earl of Southampton (includes a section reprinting the *Poetical Essays* of *Love's Martyr*); Walter Thomson; Oxford (Blackwell), 1938.

Shakespeare's Sonnets Dated; Leslie Hotson; London, 1949.

The Portrait of Mr. W. H.; Oscar Wilde; orig. 1889.

The True History of Shakespeare's Sonnets; Lord Alfred Douglas, London, 1933.

Oxford Lectures on Poetry; A. C. Bradley; London, 1909.

Shakespeare and Spiritual Life; John Masefield; Romanes Lecture, Oxford, 1924.

The Lion and the Fox; Wyndham Lewis; London, 1927.

The Sense of Shakespeare's Sonnets; Edward Hubler; Princeton (New Jersey), 1952.

Countries of the Mind; J. Middleton Murry; 2 vols., London, 1931.

The Sonnets of Michelangelo, trans. J. A. Symonds; London, 1950.

Love's Martyr, or Rosalin's Complaint (with the *Poetical Essays*); Robert Chester and others; ed. Alexander B. Grosart, for the New Shakespeare Society; London, 1878.

Poems by Sir John Salusbury and Robert Chester; ed. Carleton Brown; Early English Text Society, London, 1914.

The Phoenix' Nest (1593); Matthew Roydon and others; ed. Hyder Edward Rollins; Cambridge (Mass.), 1931.

Four Birds of Noah's Ark; Thomas Dekker; ed. F. P. Wilson; Oxford (Shakespeare Head Press), 1924.

A New Variorum Edition of Shakespeare: the Poems; ed. Hyder Edward Rollins; Philadelphia, 1938.

The Arden Shakespeare: the Poems; ed. C. Knox Pooler, 1911.

The Phoenix and Turtle, ed. Bernard H. Newdigate; Oxford (Shakespeare Head Press), 1937.

Discoveries; J. Middleton Murry; London, 1924.

16

Towards the Stars; Ranjee (Ranjee G. Shahani); Rouen, 1931.
Phönix und Taube; Heinrich Straumann; Zurich, 1953.

The Voyage to Illyria; Kenneth Muir and Sean O'Loughlin; London, 1937.
On the Literary Genetics of Shakespeare's Poems and Sonnets; T. W. Baldwin; University of Illinois Press, Urbana, 1950.

INDEX A. SHAKESPEARIAN WORKS

(i) *Sonnets*

Sonnet
1 13, 35, 60, 72, 79
2 8, 9, 13, 72, 79, 174
3 9, 13, **35**, 39, 62–3, 74, 79, 172
4 13, 79
5 13, 70, 72, 74, 79, **88,** 92, 172
6 13, 75, 79, 80
7 13, **63,** 70, 79
8 13, 16, **27,** 79, 94
9 13, 79
10 13, 79
11 13, 39, 79, 92
12 13, 70, 73–4, 79
13 13, 39, 70, 75, 79, 96
14 13, 38, **45,** 61, 66, 79
15 13, 44, 63, 66, **71–2,** 74, 79, 87, 92
16 10, 13, 39, 43, 74, 79, 86, **100,** 172
17 13, 38, 67, 79, 80, 83
18 63, 70, 72, 75, **90,** 96, **99**
19 39, 72, **74–6,** 81, 83, 94, **196**
20 7, 9, 17, **25,** 34, **35–6,** 38–9, 62, 177
21 19, 39, 62, 66, 72
22 9, 37, **44,** 72, 74
23 17, 20, **37,** 38, **126,** 182
24 39, **40–2,** 61–2, 121–2, 200
25 6, 7, 8, 61, 63, **133–4**
26 6, 60, 66, 134
27 39, 66
28 63
29 8, 13, 61–2, **110,** 139, 173
30 9, 82
31 9, 39, 67, **108,** 118, 182
32 8, 10, 12, 14, 19, 75
33 12, 14, 38, 62, 63
34 66
35 11, 13, 43, 60, 62
36 8, 13, 17, **25,** 34, 42
37 6, **8,** 13, 37, 61
38 96, 99, **107**
39 25, 42–3, 46
40 11–13
41 11–13
42 11–13, 42

Sonnet
43 39
44 **46,** 92
45 6, **46,** 89, 92
46 38
47 39, 46
48 42, 66, 172
49 38, 62
50 46
51 46
52 66
53 8, 20, 35, 39, 70, **118,** 182
54 47, 60, **88,** 181, 183
55 63, 75, 82, **85,** 90–1, 95, **100–2**
56 38, 44, **47,** 70, **126,** 182
57 6, 31, 60
58 6, 31
59 **39, 40,** 59, 68, **83**
60 45, 59, **72–3,** 74, 81, 92
61 39
62 10, 42, **44,** 128
63 **10,** 61, 74, **86**
64 66, 74–5, 92, 95–6
65 5, 63, 66, **72,** 74–5, 81, **86,** 92, **95,** 97, 114
66 62, **110,** 131
67 8, 13, **20,** 27, 39, **59,** 60, 67, 68, 82
68 19, 20, 62, **82,** 171
69 8, 13, 43, 67, 173
70 13, 35, 43, 61, 67, 72, 74, 173
71 13
72 13
73 10, 63, **71,** 92
74 43, **68,** 75, **89,** 92, 171
75 67
76 62, 74, **83,** 92, 172
77 73, 75, 96
78 8, 14, 19, 27, 45, 61, **107**
79 14, 87, 107
80 14, 66, **94**
81 **89**
82 8, 19
83 14, **20,** 43, 85, 86, 112
84 9, 27, 35, 43, **86,** 112, **120,** 182
85 19, 20, 43, 62, 112

Sonnet
86 **13–14,** 43, 66–7, **90,** 111
87 13, 61, 66
88 13, 52, 111, 166
89 13
90 13, 17
91 9, 13
92 13
93 13, 43, 67, 110
94 9, 13, 17, 22, 27, **35, 43,** 55, 60, 109, 173–4
95 13, 22, 43, 60, 173
96 13, 22, 35, 43, 61, 66
97 14, **70,** 173
98 39, 60, 71, **118,** 182
99 60
100 14, 44, 54, 72, 75, 107, **112–13**
101 19, 20, 27, 44–5, 47, 62, 81, 95, 107, **113**
102 5, 19, 44, 67, **113–14, 126–7**
103 19, 44, 114
104 10, 43, 68, **71,** 73, **114**
105 20, **67,** 114
106 15, 39, 62, 82, **84, 100,** 114–15
107 **3–5,** 75, 77, 82, 85, 87, 91, 95, 102, 111, **114–15**
108 10, 14, **47,** 68, **84–5,** 96, **115,** 172, 200
109 13, 42, 47, 60, **115–16,** 118–19, 172, 182
110 9, 13, 15, 45, 53, 68, 96, **116–17**
111 9, 13, 15, 17, 48, 53, **117,** 135
112 13, 47, **117–19,** 182
113 47, **119–20, 126,** 139, 182
114 38, 61, **120–2,** 123, 139–40, 172, 182
115 61–2, 67, 68, 73–4, 77, 85, **122–3, 126,** 139, 172
116 23, 66–8, 75, **91,** 94, **100, 123–24,** 130
117 **124,** 135
118 47, **125–7,** 182
119 16, **127–8,** 166
120 13, 43, 128

227

(ii) Plays and Poems

INDEX B. GENERAL

Acheson, Arthur: 14
'A. E.', see Russell, G. W.
Aeschylus:
  Oresteia, 26, 27
Agathon: 214
Alcibiades: 37
Alexander, Peter: 76, 82
Aristophanes: 191, 221;
  The Clouds, 191
Arnold, Matthew:
  Thyrsis, **69**

Baldwin, T. W.: 5, 114, 118, 152, 193,
  198–9, 200, 203, 221
Barnfield, Richard:
  The Affectionate Shepherd, 10, 18
Bateson, F. W.: 5
Bedford, Countess of: 148, 190
Benham, Sir Gurney: 175, 183–5,
  189
Benson, John: 137
Berkeley, Bishop: 120
Berry, Francis:
  The Galloping Centaur, 223;
  Phoenix, **223–4**
Blake, William: 52;
  The Mental Traveller, 204
Boccaccio, Giovanni:
  The Decameron, 29
Bozman, M. M.: 180
Bradley, A. C.: x, 8, 9, 124
Bridges, Robert:
  The Testament of Beauty, 52, 56
Brontë, Emily:
  Wuthering Heights, 26, 42
Brooks, Cleanth: 193
Brown, Carleton: 146–7, 149, 160,
  174–5, 194–5
Browne, Sir Thomas: 24
Browning, Robert: 93, 206;
  Abt Vogler, 93, 98;
  An Epistle of Karshish, 93;
  The Ring and the Book, 215;
  Saul, 24
Bullen, A. H.: 220
Burns, Robert: 49
Butler, Samuel: 3–17, 80, 88, 107,
  112, 130, 132

Byron, Lord: 10, 13, **24**, 26, **35**, 49, 52,
  65, 77, 108, 117, **125–7**, 138, 141;
  Don Juan, **30–3**, **35–6**, 56, 187;
  Don Leon, see Colman, George
  Manfred, 127;
  On Completing My Thirty-Sixth Year,
  10;
  Sardanapalus, 36, **204**

Capell, Edward: 20
Cary, H. F.: 103–4
Castiglione:
  The Courtier, 153
Cavafy, C. P.:
  Days of 1908, 167;
  To Remain, 167
Chapman, George: **14;**
  Peristeros: or the Male Turtle, 145,
  179, **184–5**, 223
Chaucer, Geoffrey:
  Prologue to The Canterbury Tales, 59
Chester, Robert: 146, **174–6**, 178, 189,
  195, 205, 210–11;
  Love's Martyr, or Rosalin's Complaint,
  145–51, 153, 155, **156–78**, 188,
  190–1, 195, 202
Christ, Jesus: 27, **34**, 150, 212, **222**
Churchyard, Thomas:
  Challenge, 146, 150
Chute, Marchette: 6
Coleridge, Samuel Taylor:
  Kubla Khan, 64, 182;
  Zapolya, 65
Colman, George (?): *Don Leon*, **24**
Crashaw, Richard: 153
Cunningham, J. V.: 200

'Danielle': 147, 153
Dante: 25, 49, 52, **120**, 138, 154–5,
  206;
  Divina Commedia, 68, **103–4**, 123,
  200, 204, 221;
  Vita Nuova, 212
Darley, George:
  Nepenthe, 221
David: 24
Dekker, Thomas:
  Four Birds of Noah's Ark, 222

229